Stephen Najda

LIFE

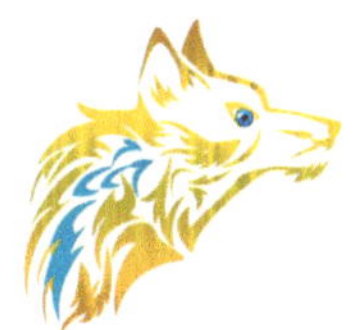

On the cover:
"Matilda resting against a wall-detail"

*** * ***

Layout Cover and Internal by: Wolf Graham

ISBN 978-1-913964-18-4
Publishing Company:
Black Wolf Edition & Publishing Ltd.
Scotland (UK)
www.blackwolfedition.co.uk

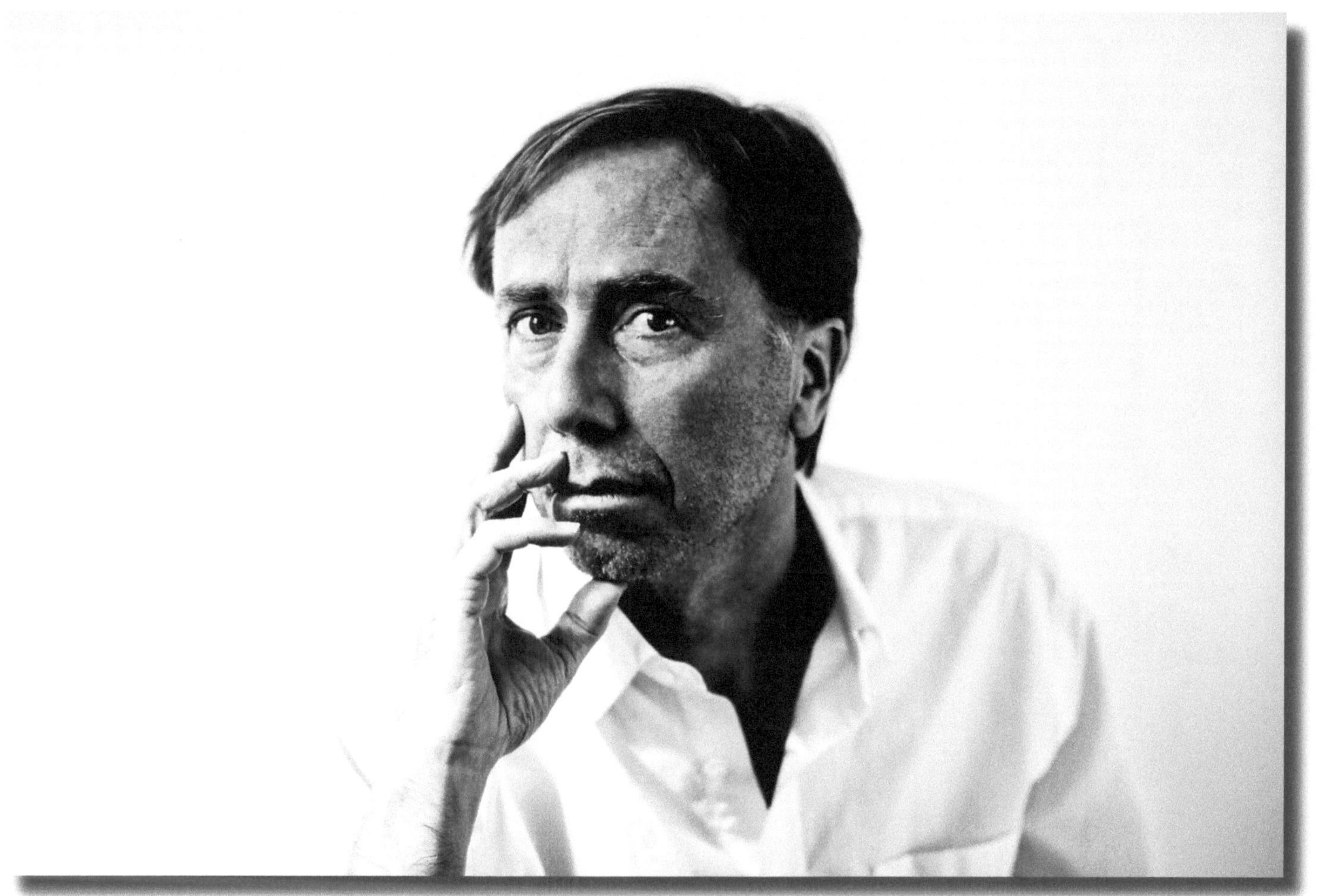

Stephen Najda was born in a Glasgow tenement of Scottish-Polish parentage. The Scottish mountains were an early lure. Since then, Stephen has climbed extensively in the wilderness mountain areas of Europe, the Middle-East, Africa, Asia and the Americas.

Stephen graduated with a PhD in physics from St. Andrews University. Followed by research posts in physics at Tokyo University, CNRS Grenoble and Oxford. Stephen returned to Glasgow to work with a photonics high-tech company and has been 're-born' in Poland with another high-tech venture.

Stephen discovered art by chance and good fortune, pre-empting a 'new path' of discovery and self-expression. Najda's art spans the complete spectrum of human emotion from simple beauty of sensual curvaceous women; through captured moments from the artist's travels; through a wide range of scientific, social, political, philosophical and intellectual questions and debates; to the provocative and challenging brutal reality of war, disease and human tragedy. These theoretical concepts are brought into focus through the medium of oil on canvas to create a unique visual experience. The art is both, wonderful and enlightening, pleasurable and challenging, beautiful and harrowing, complex and terrifying, producing powerfully evocative images that are entirely relevant to the modern world and questioning our path into the future.

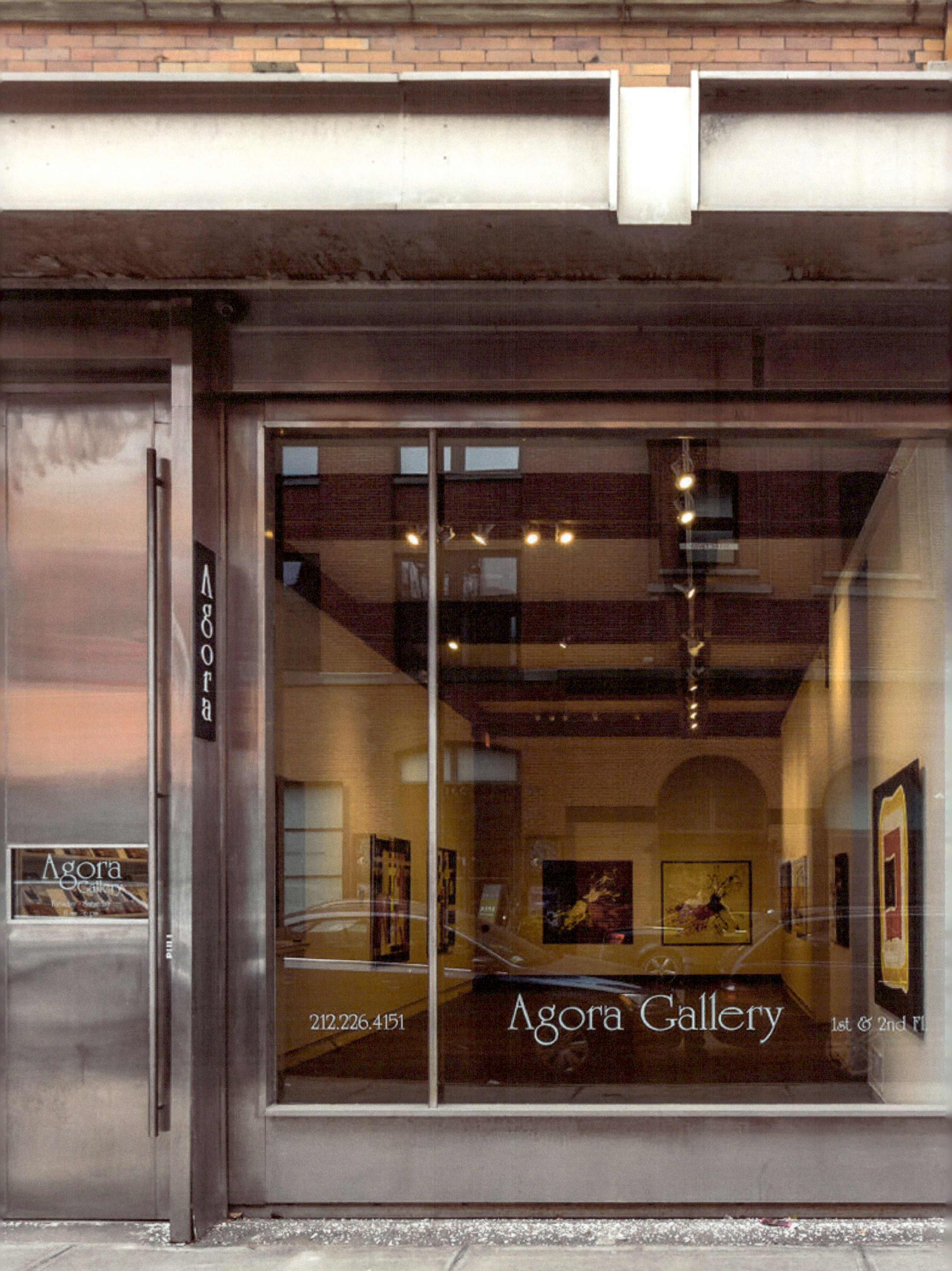

Agora
Agora Gallery
212.226.4151
Agora Gallery
1st & 2nd Fl

Najda in Life: a series of paintings by Stephen Najda

The art of Stephen Najda crosses many boundaries, over a wide spectrum of subjects, and a multitude of techniques. A complex individual with a deep curiosity and an extraordinary fertile mind that crosses a huge range of subjects that coalesce into art in an attempt to articulate the known fundamental interactions of the universe and forms of matter. Often called Renaissance man, Najda is a precociously talented and prolific artist bringing a multidisciplinary background in science, literature and art, mixed with an insatiable appetite for adventure and travel. Stylistically placed between Matisse, Picasso and de Kooning, Najda features expressionistic figures representing the primitive self in big, bold, hugely imaginative paintings.
In Life, we explore a different facet of the artist. This is a short history of the informative first few years of the artist showing a restless, radical, ever-changing aspect to his work. The life class is where Stephen Najda discovered art. Surprisingly, the artist has kept every piece of work from day-one, showing all the mistakes, struggles and dead-ends of early academic studies. This is a self-taught 'artists way' process.

The study of the classic nude is one of the most studied, traditional and fundamental academic practise following in the ancient Greek tradition. Classical Greece had no division between art and science, instead it was seen as fluid, where artists and scientists seamlessly floated between disciplines whilst exploring new ideas.

Painting the human form is the most difficult of all art forms. Najda's early style was technical fleshy nudes and self-portraits, however his style transformed dramatically into dramatic, contemplative figures visually skewed and exaggerated, with bold curvaceous lines melting into a chaotic burst of colour and vivid primary pigment Fauve flesh. Each work brings a new openness and ambiguity and shifts back and forth between representation and abstraction. For Najda this change was instinctive giving a progressive and yet accessible style.

Angela Di Bello,
Executive Director
Agora Gallery 530 W 25th St, New York, NY 10001, USA
and Editor-in-Chief of ARTisSpectrum Magazine.

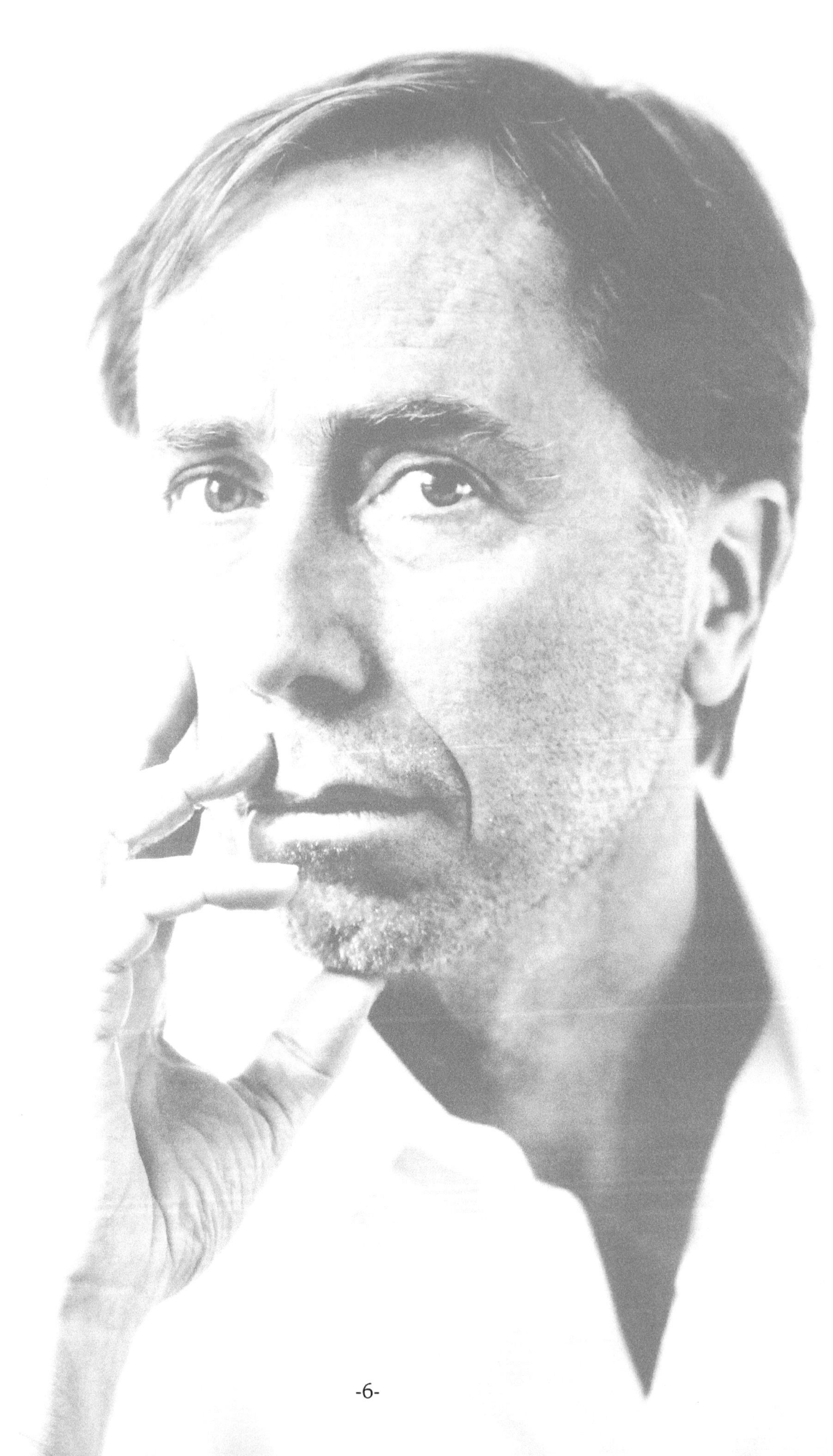

Stephen Najda

Life

- Life class & Studio-

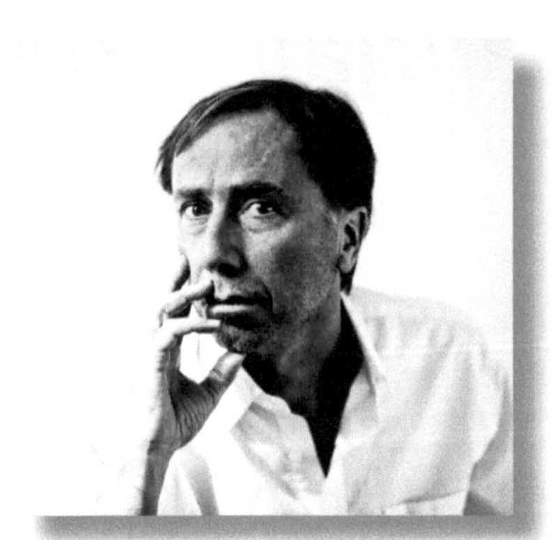

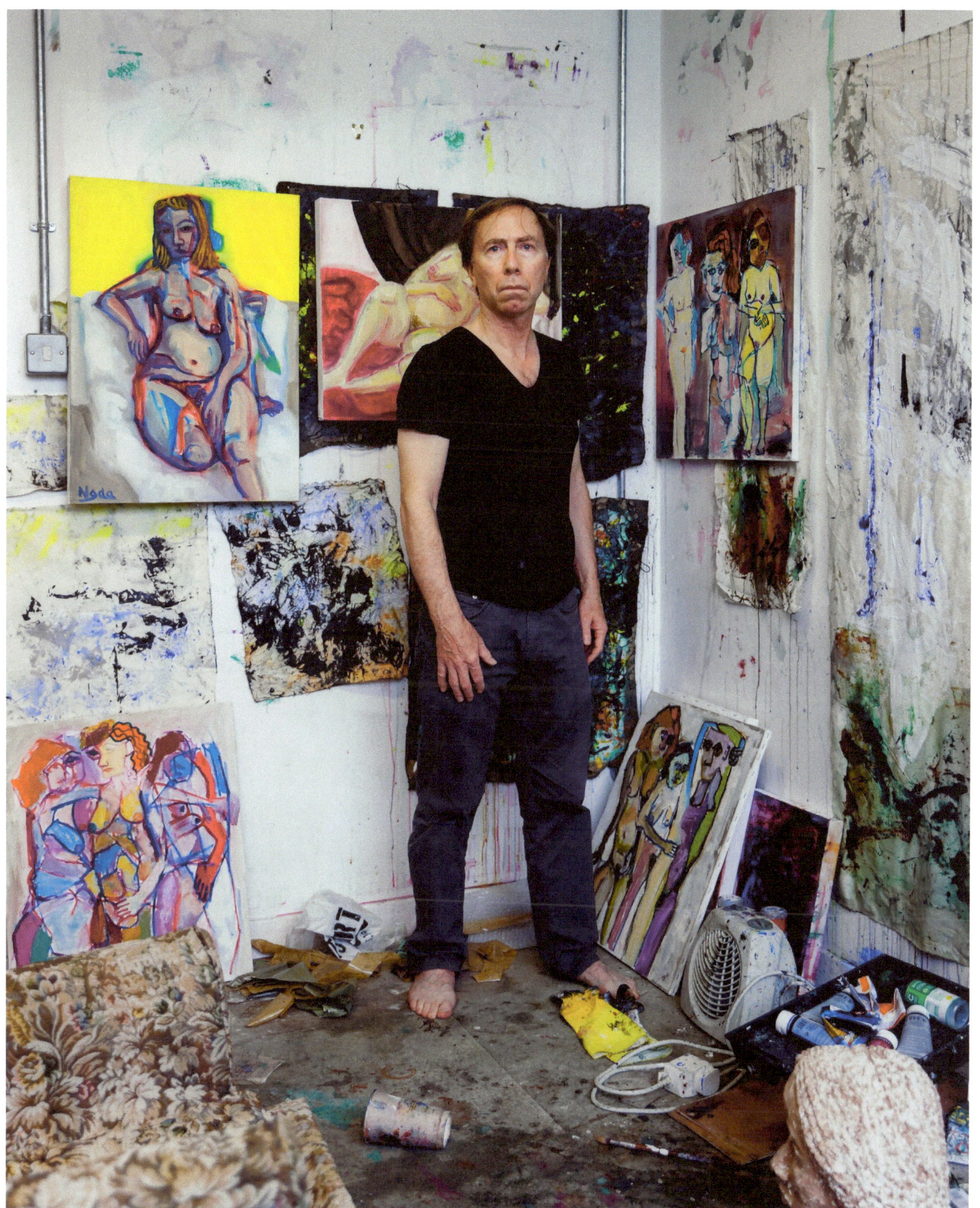

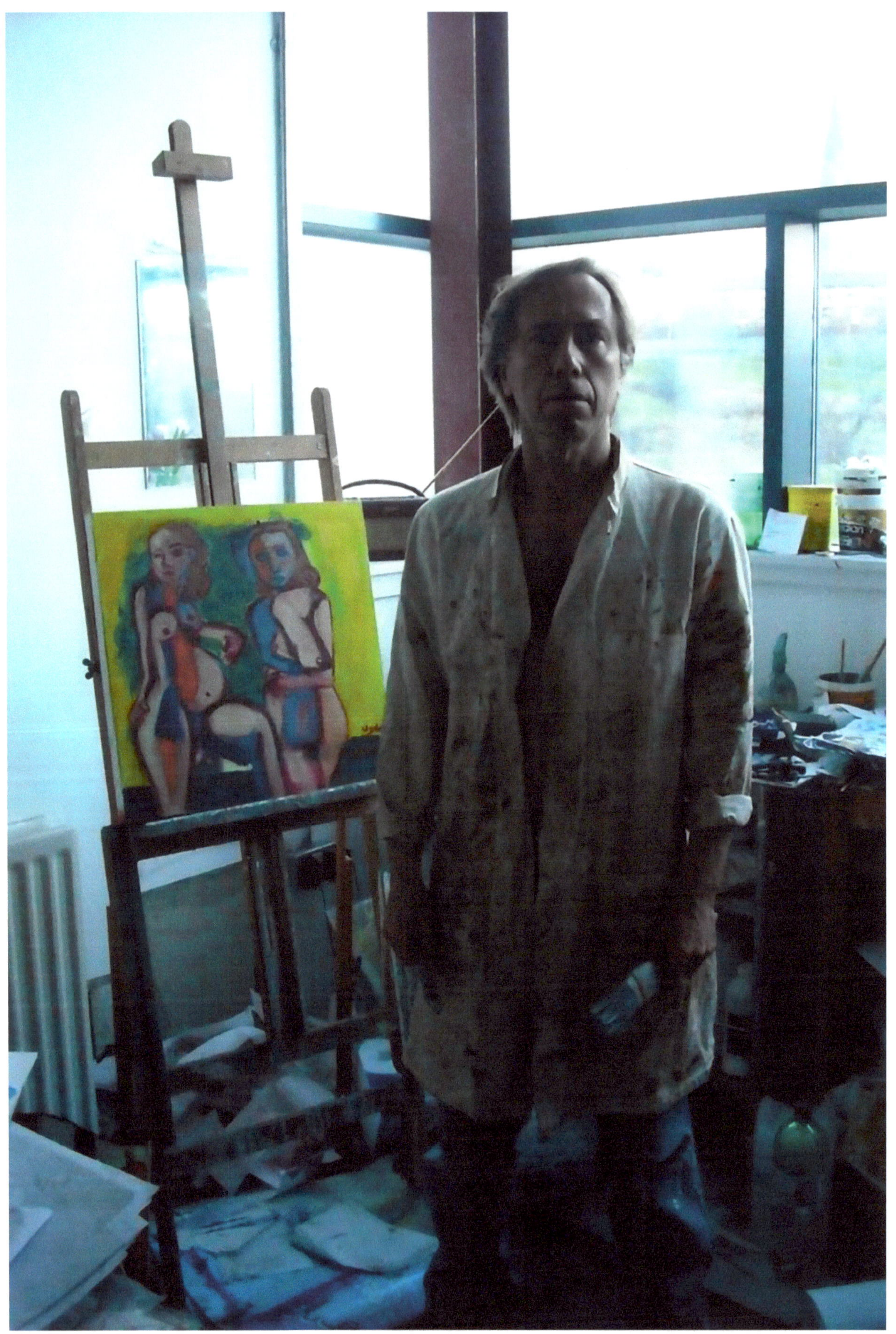

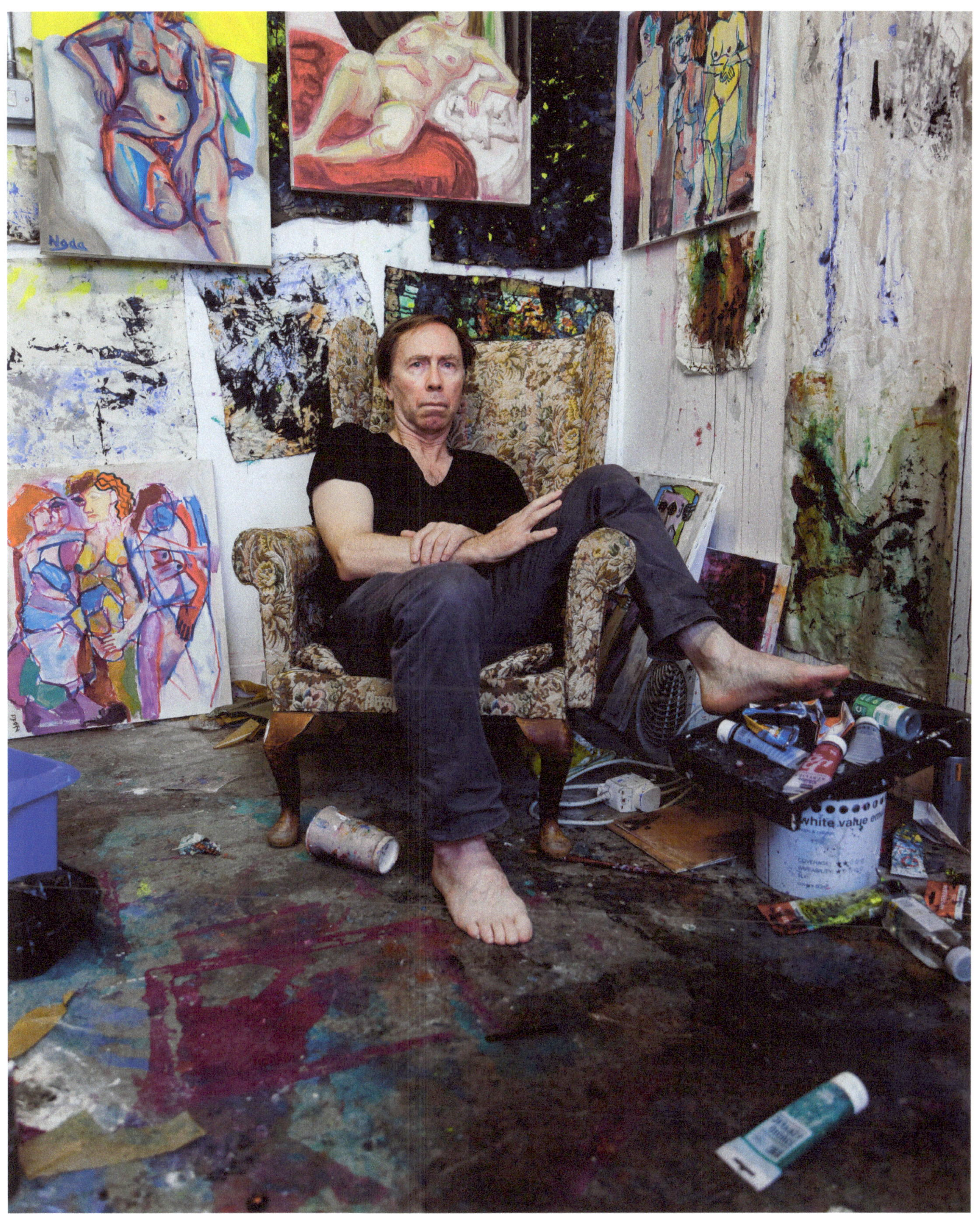

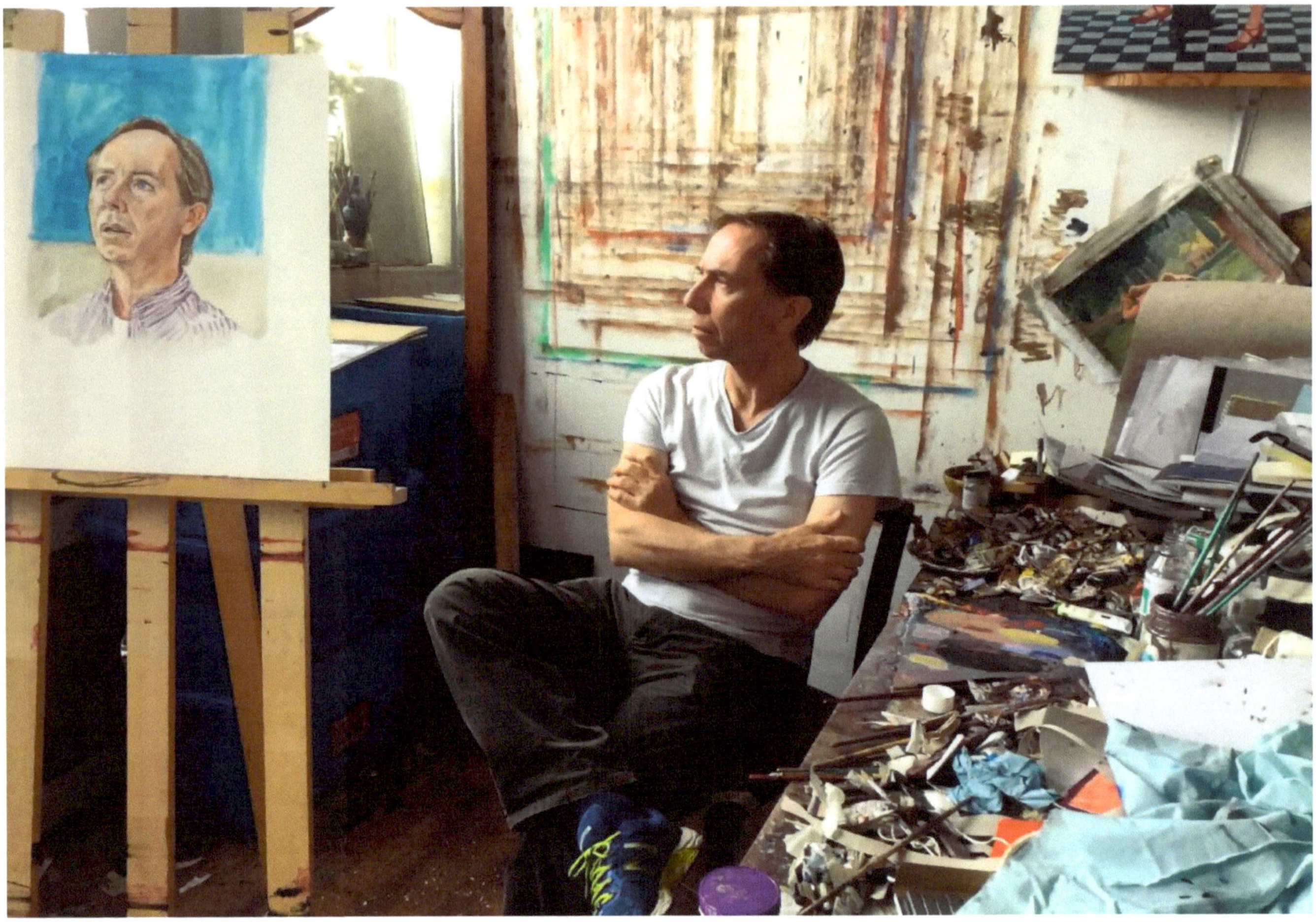

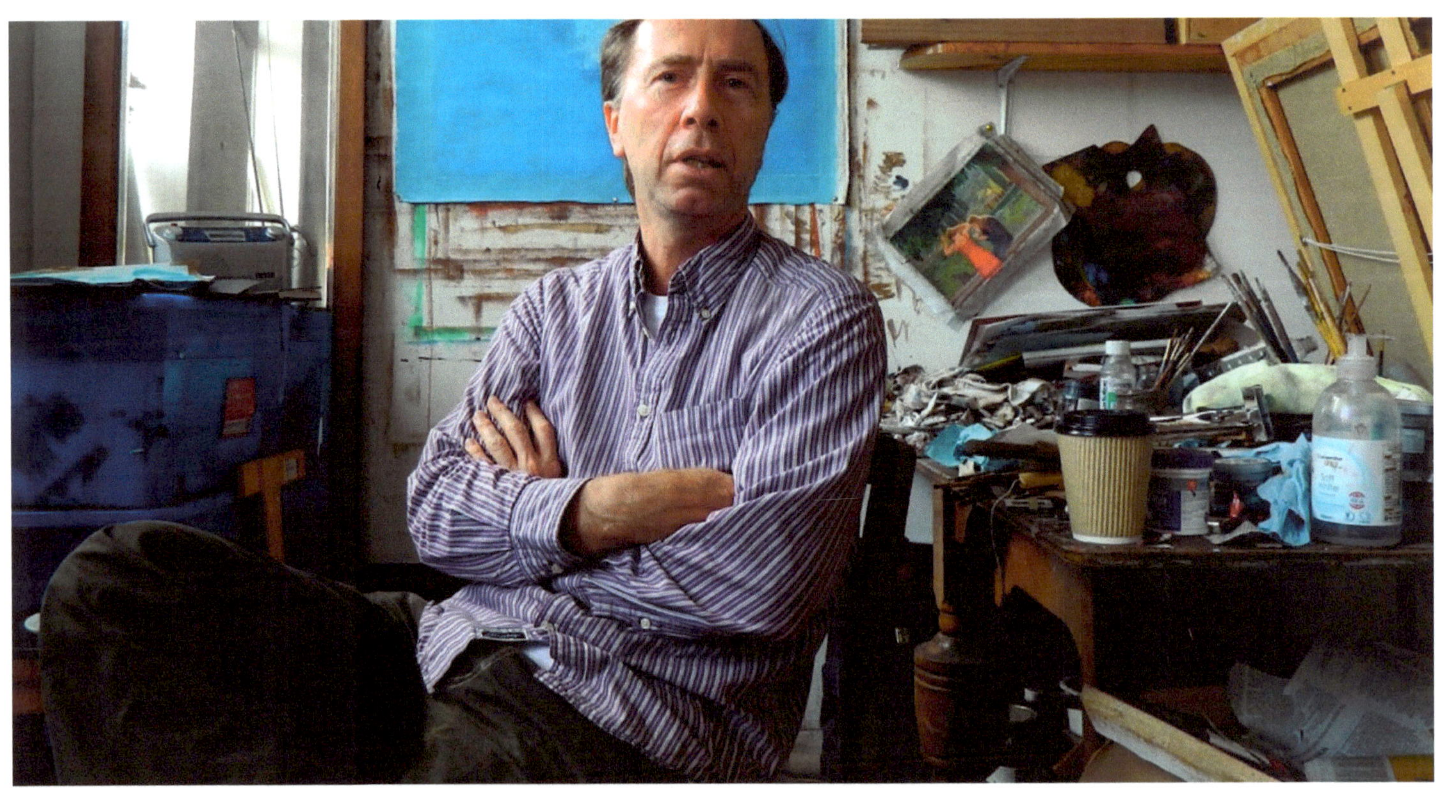

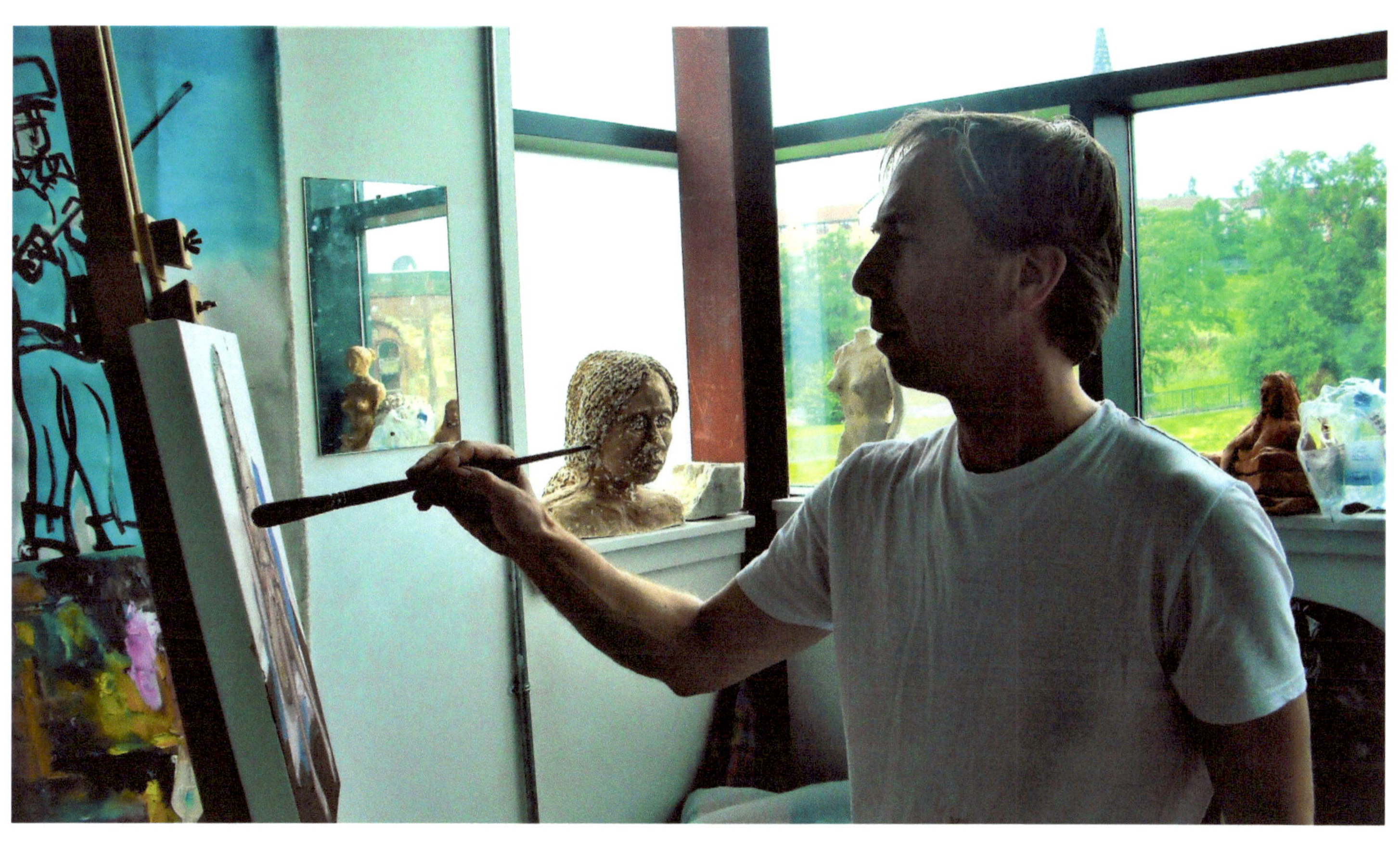

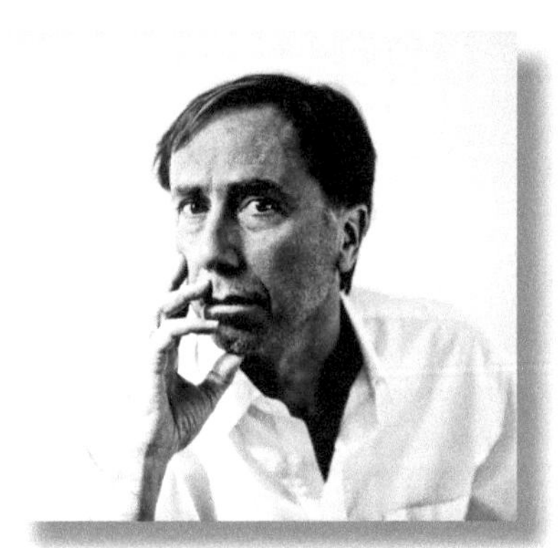

Stephen Najda

Life

- Acrylic on paper -

Agora Gallery

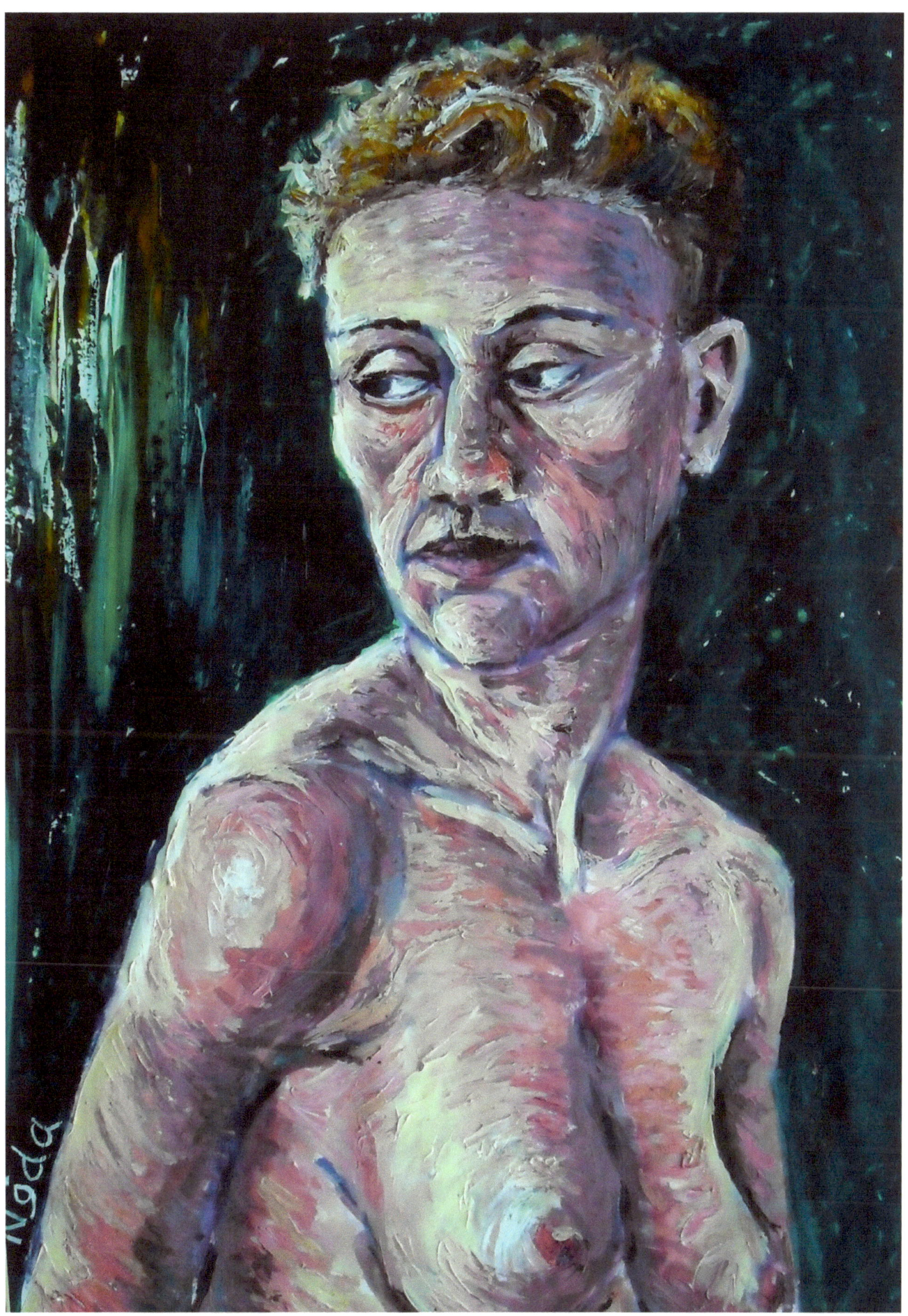

“FIONA”

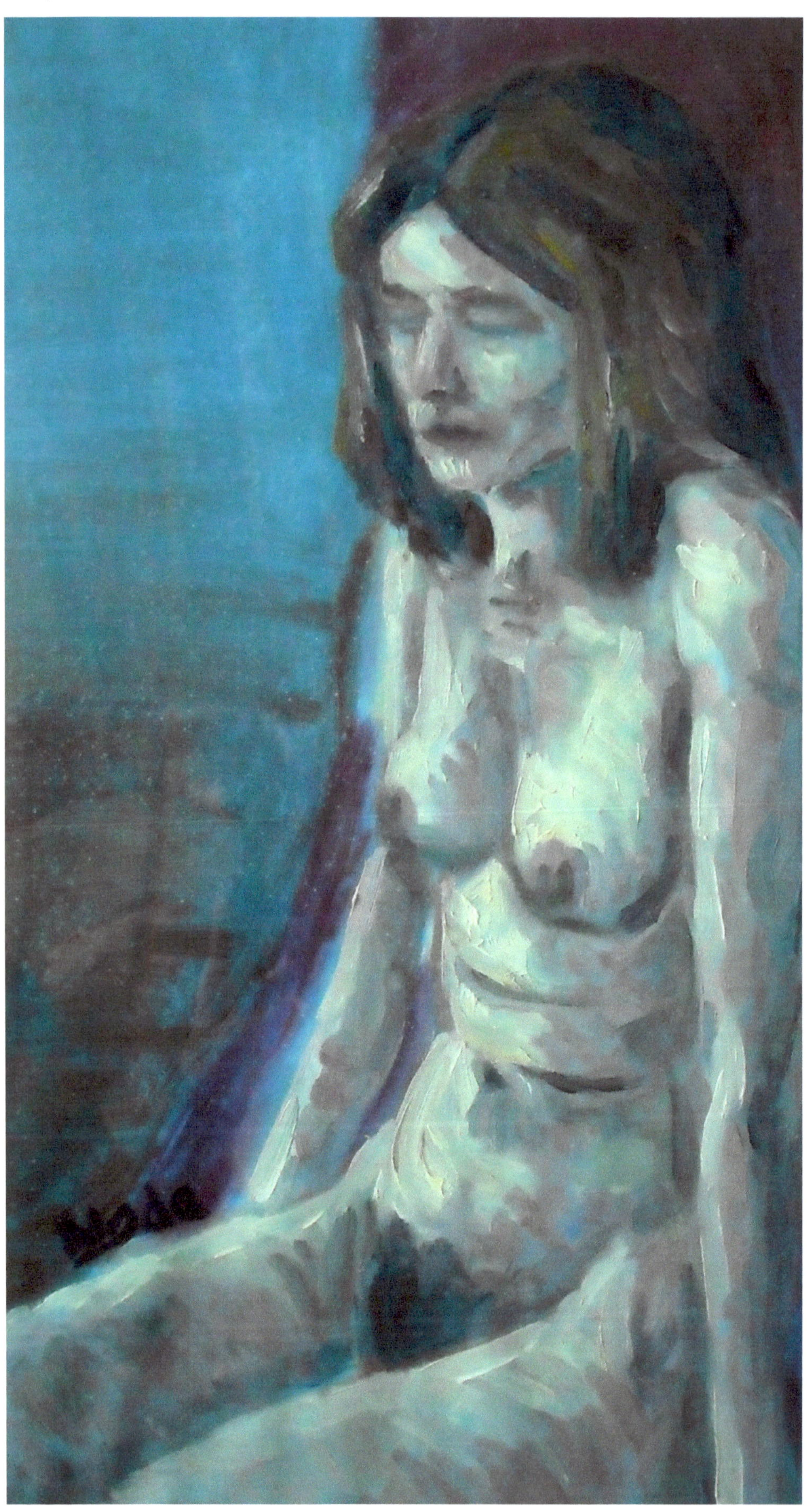

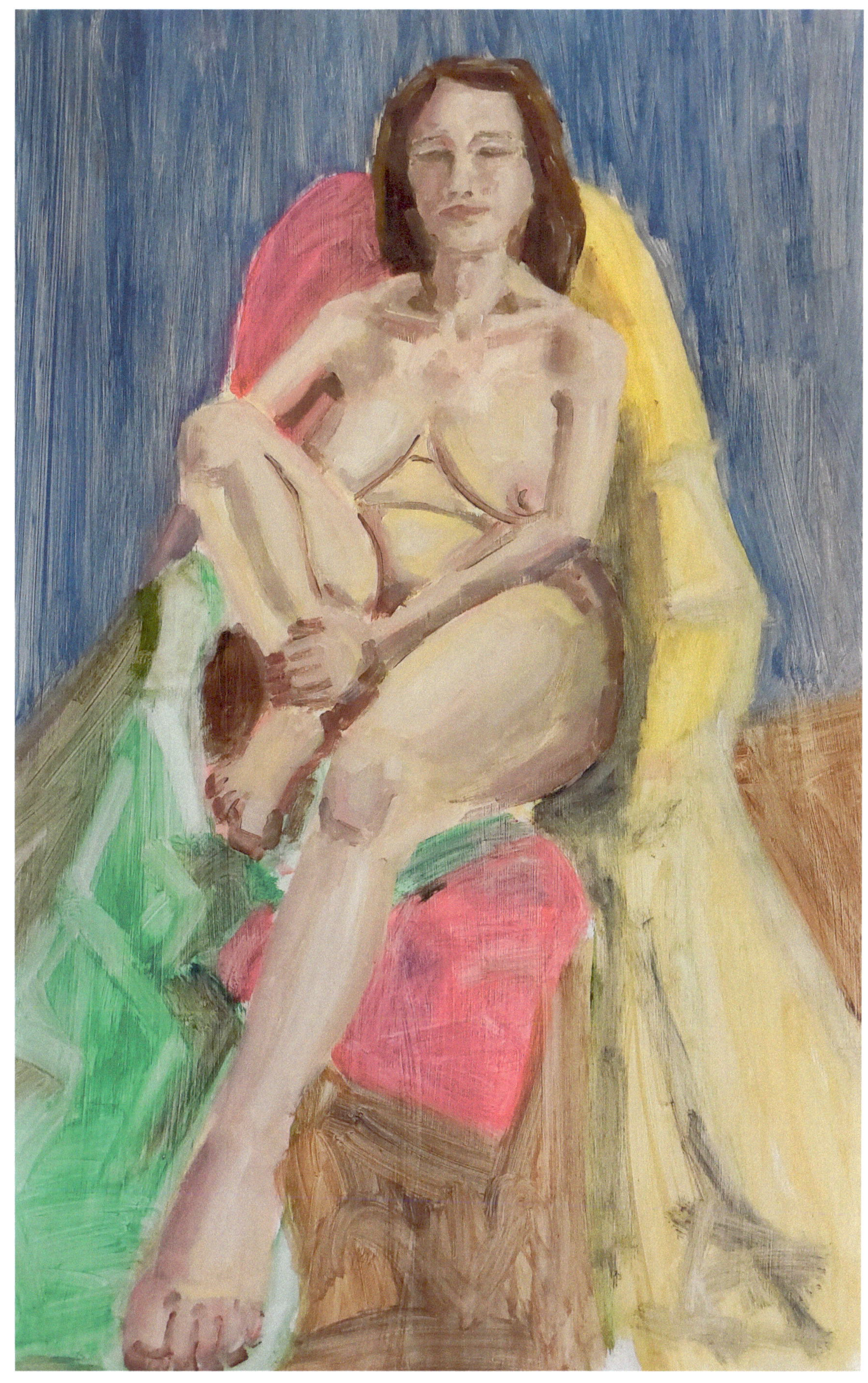

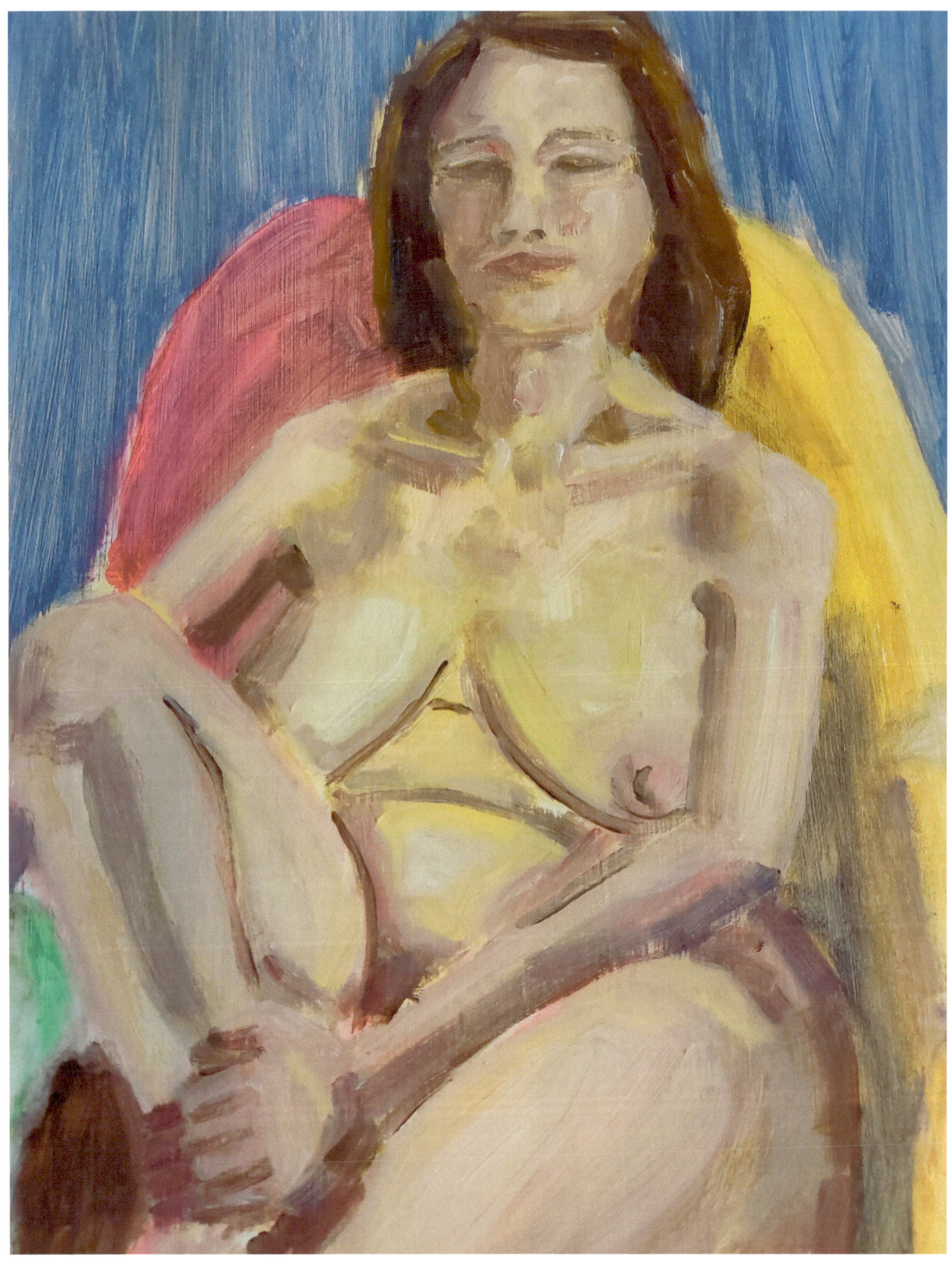

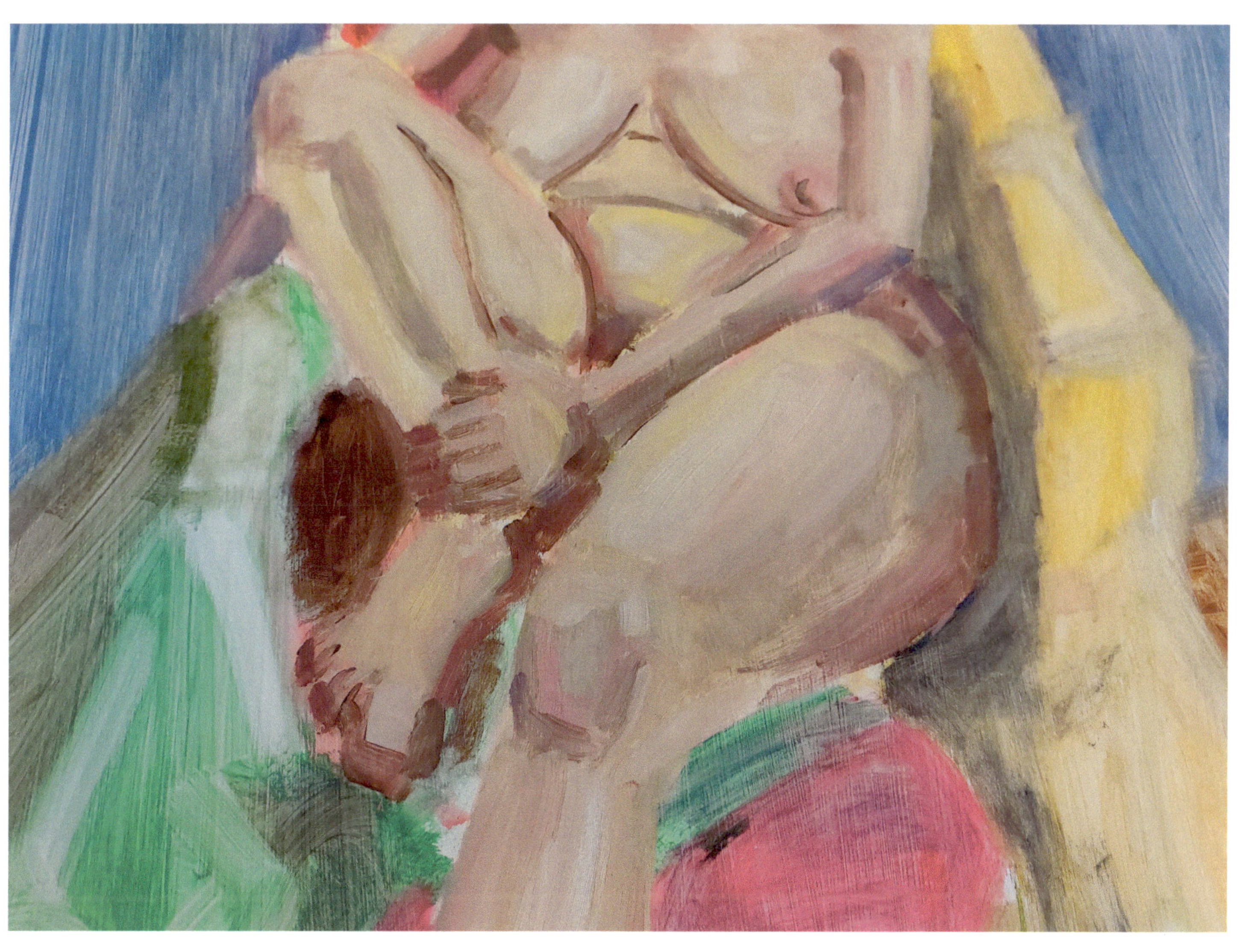

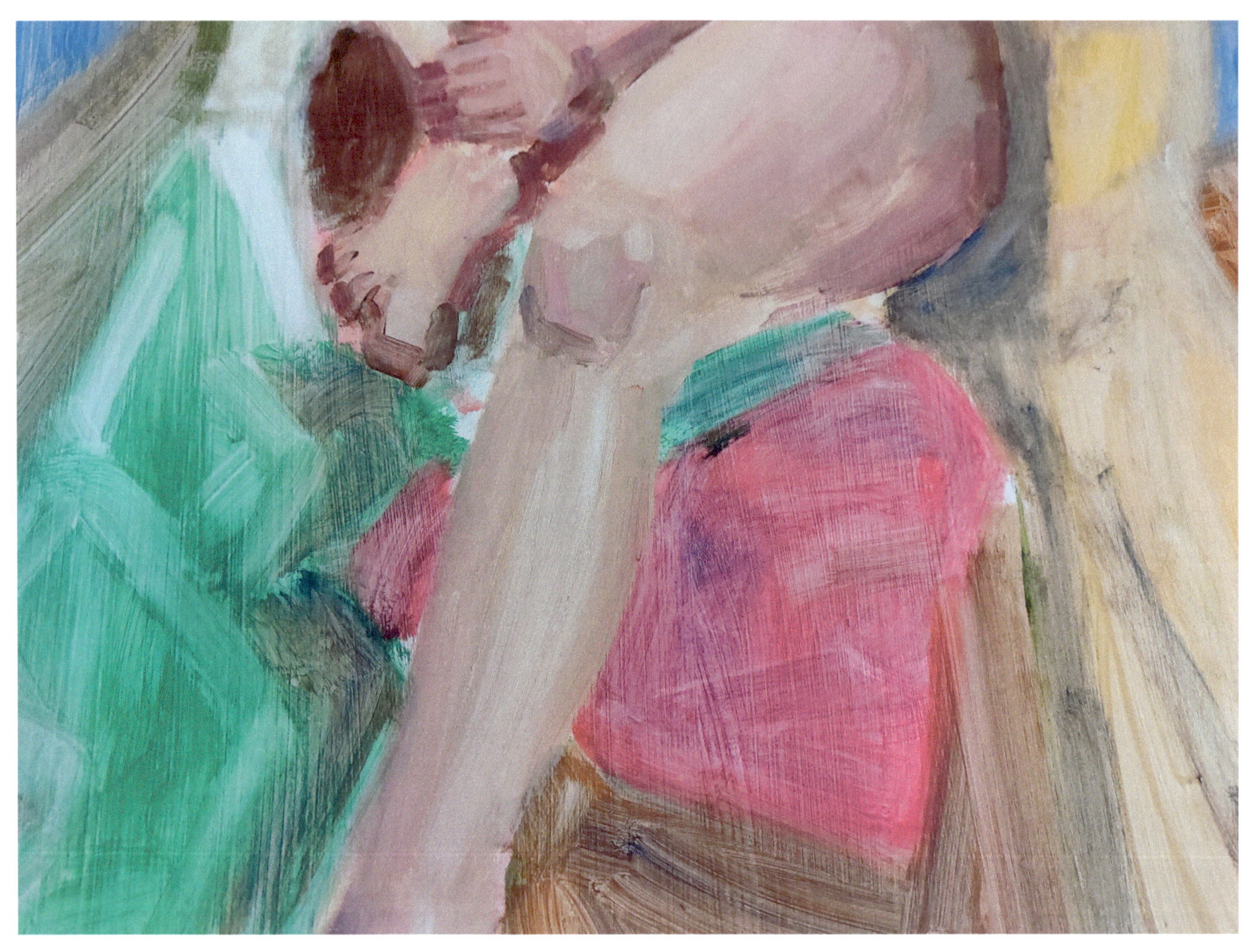

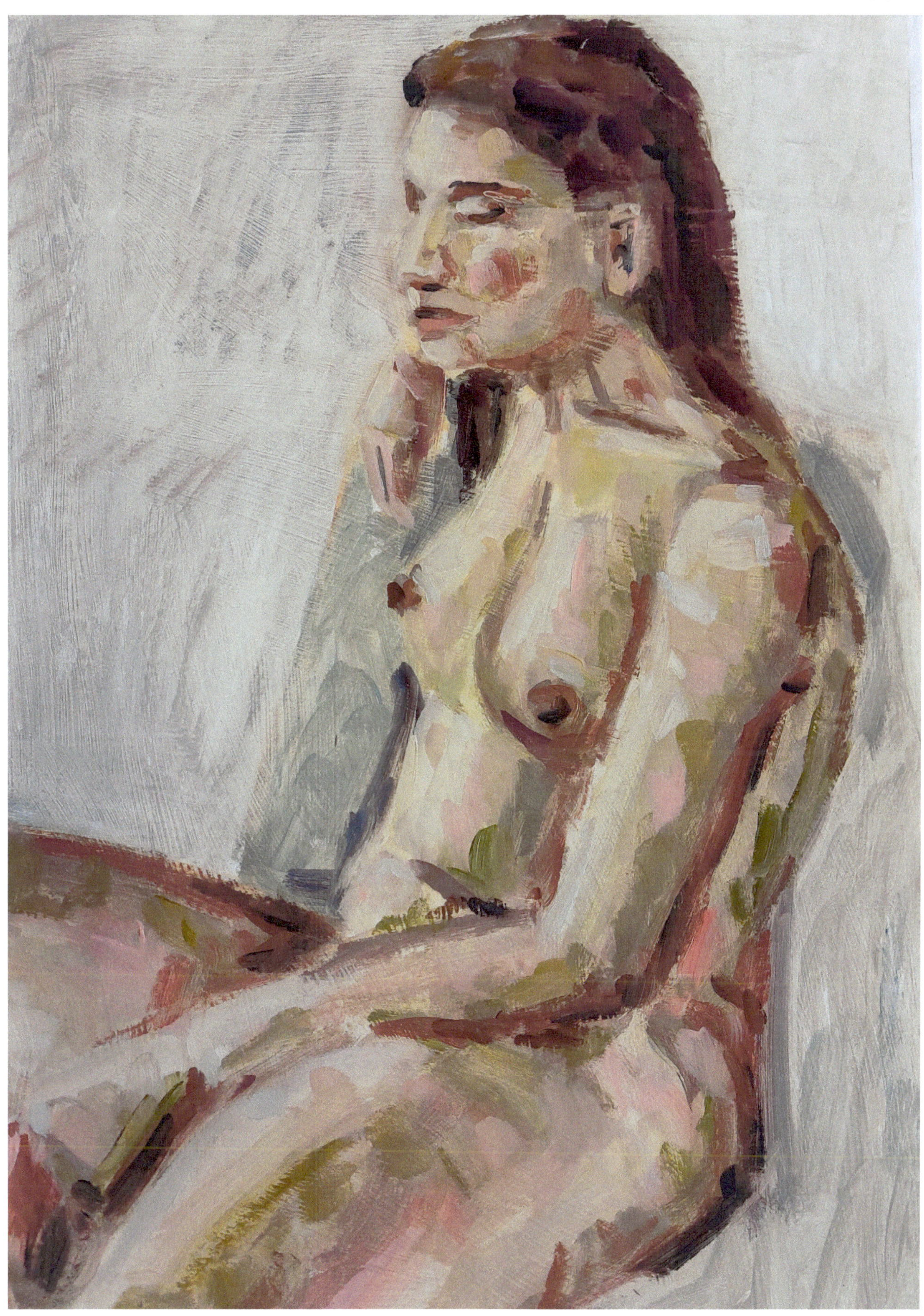

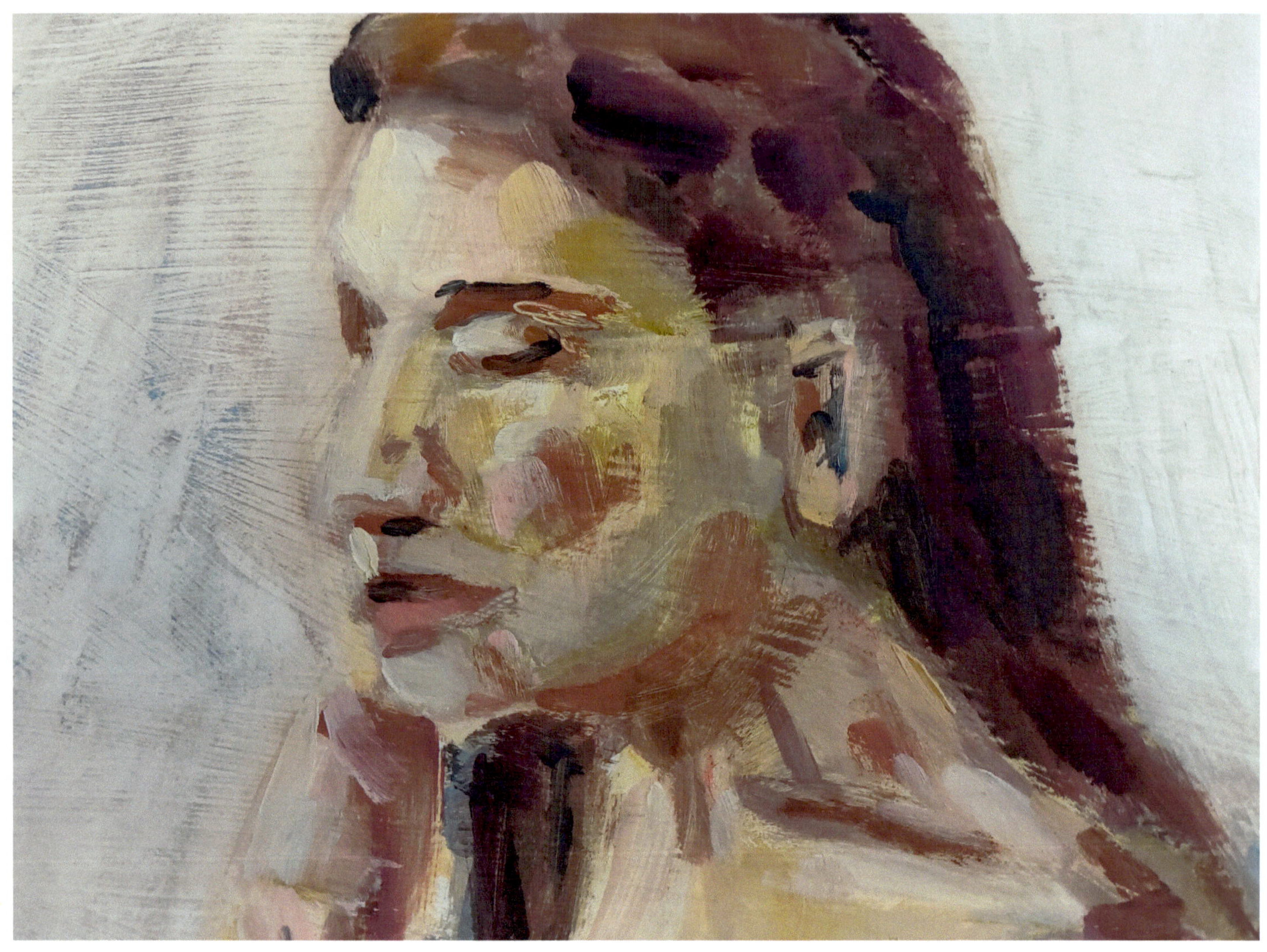

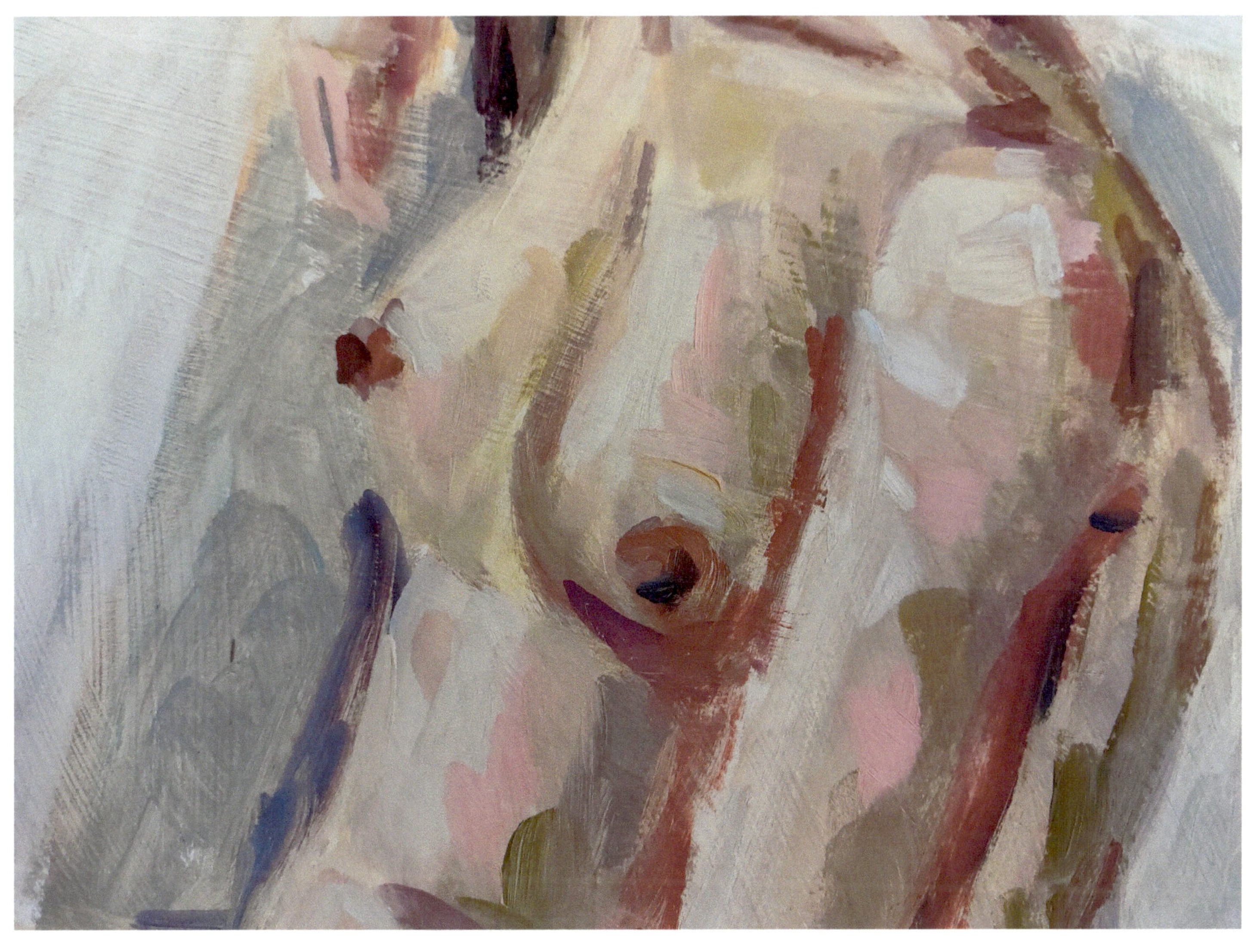

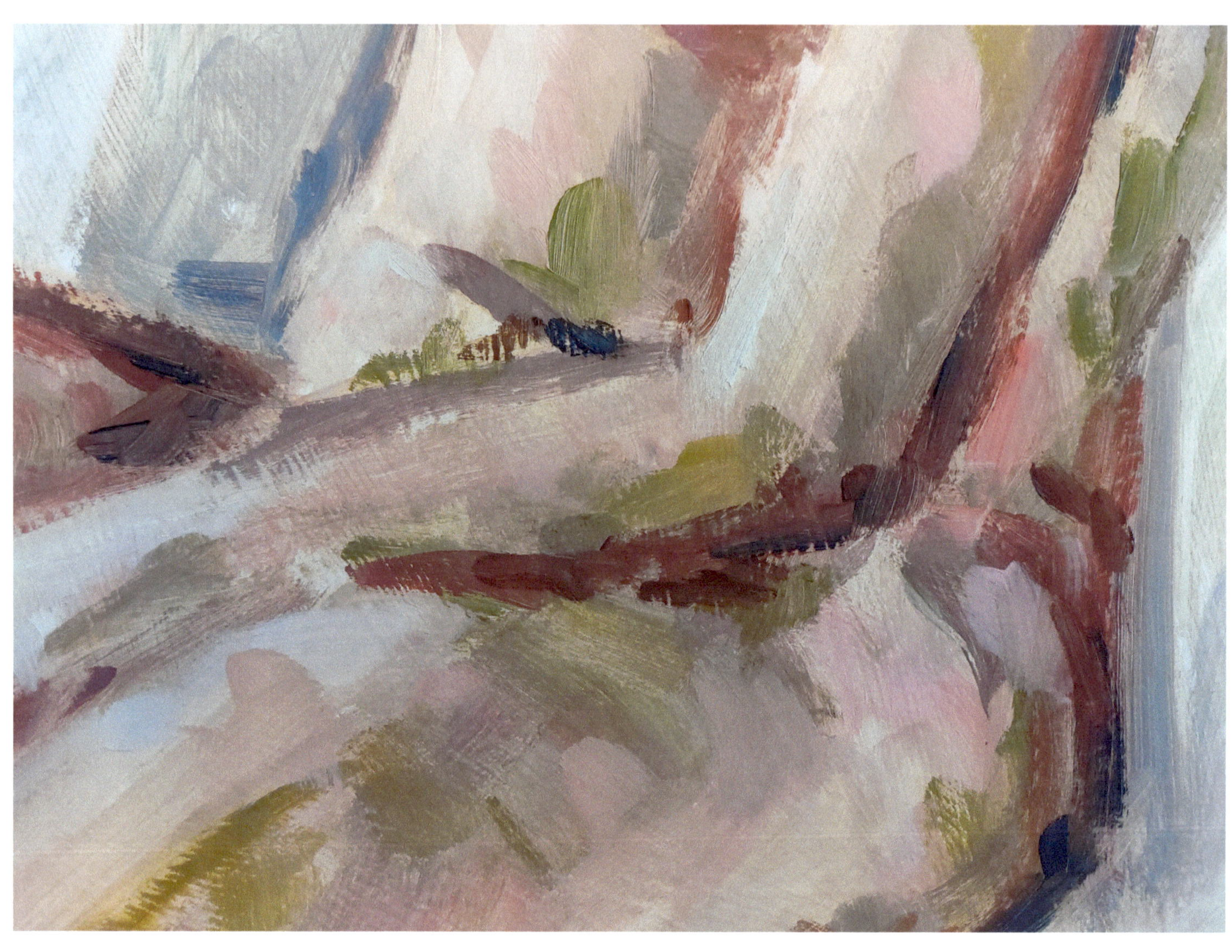

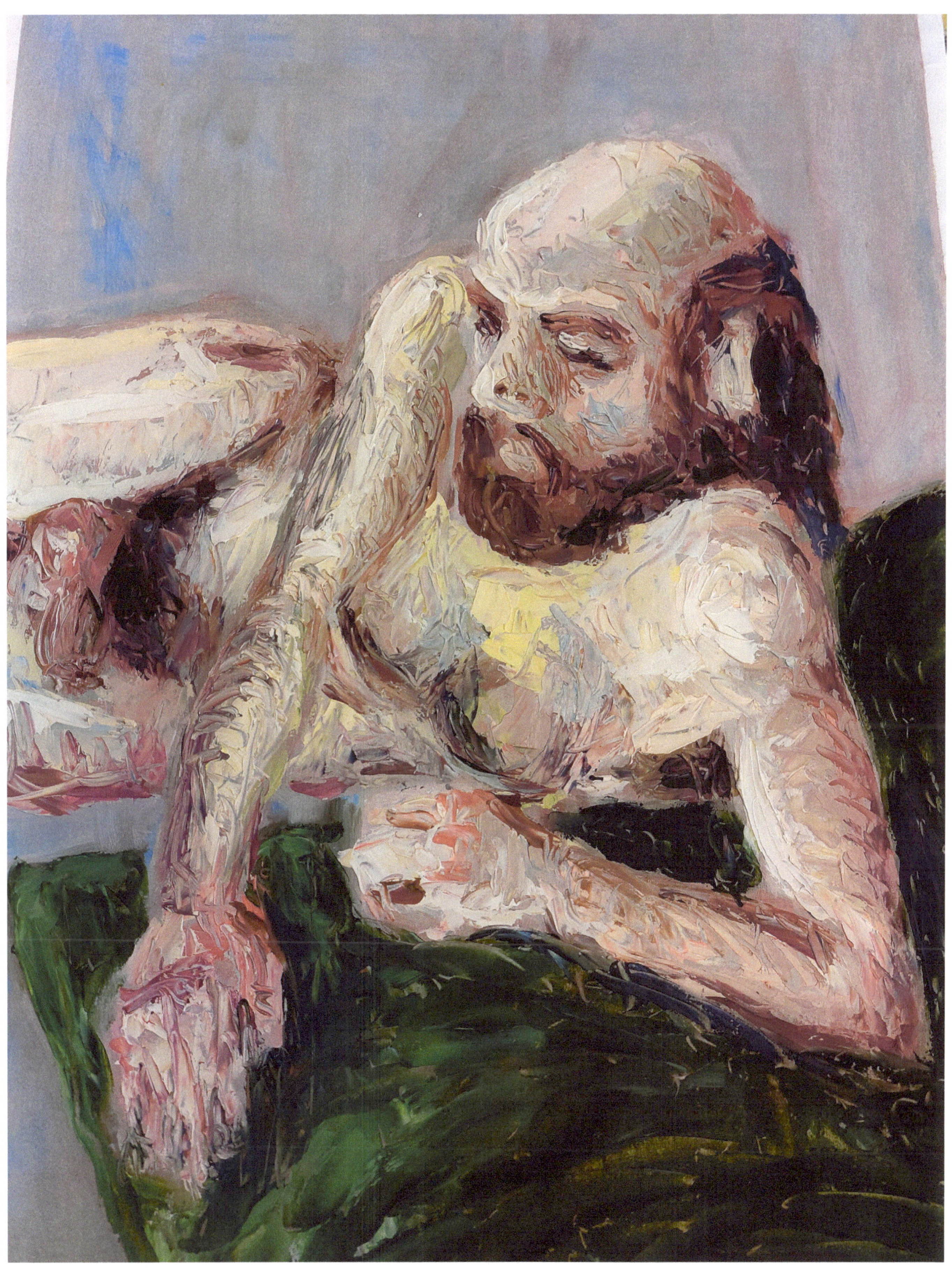

DETAIL - "OLD MAN"

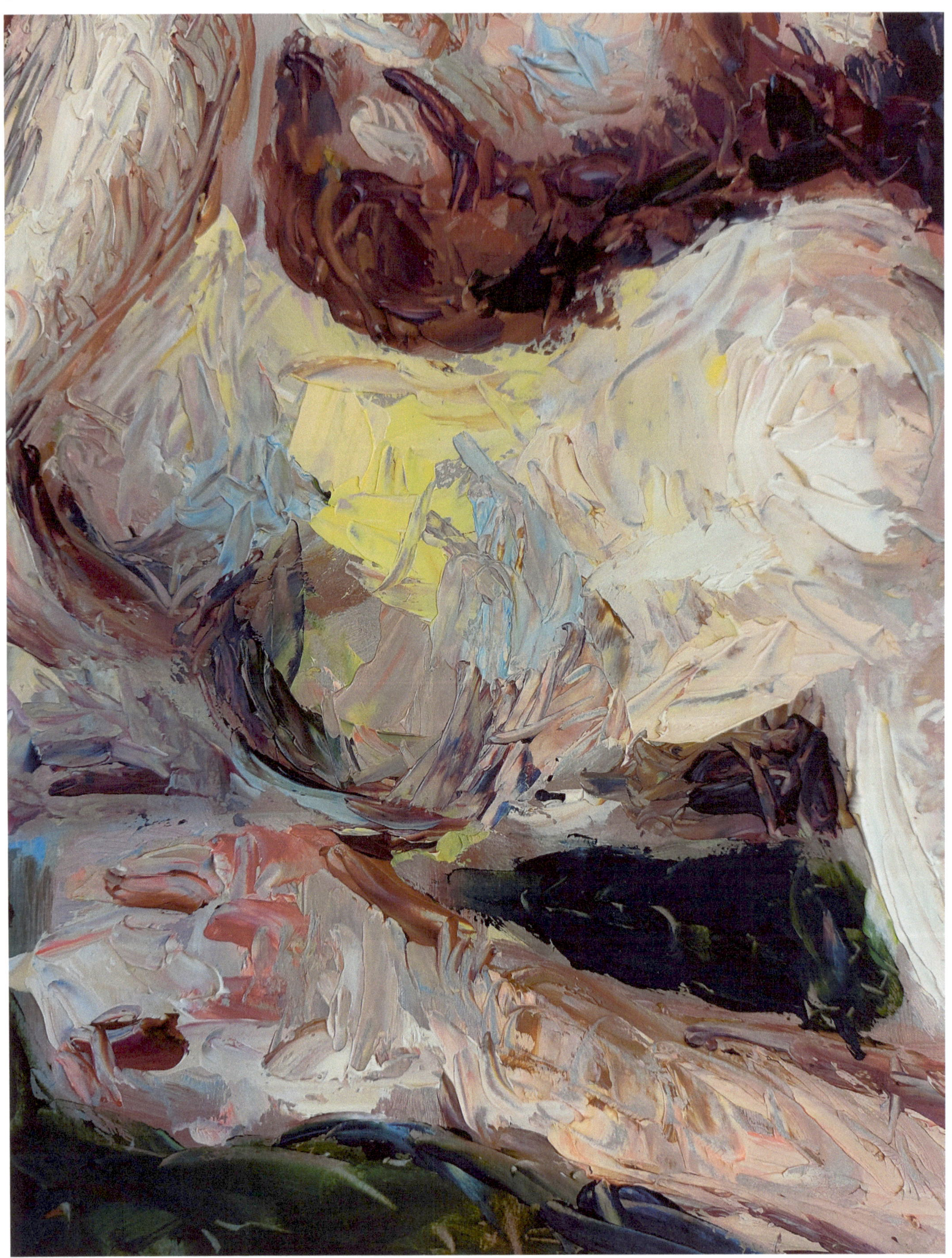

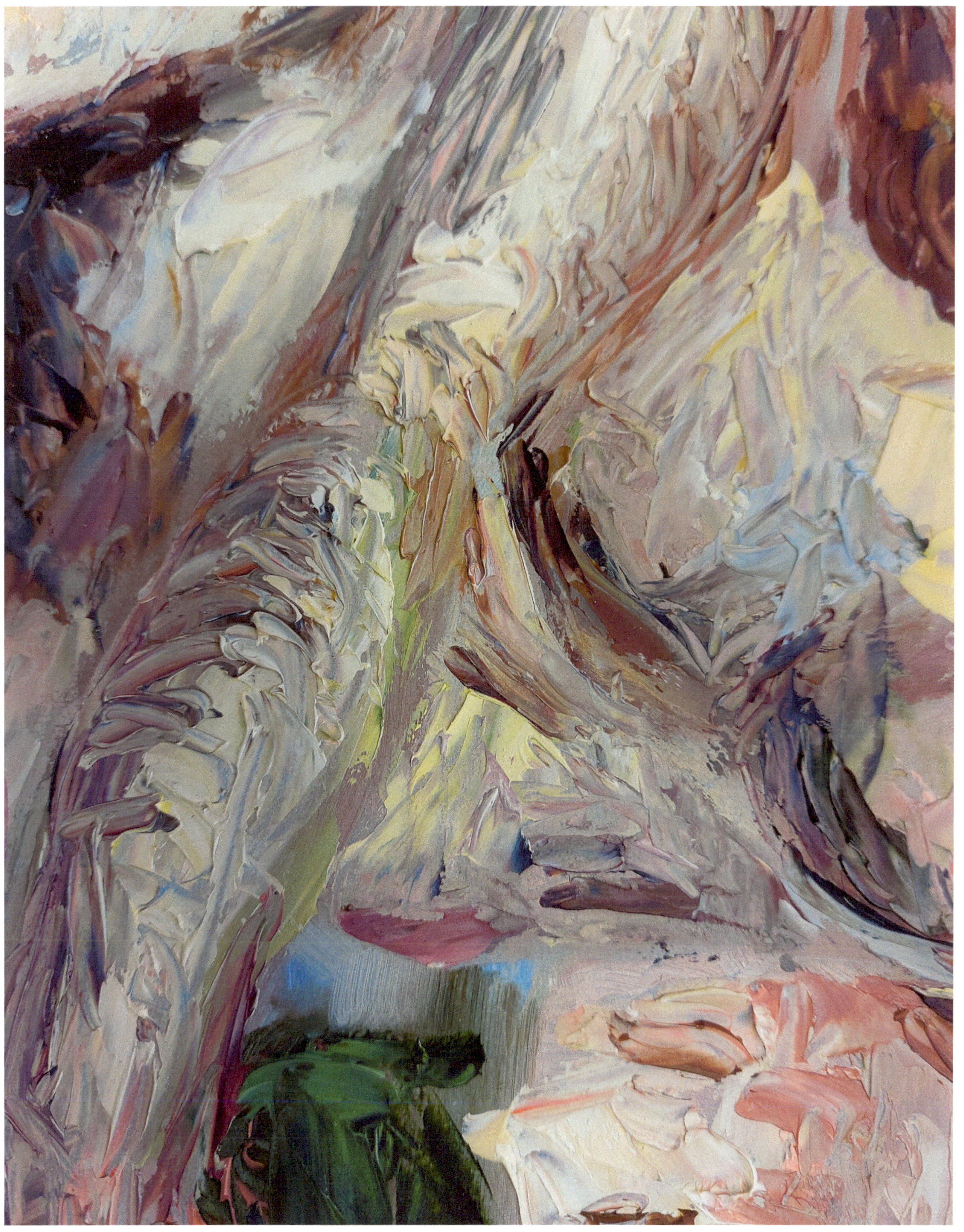

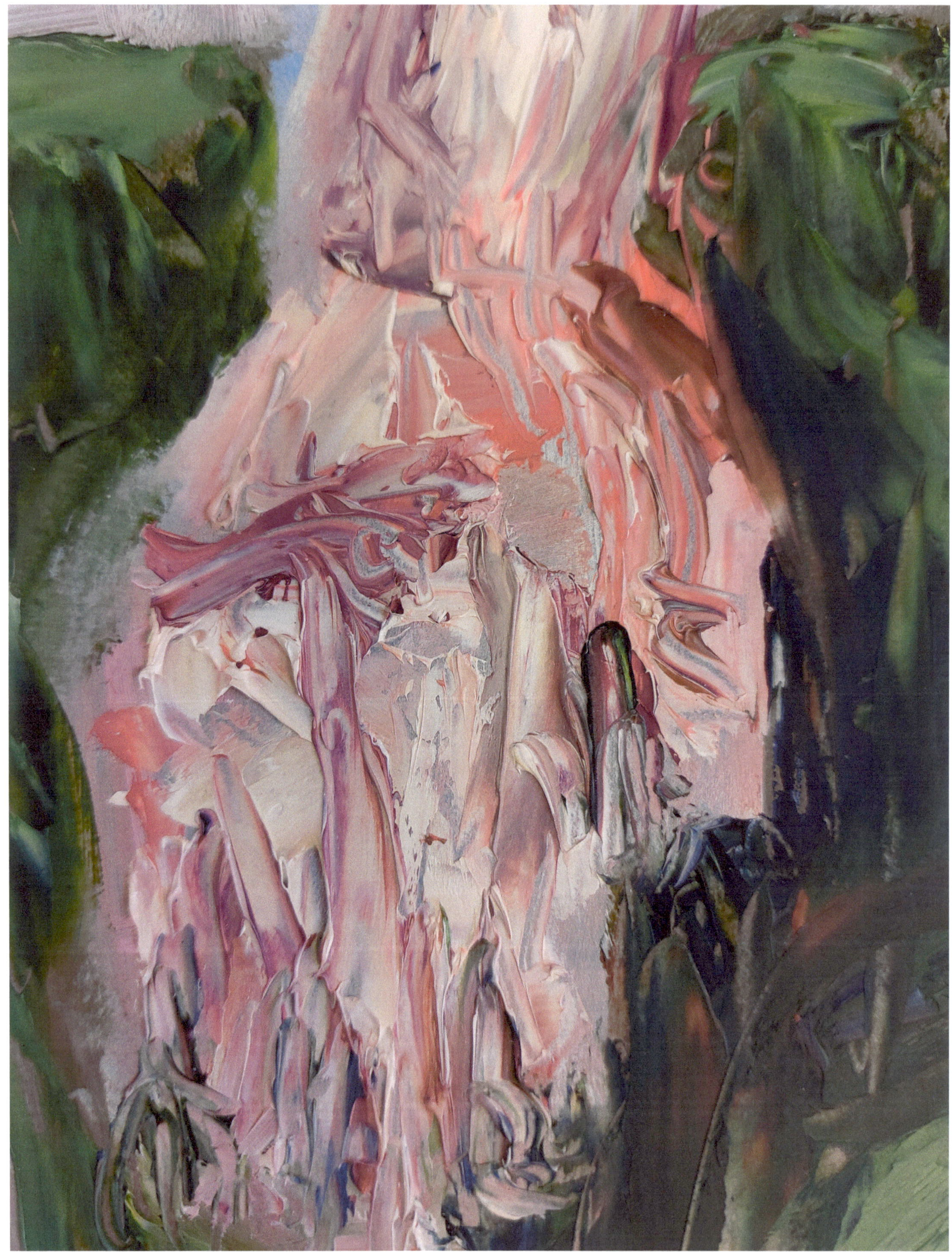

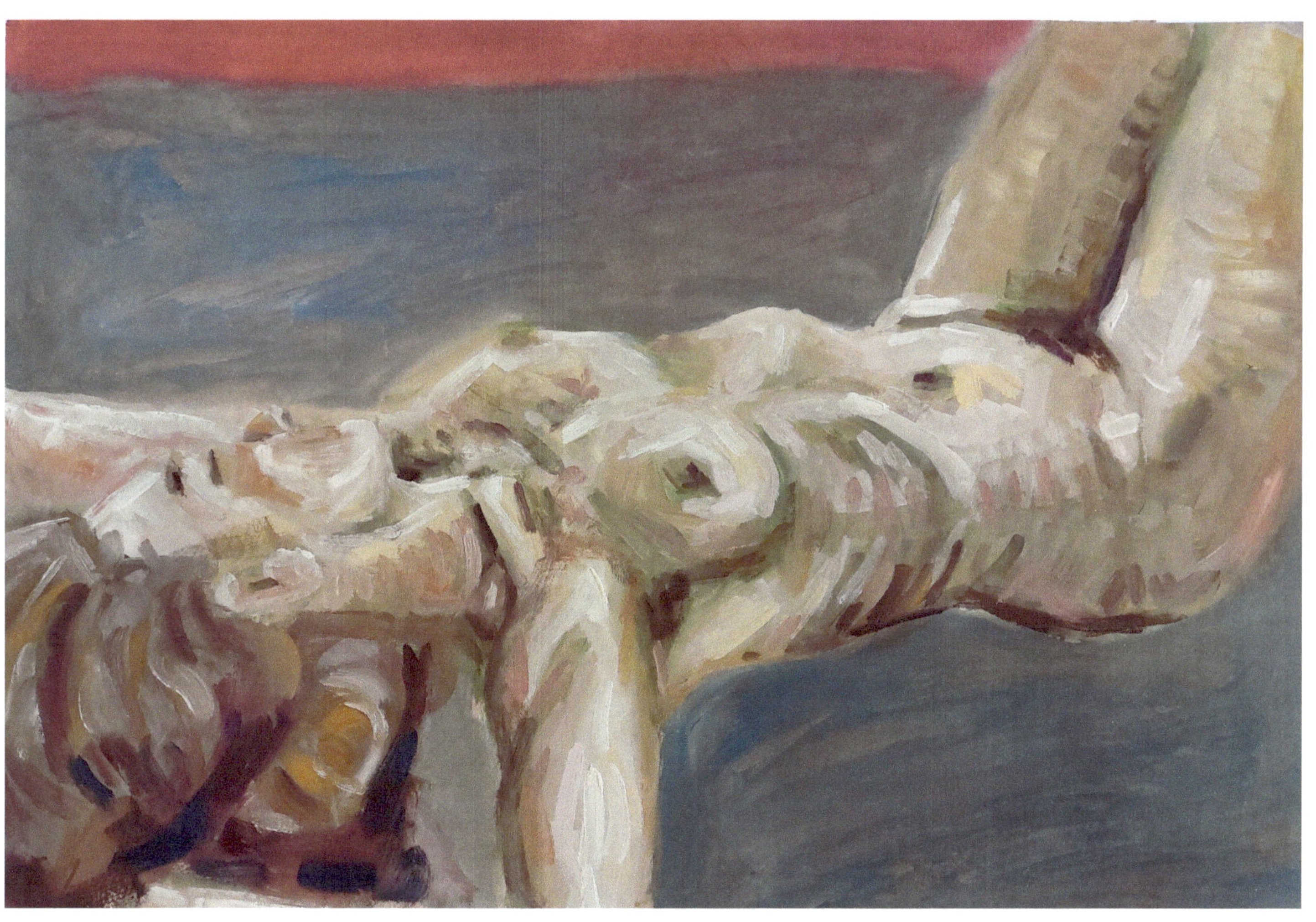

DETAIL - "GABRIELLA"

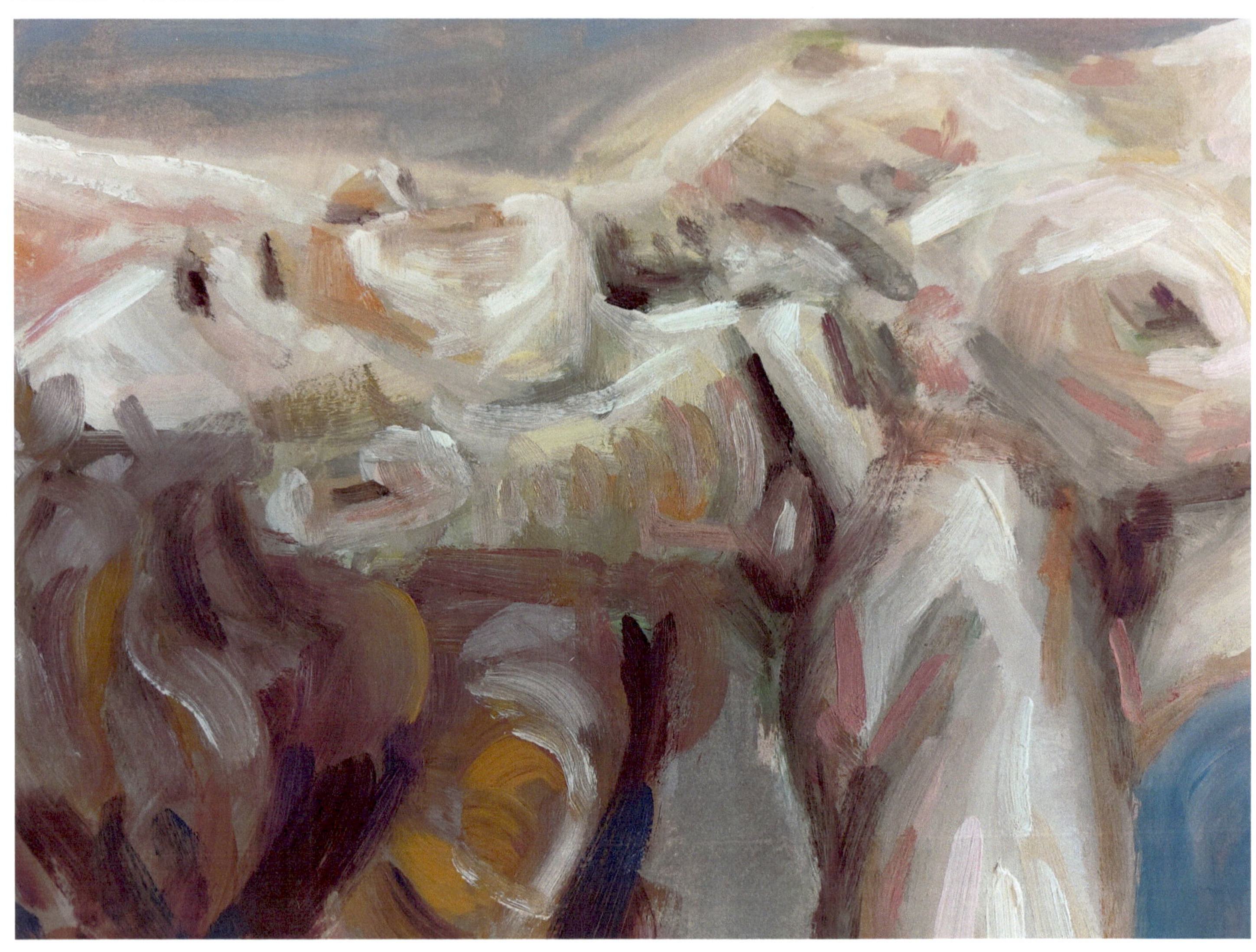

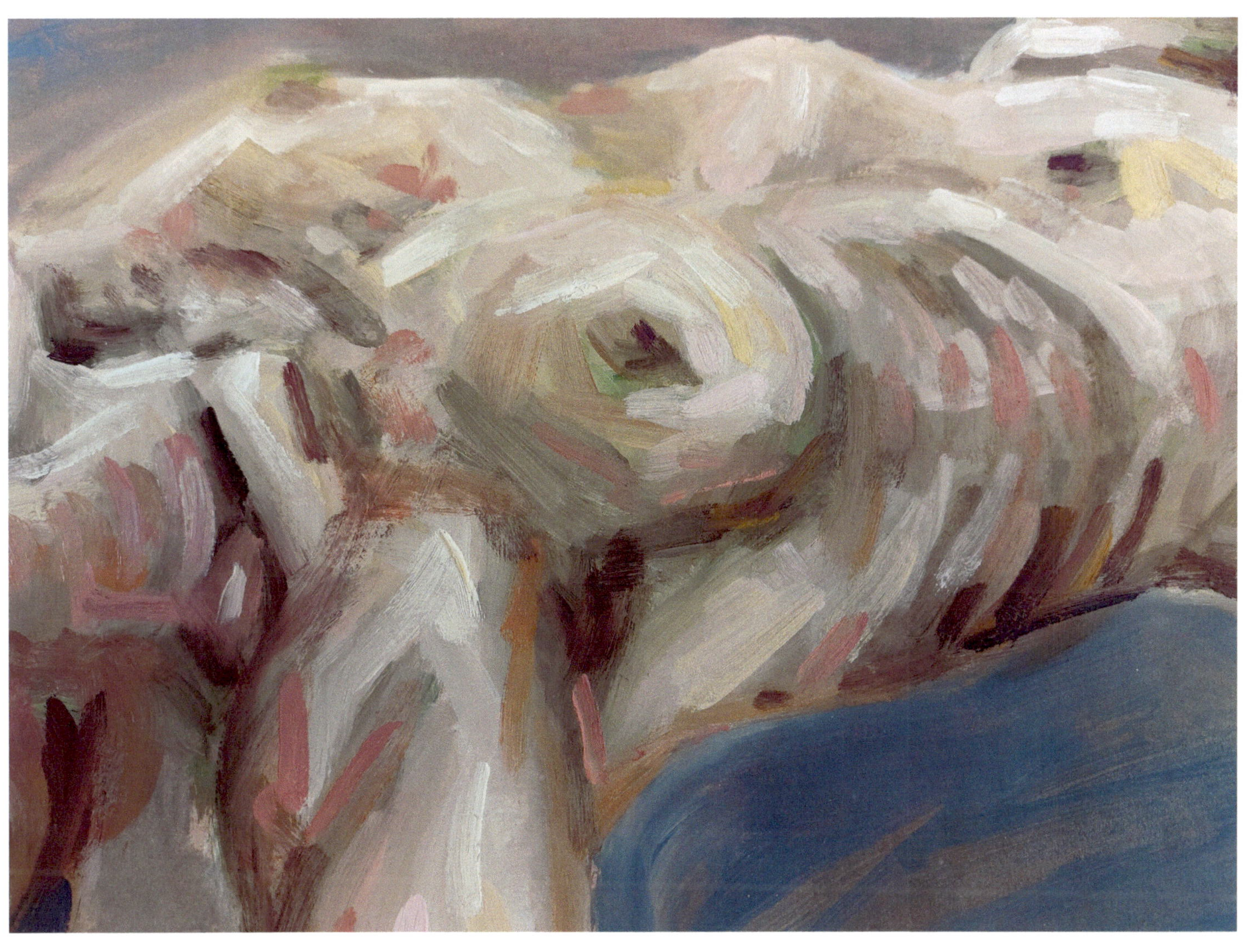

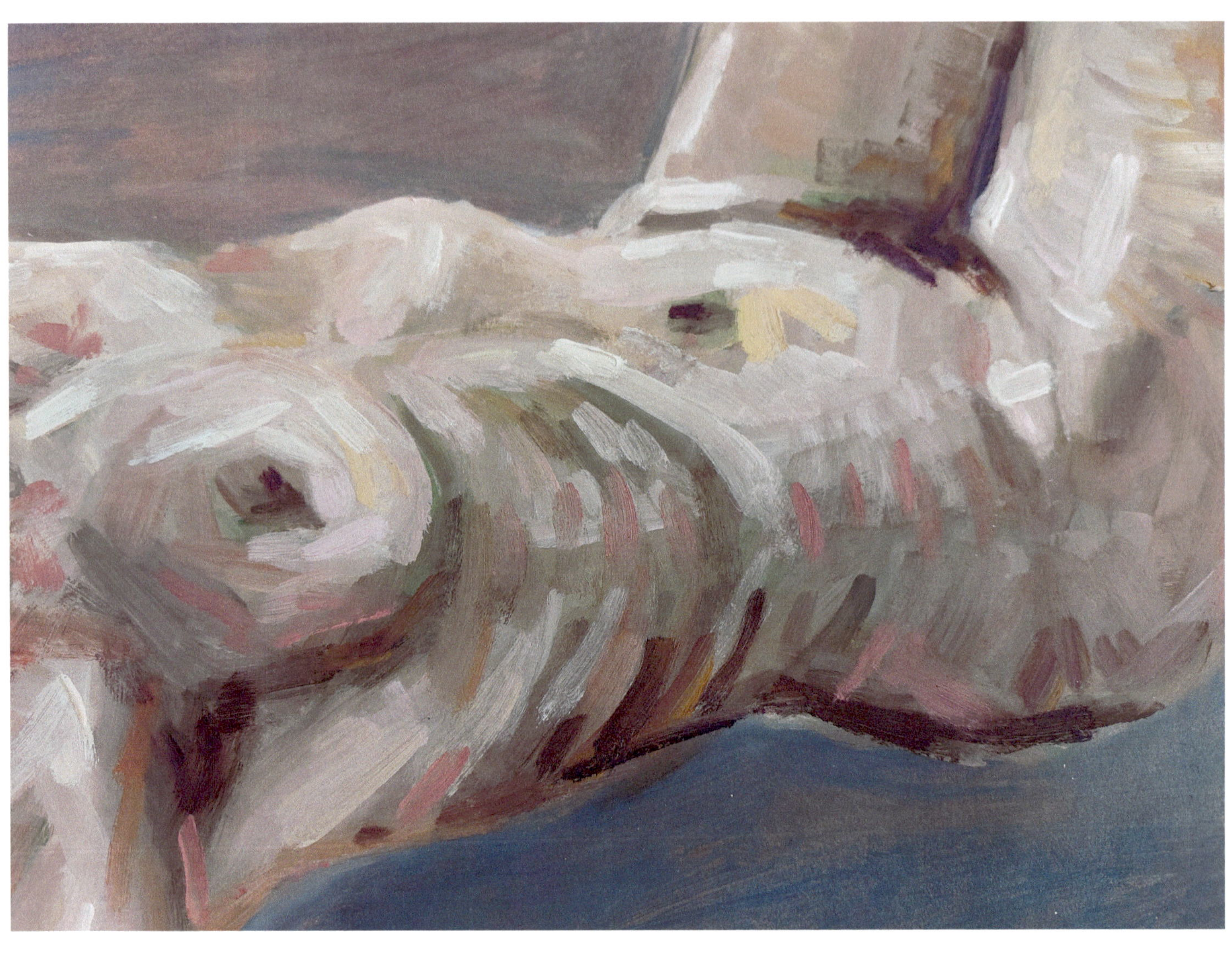

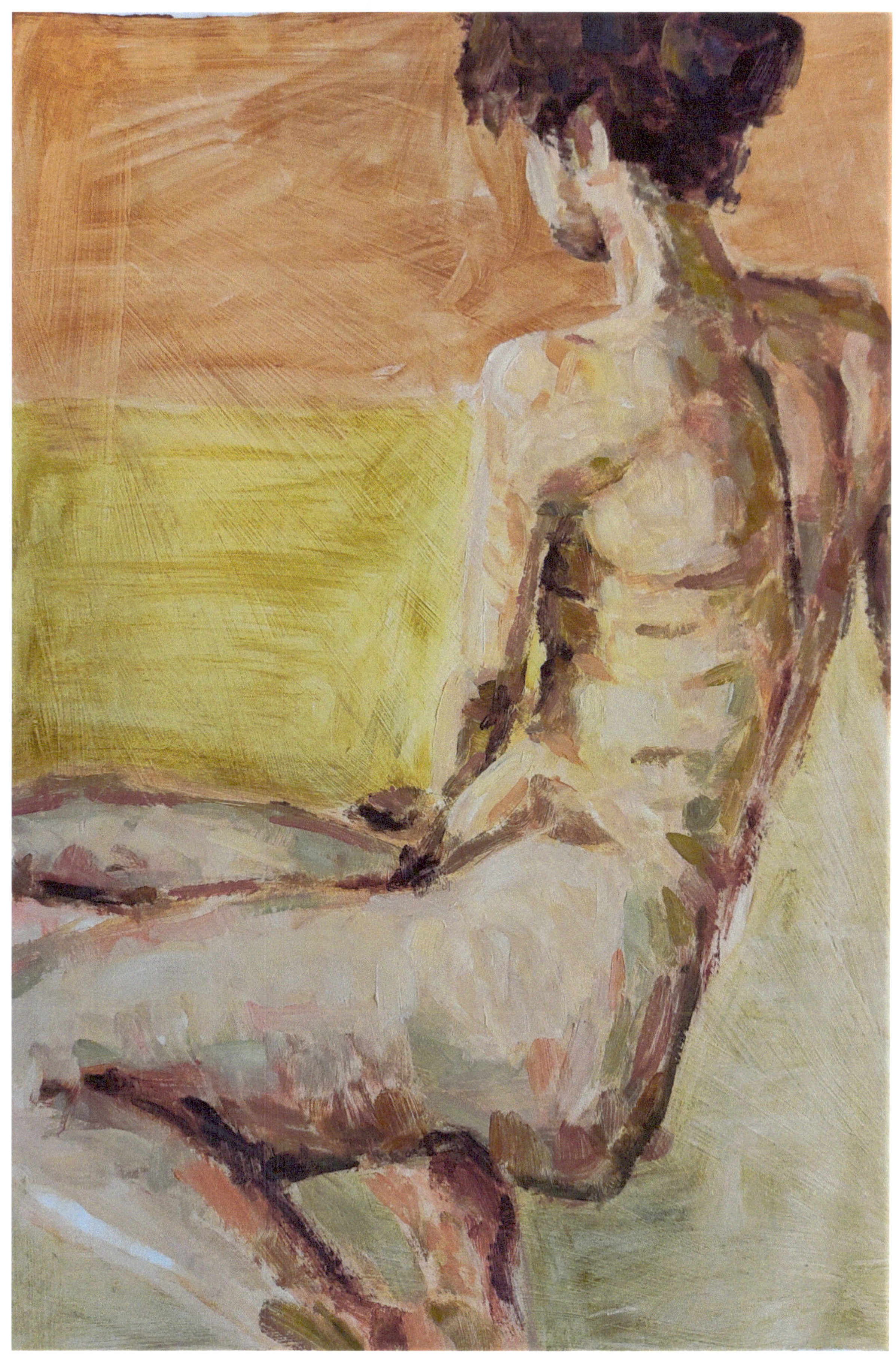

DETAIL - "ISABELLA"

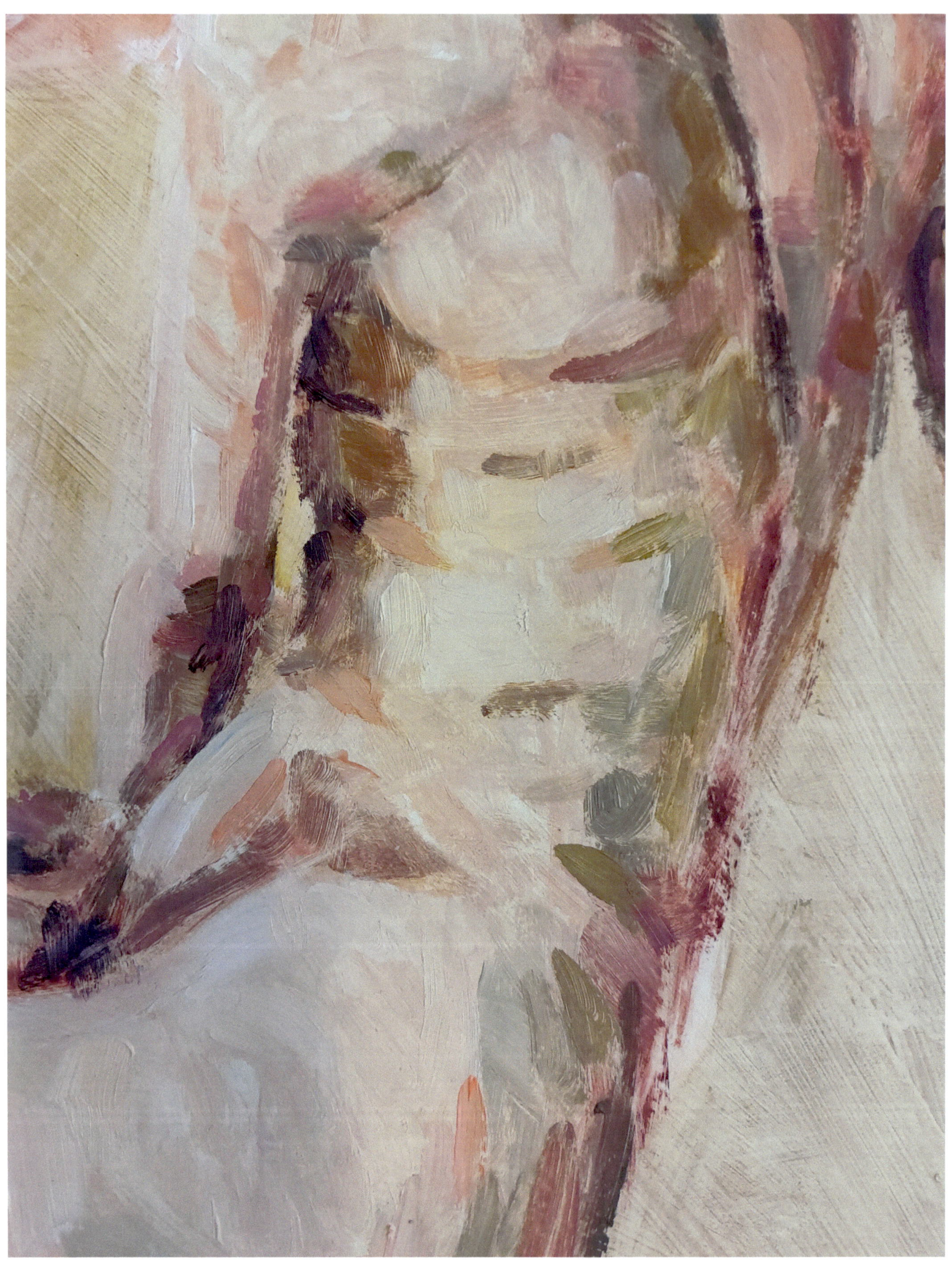

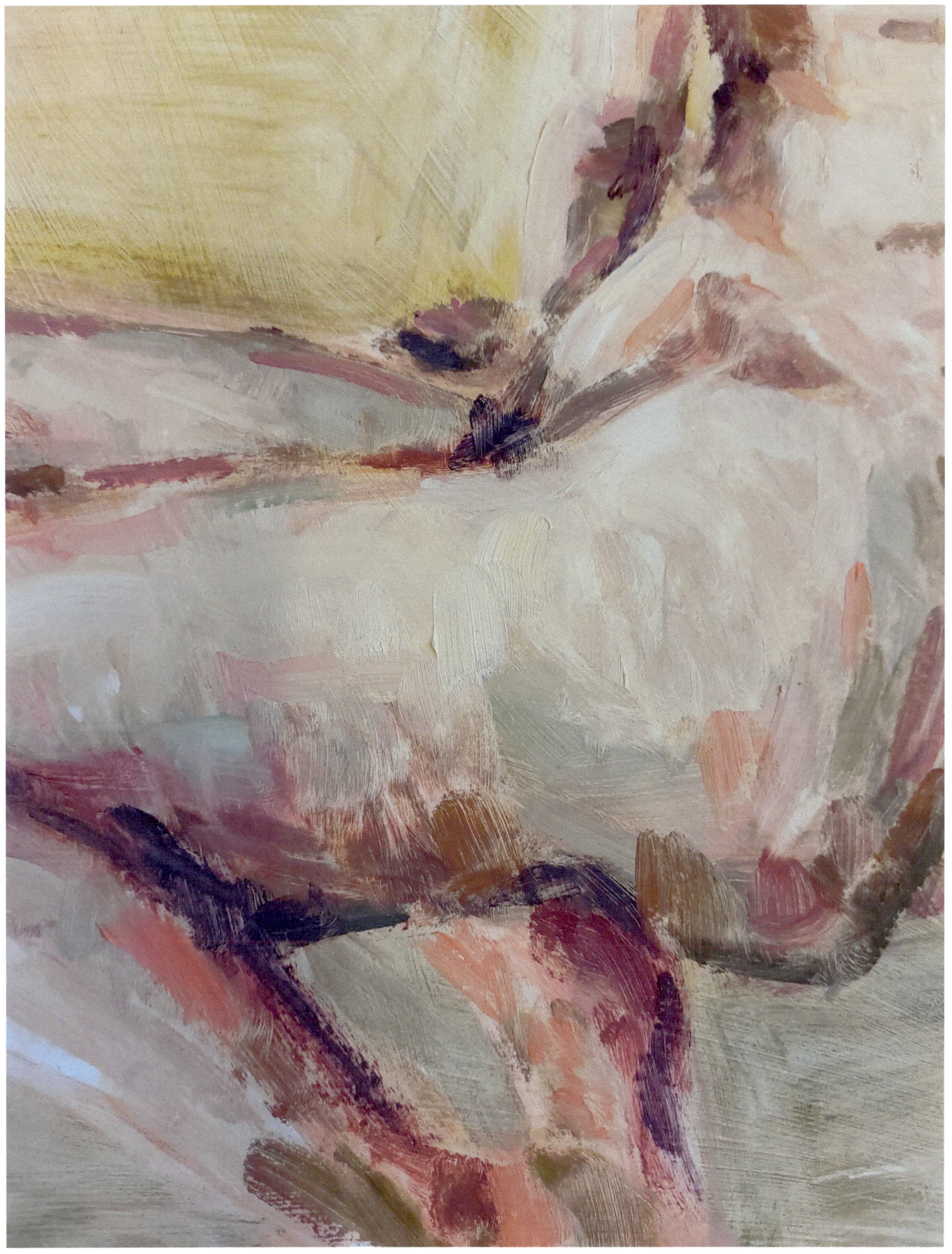

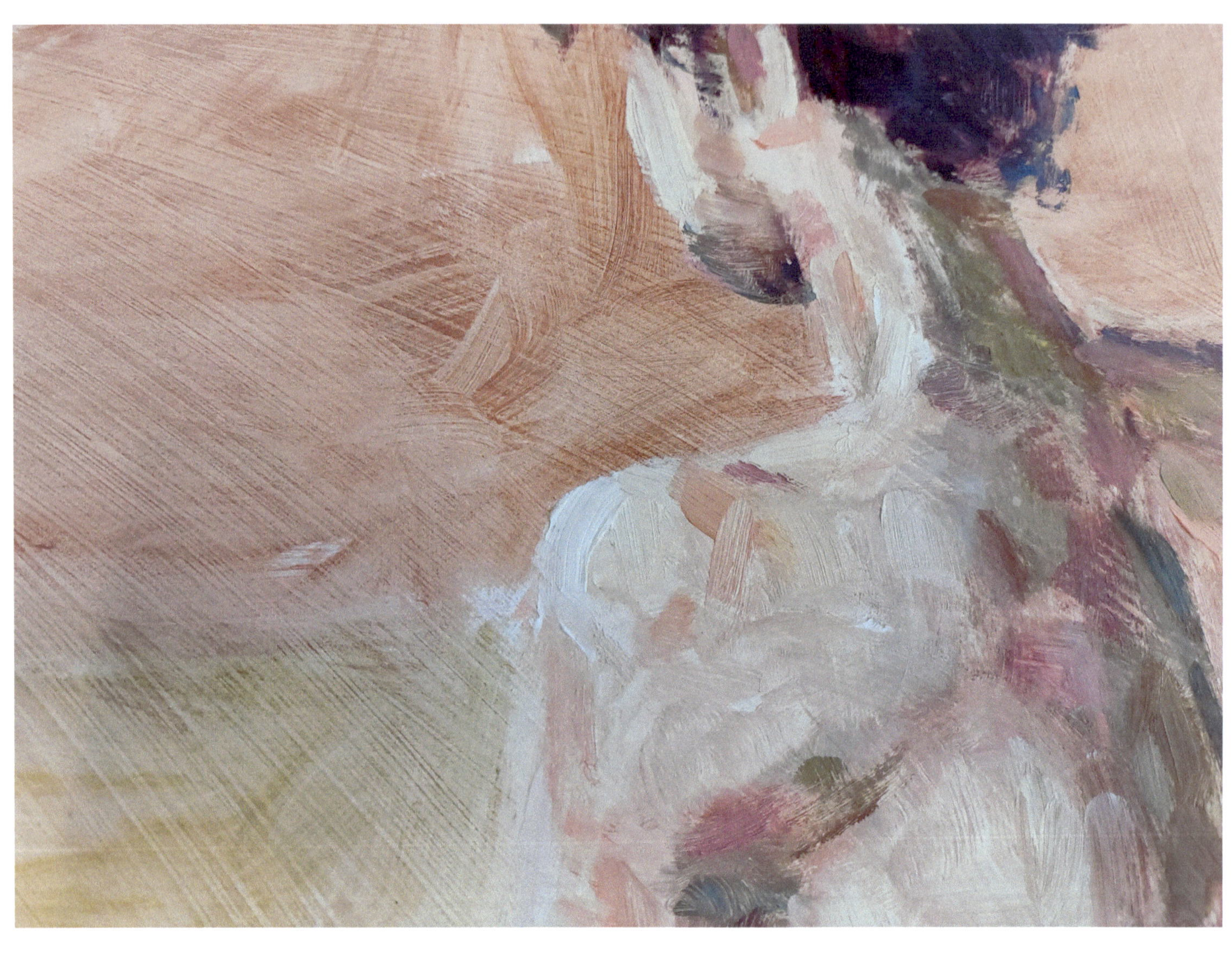

Stephen Najda

Life

- Oil on canvas -

Agora Gallery

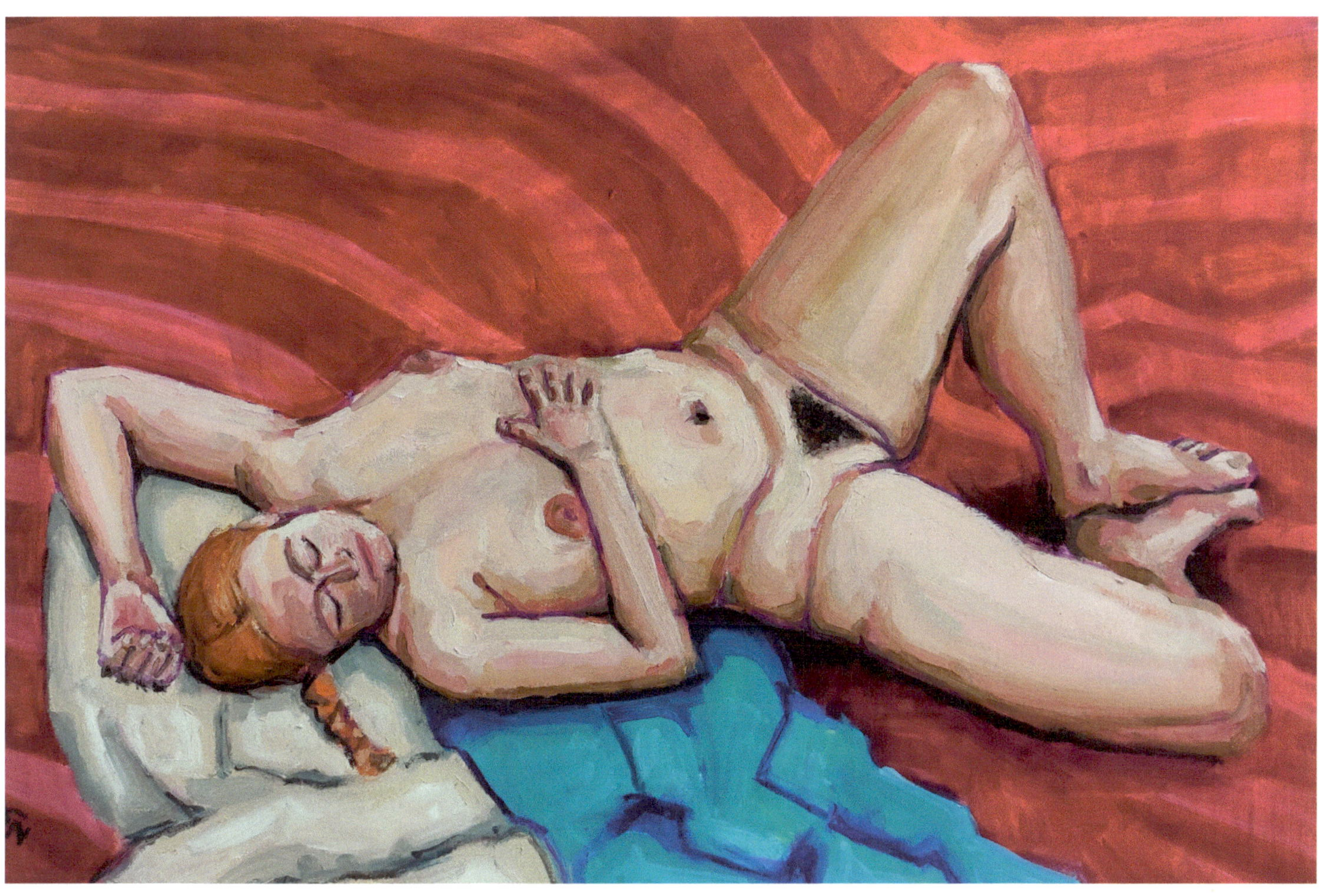

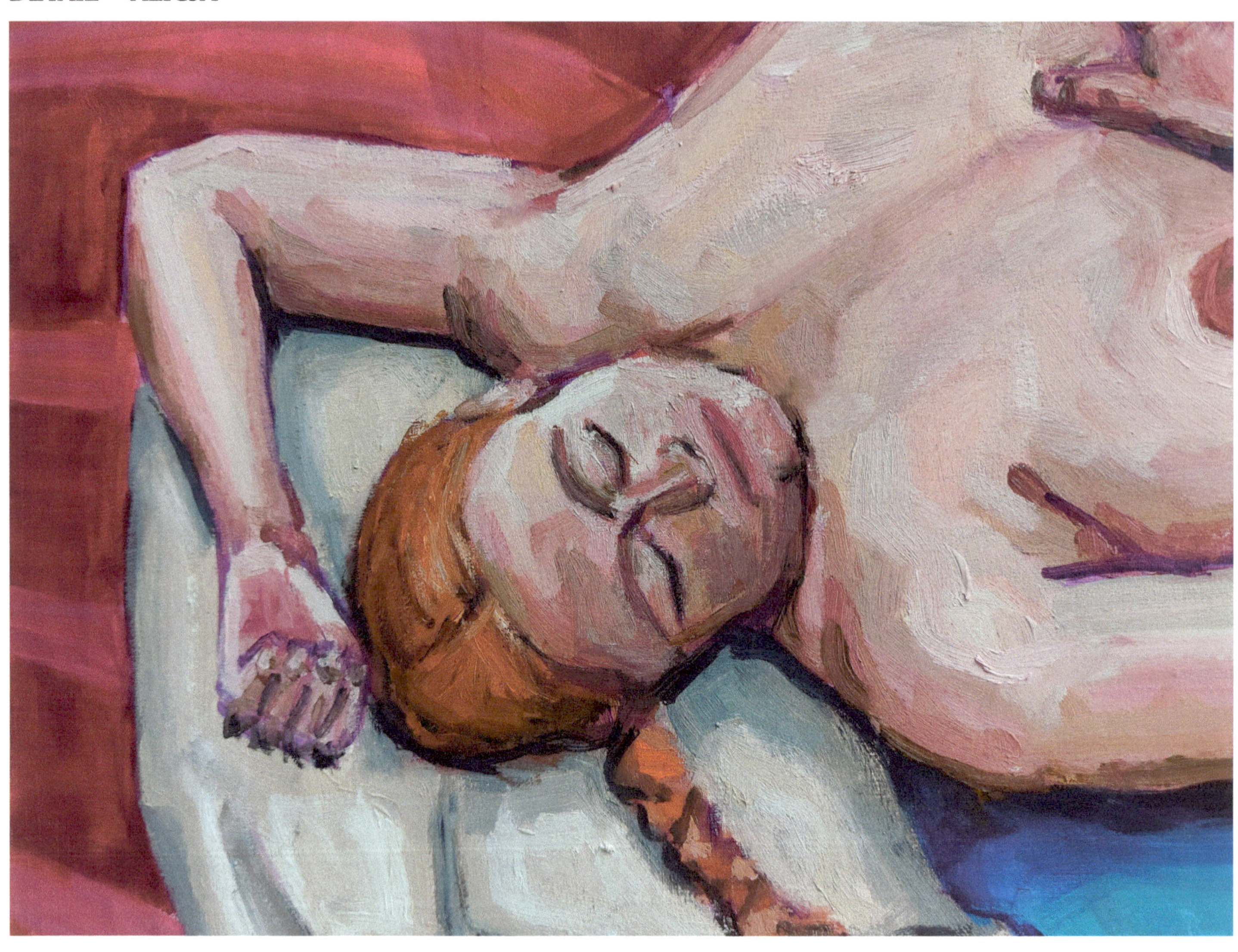

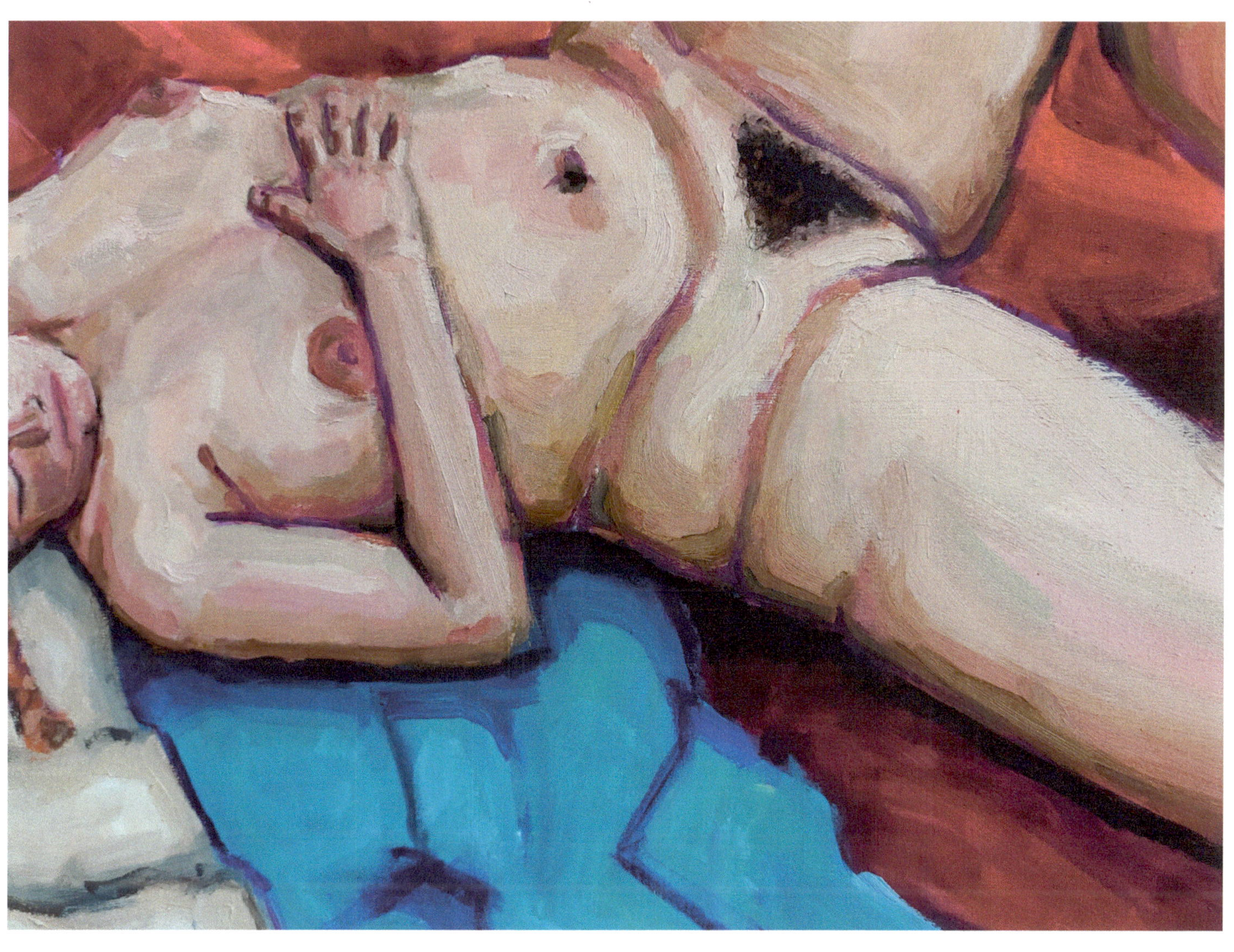

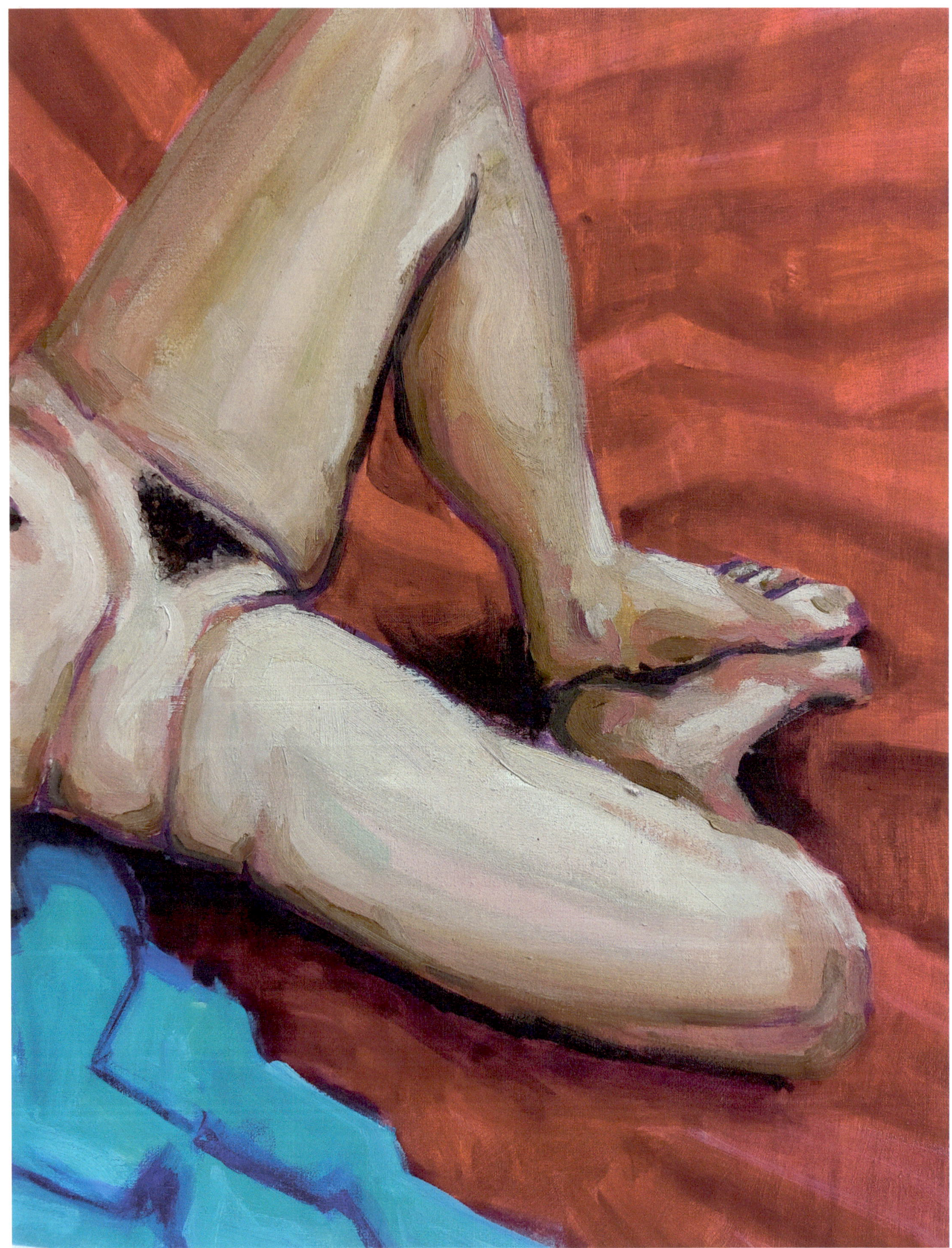

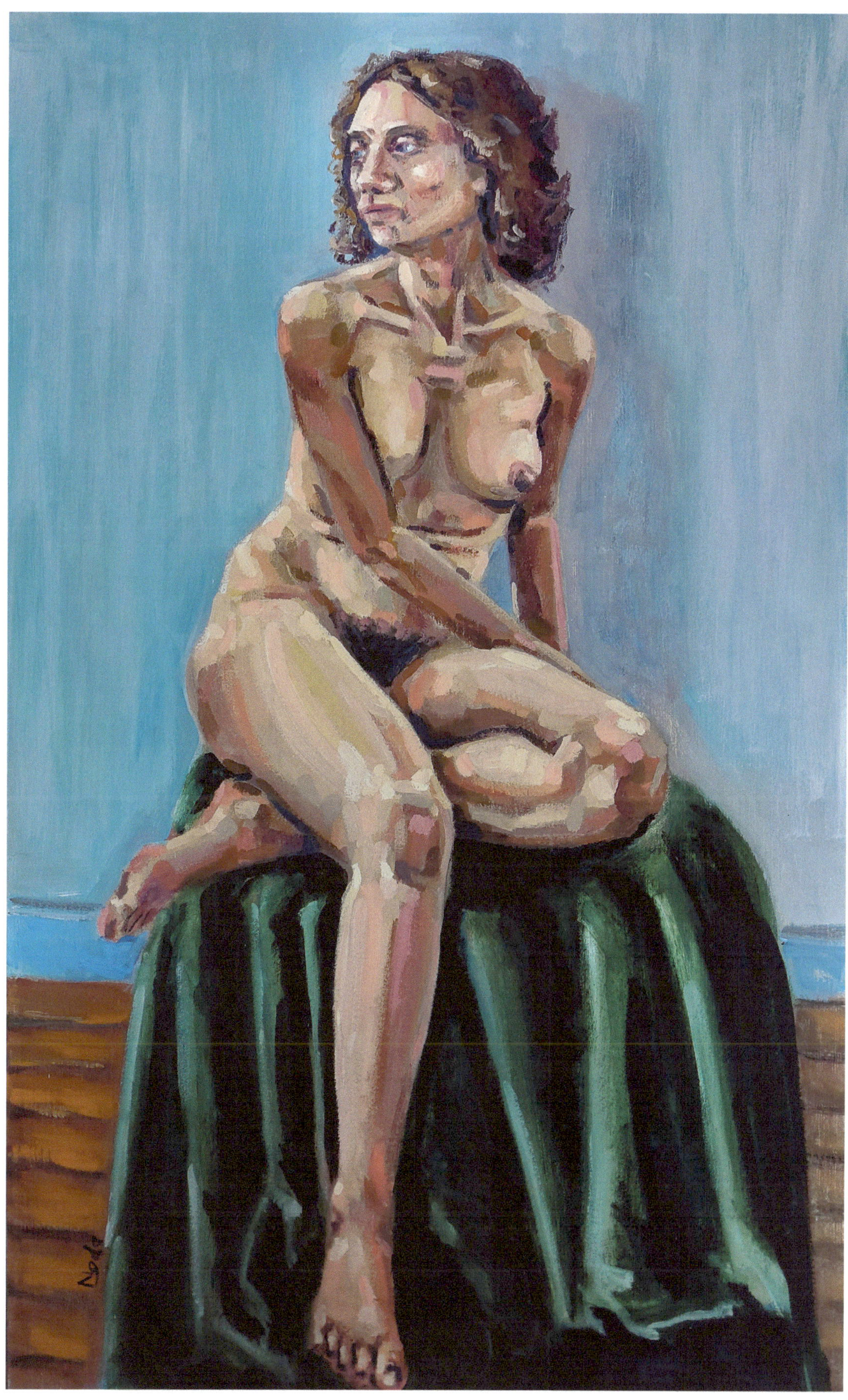

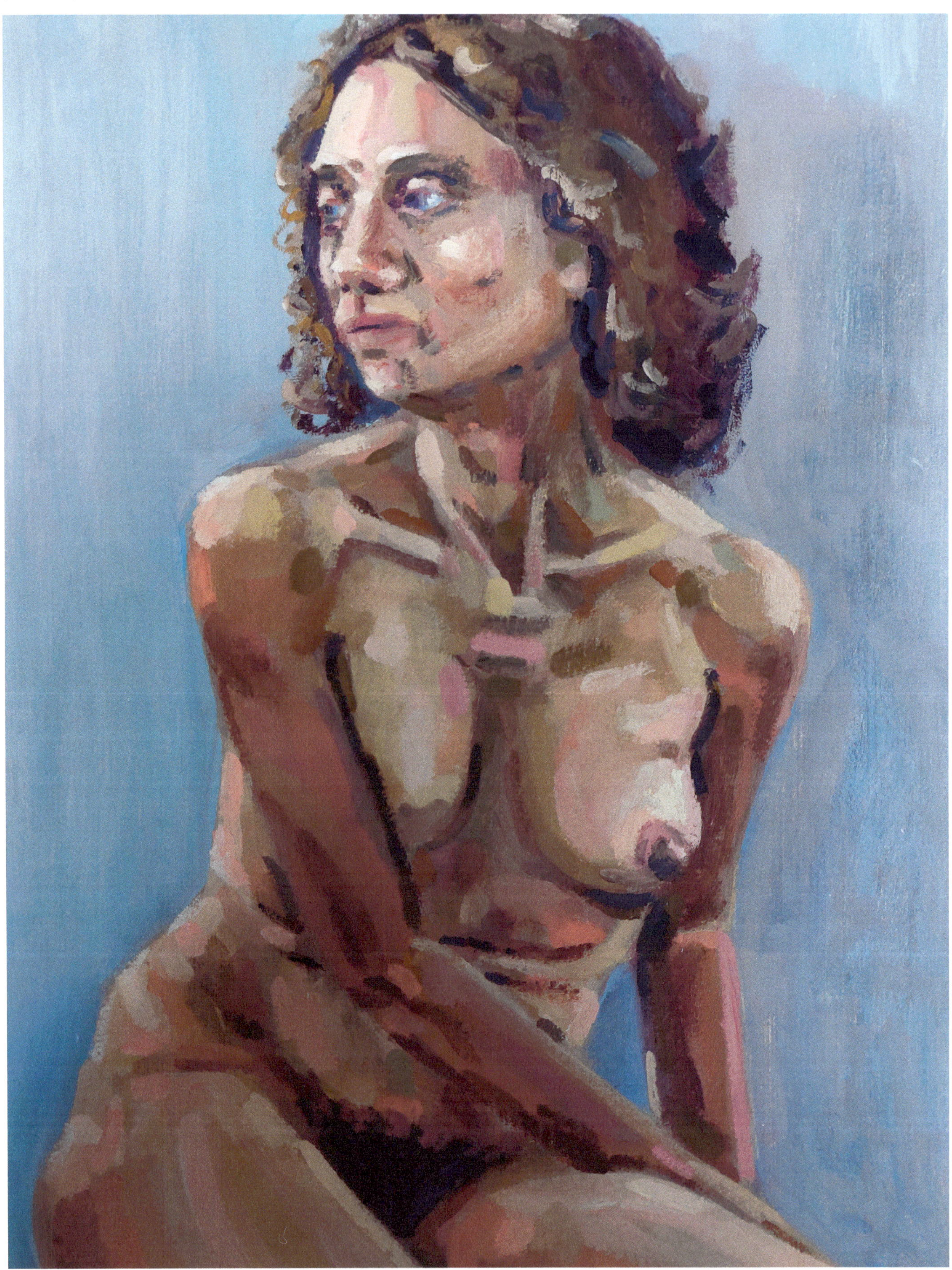

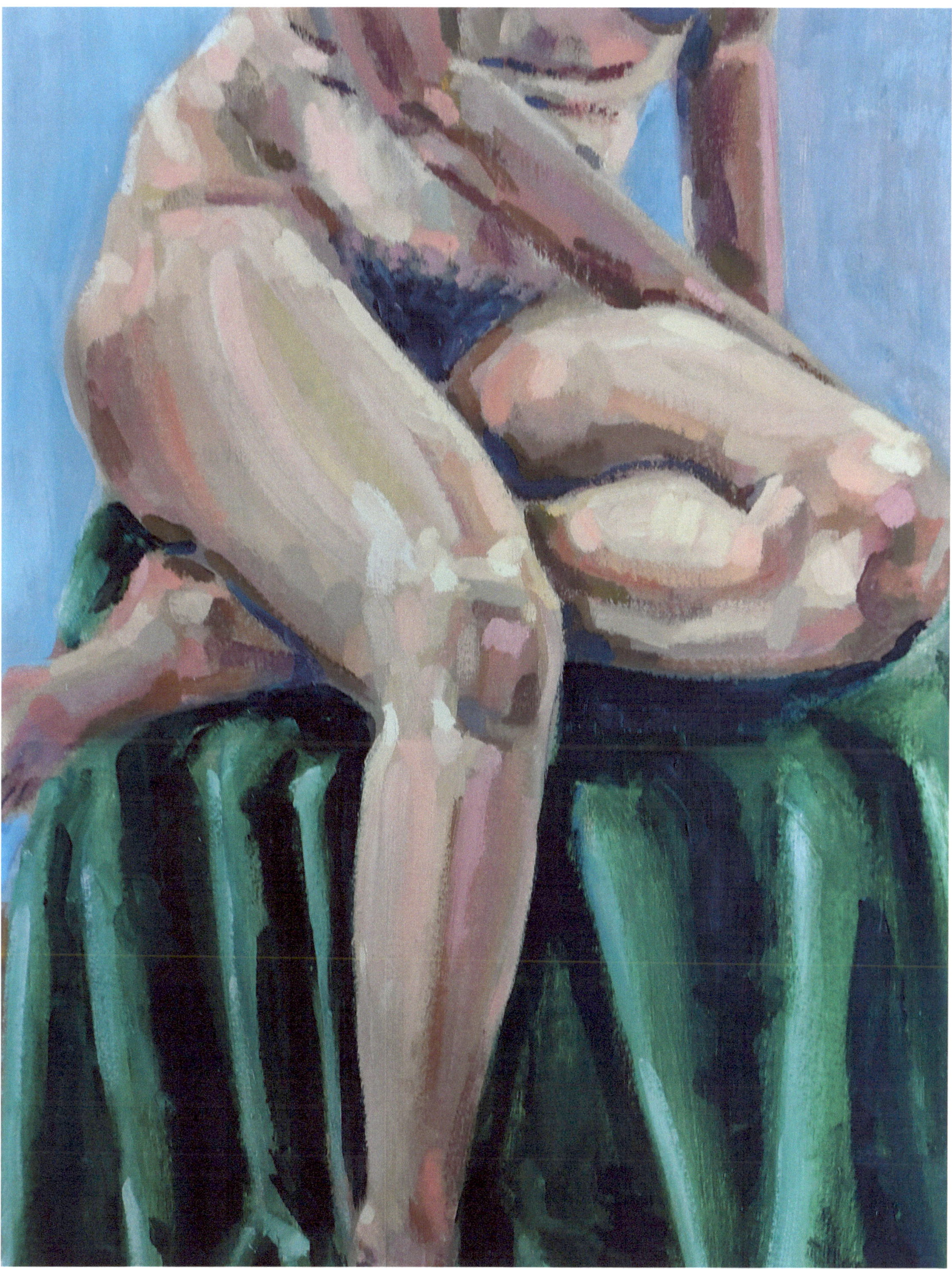

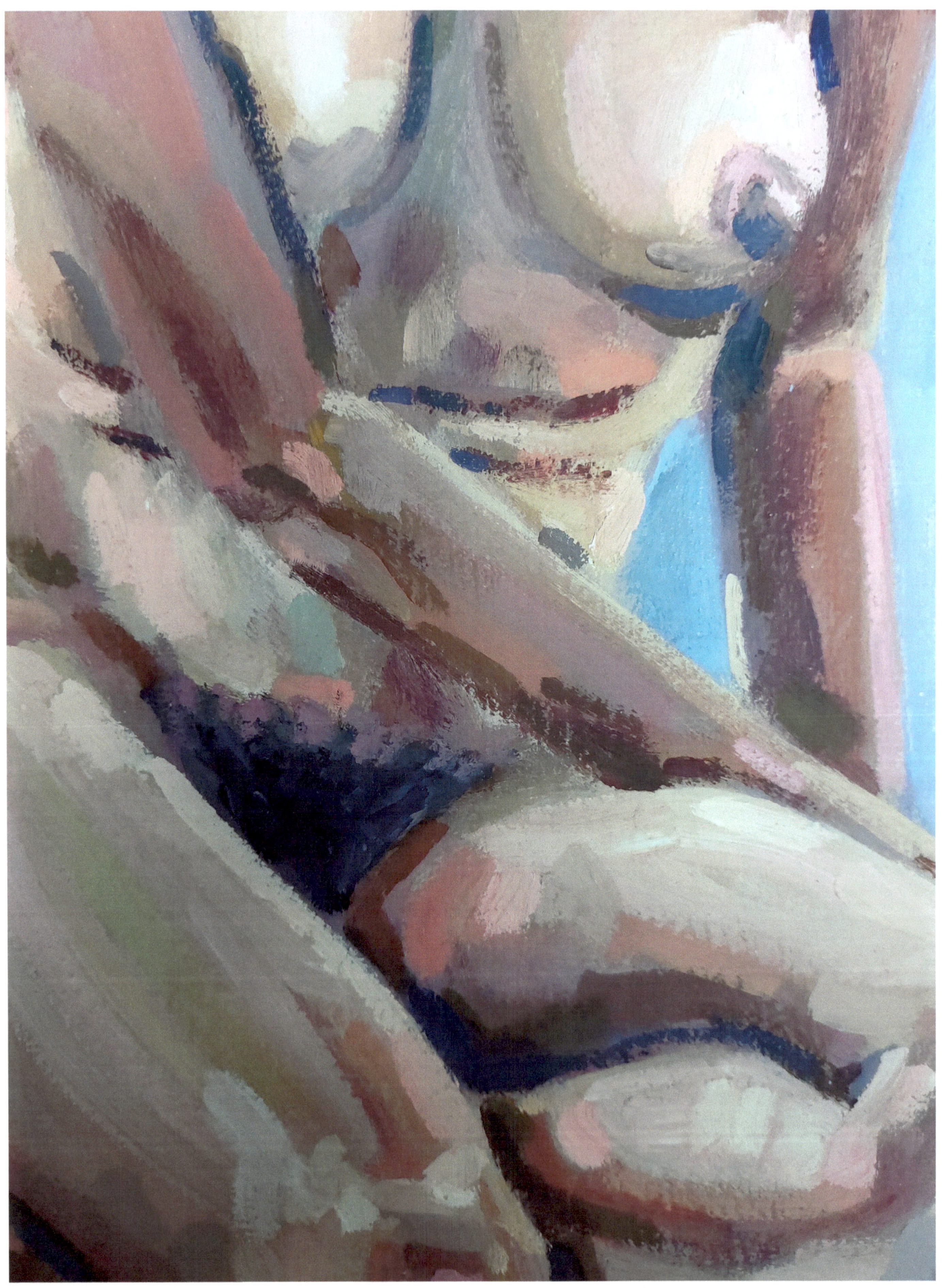

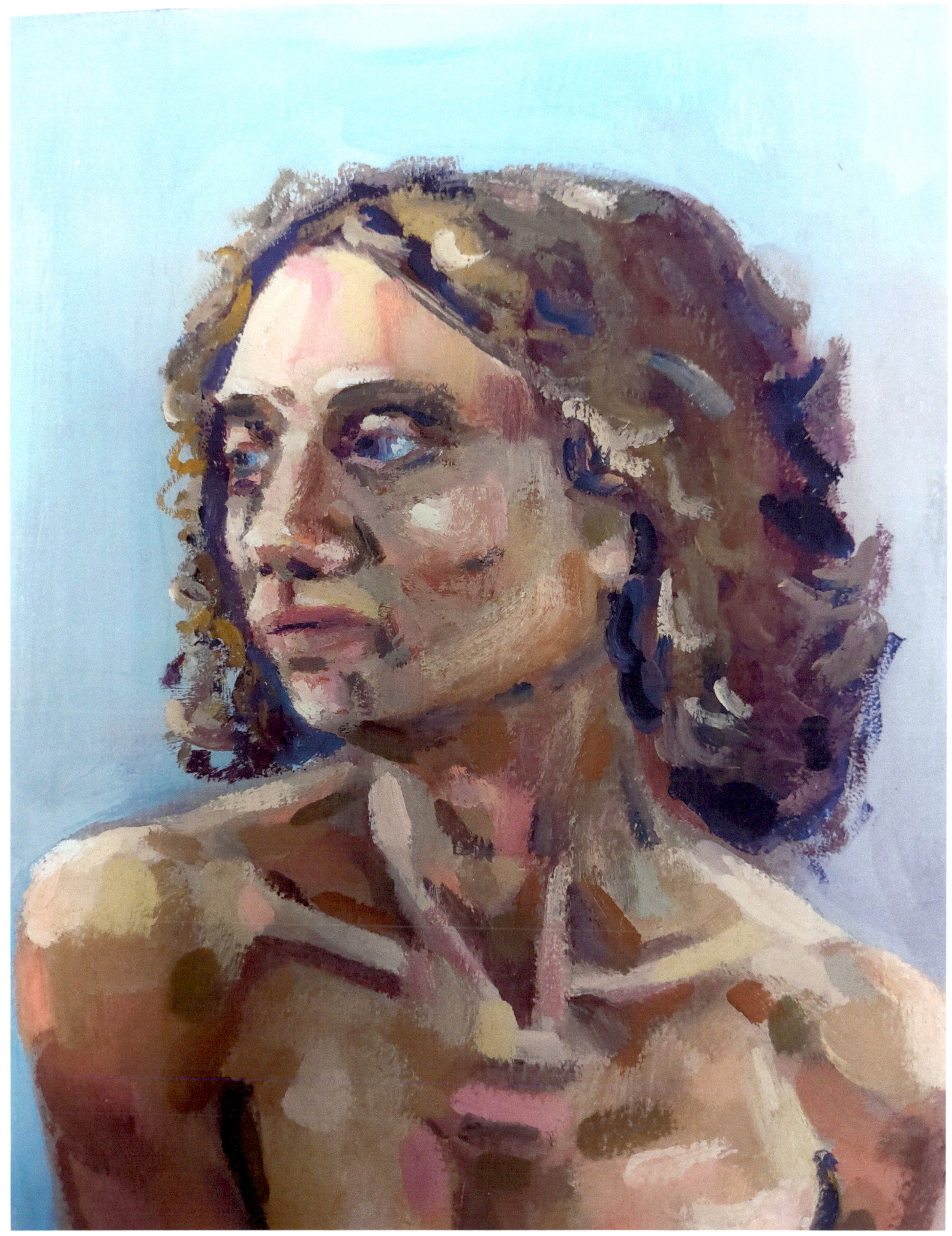

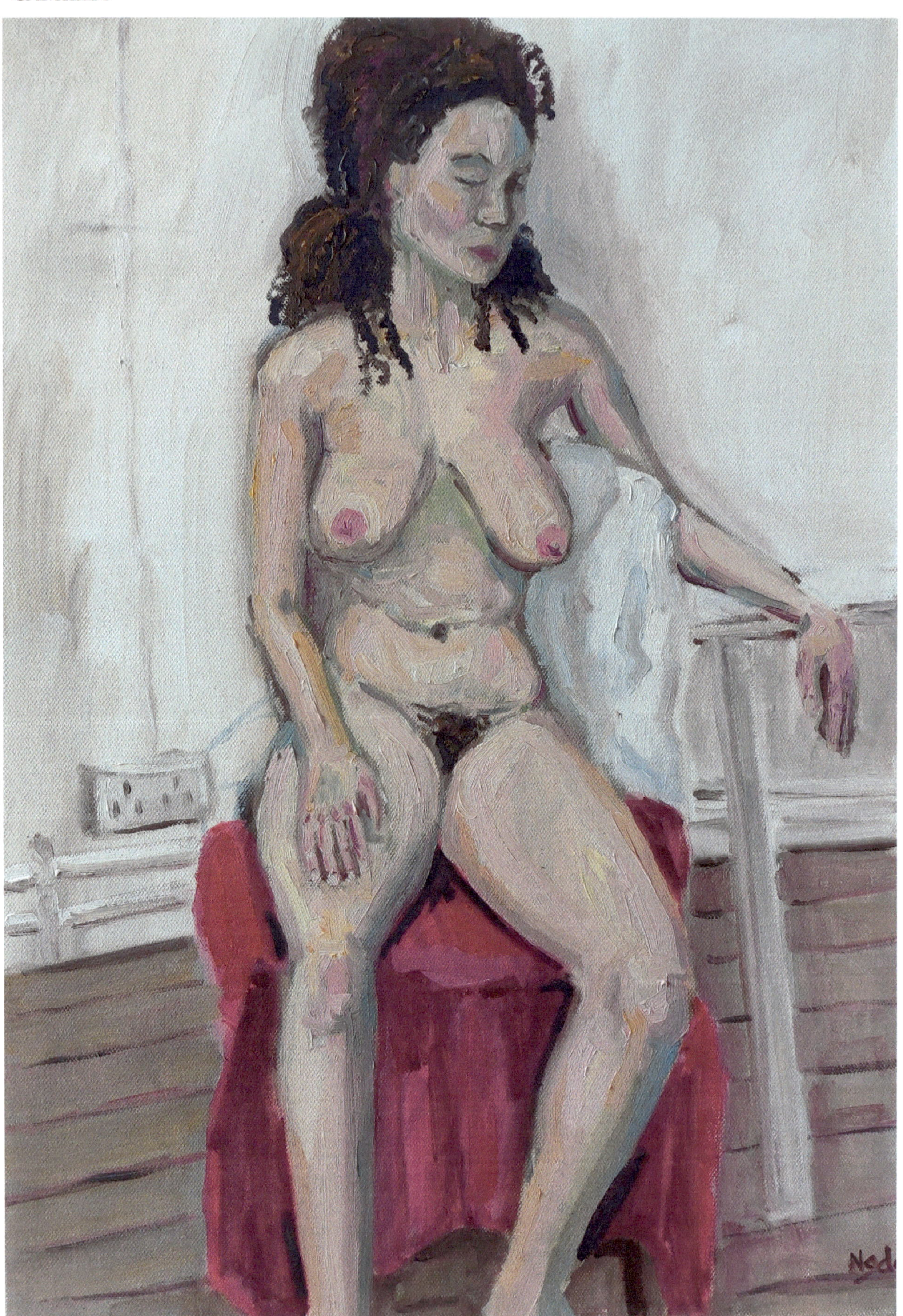

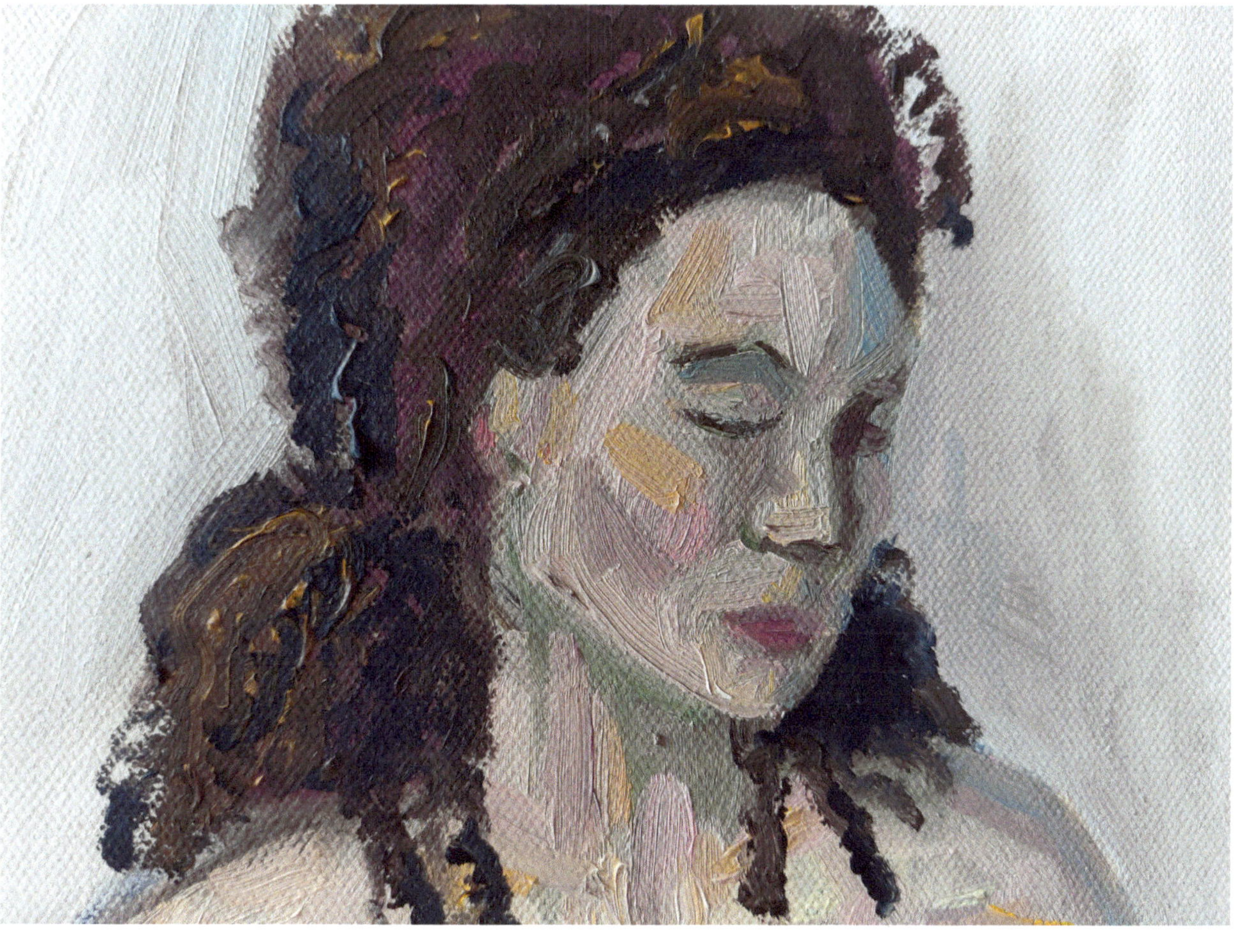

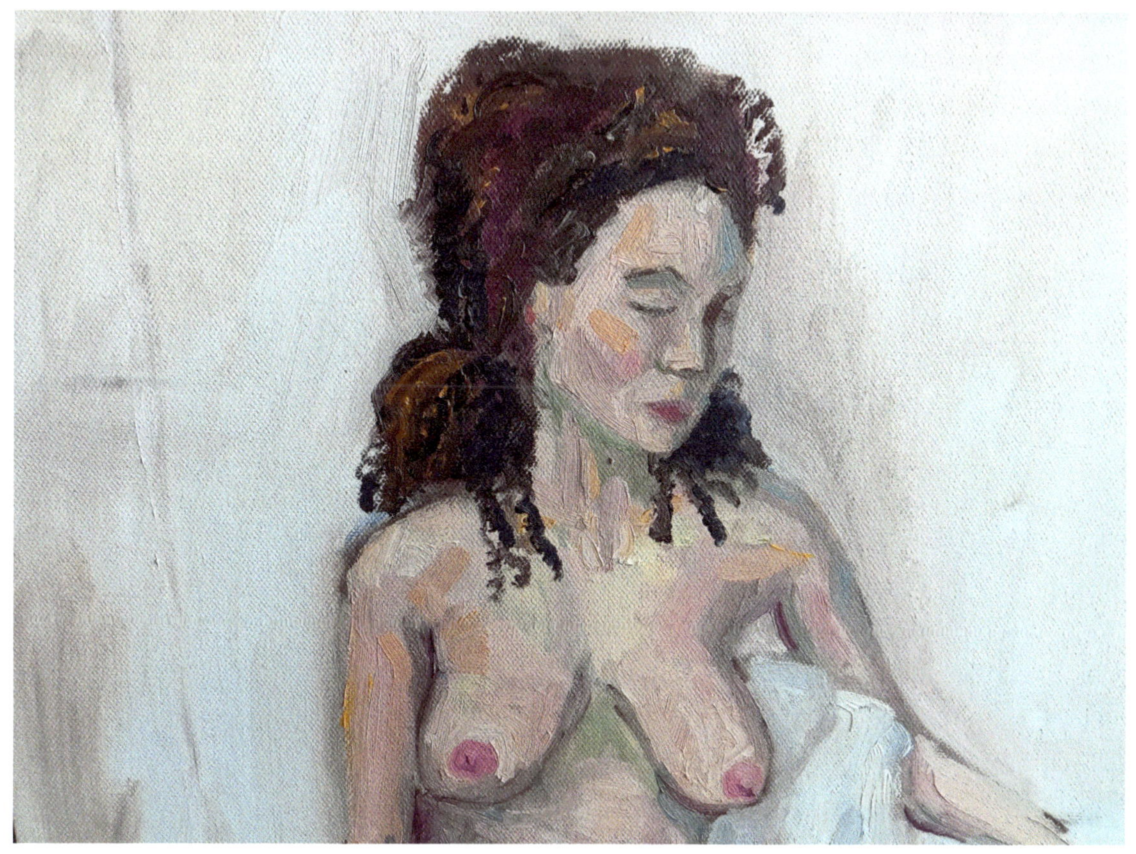

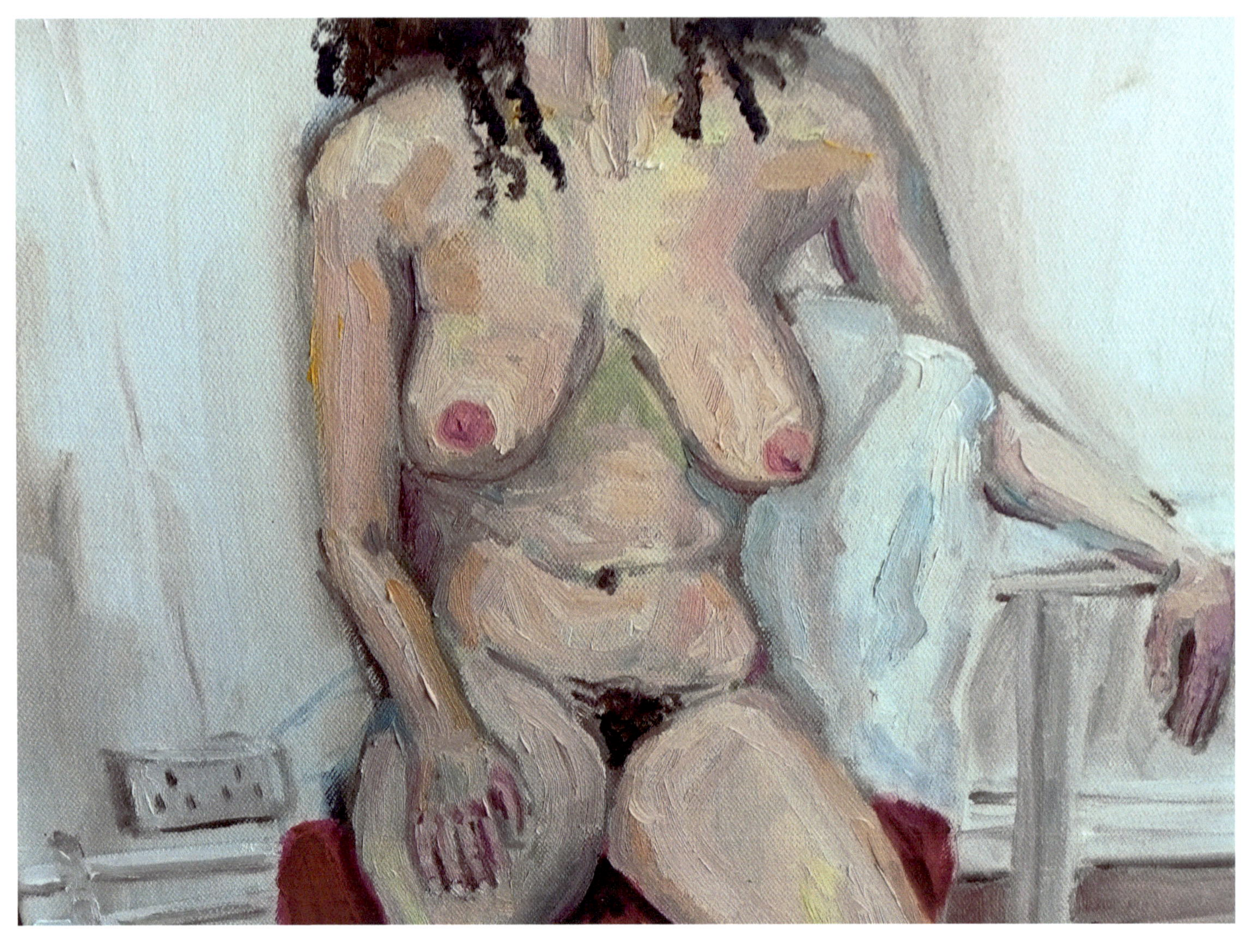

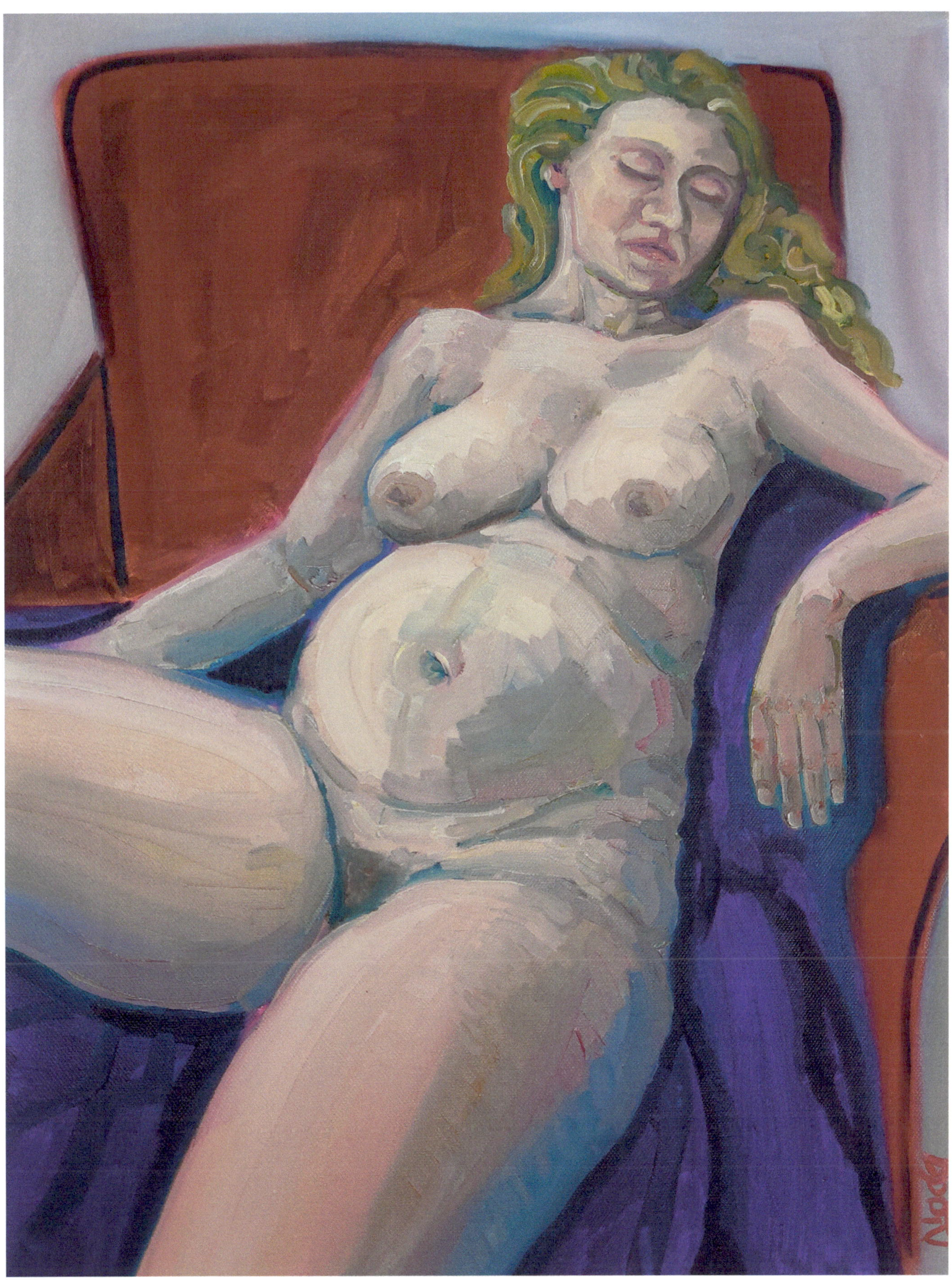

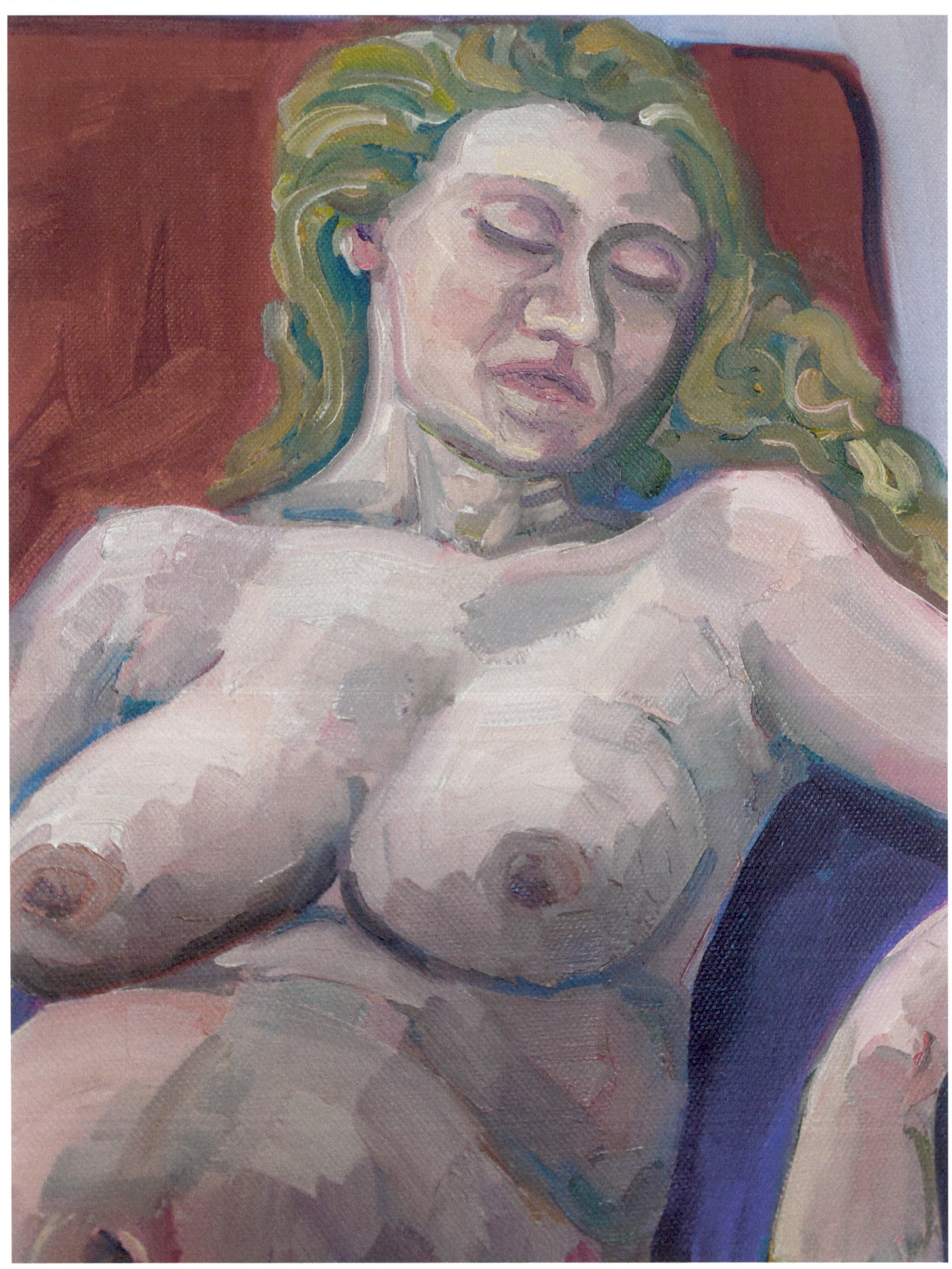

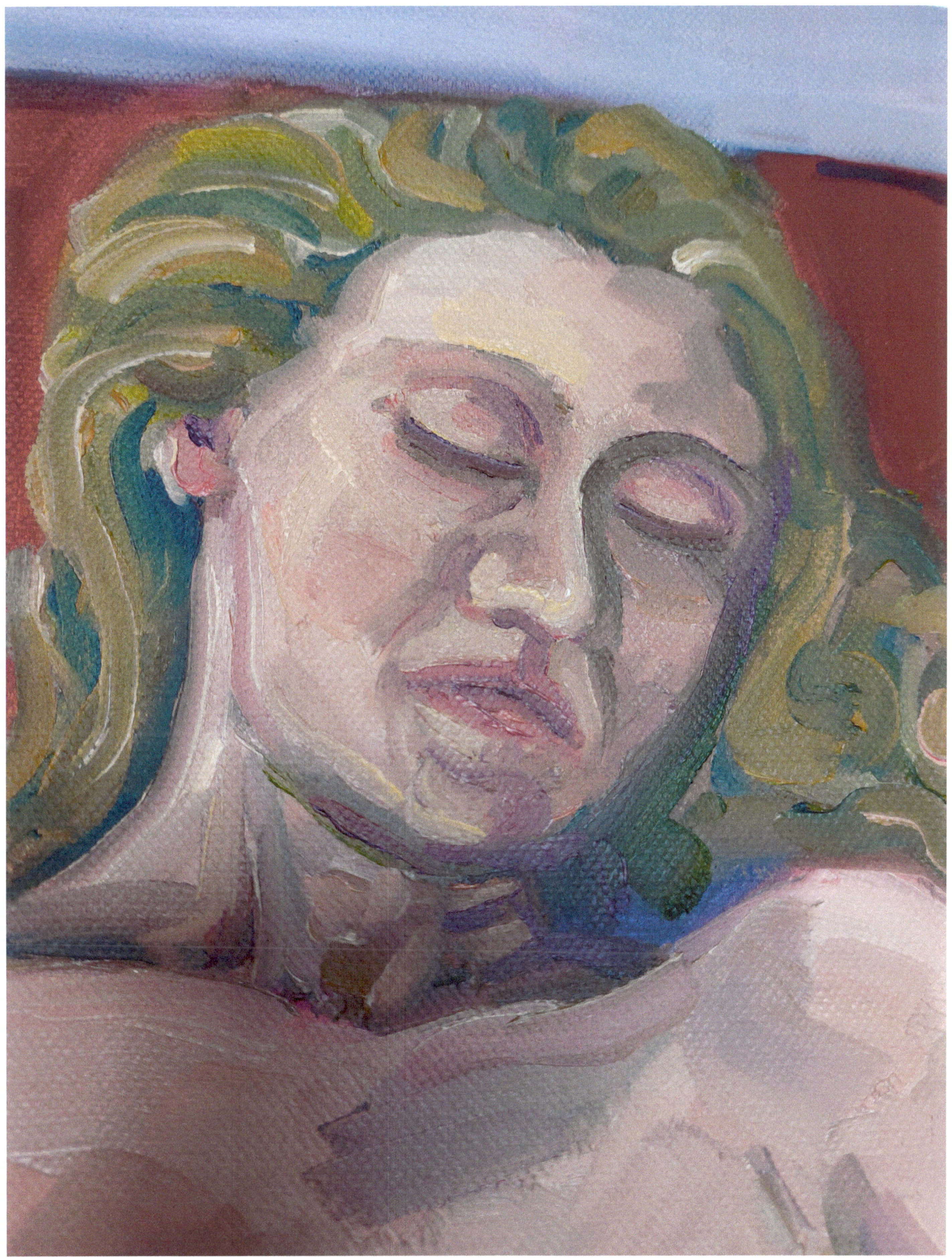

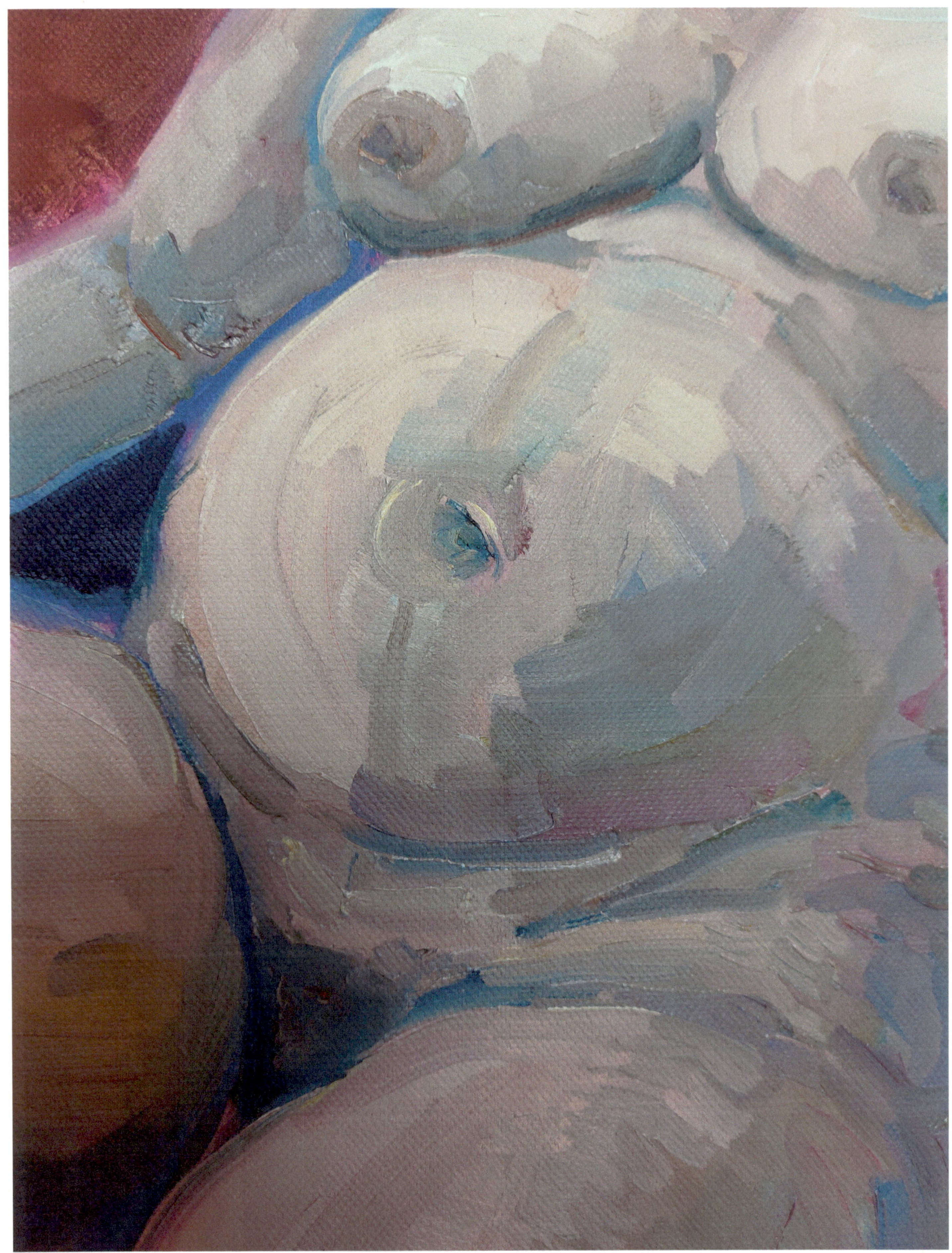

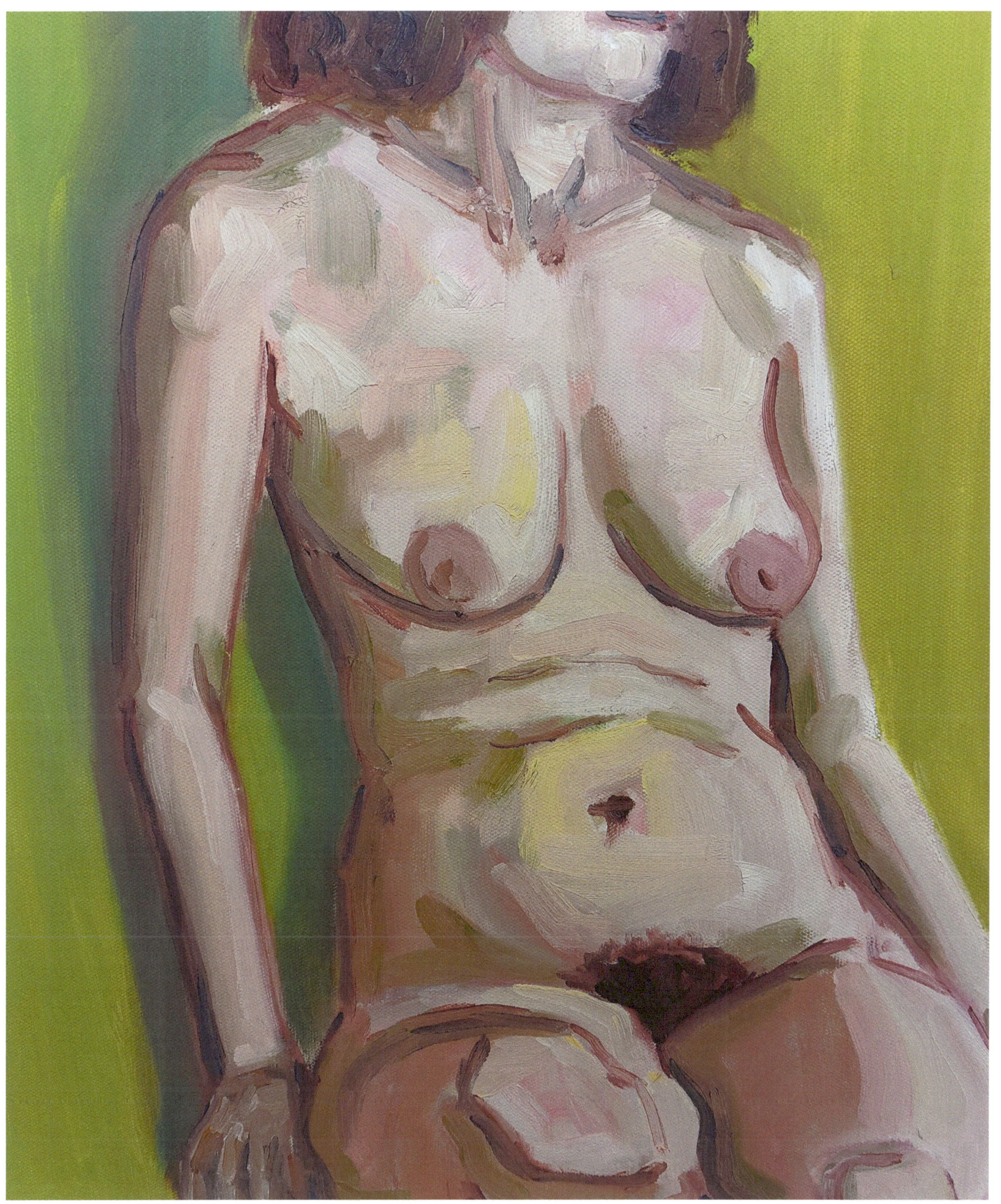

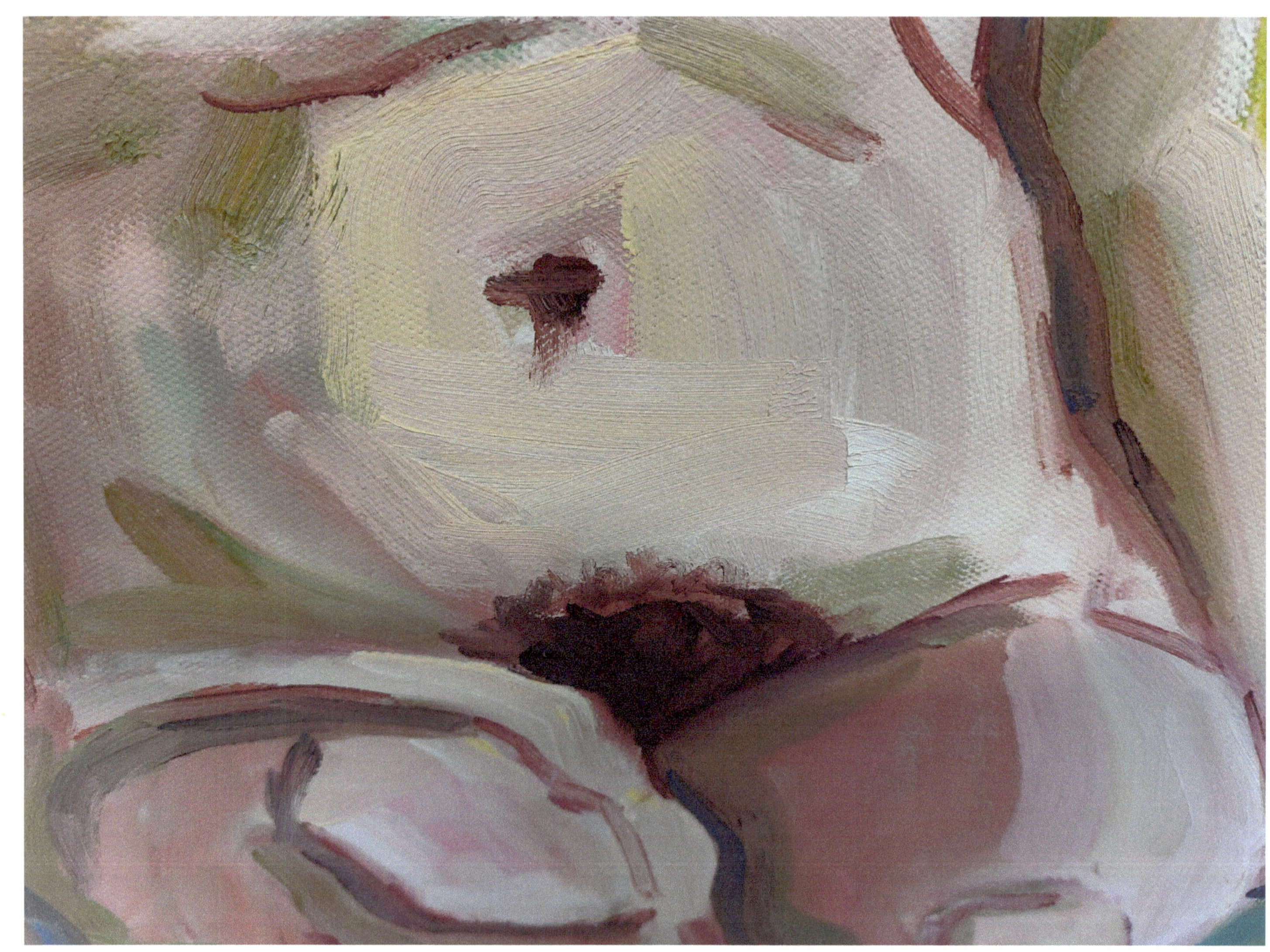

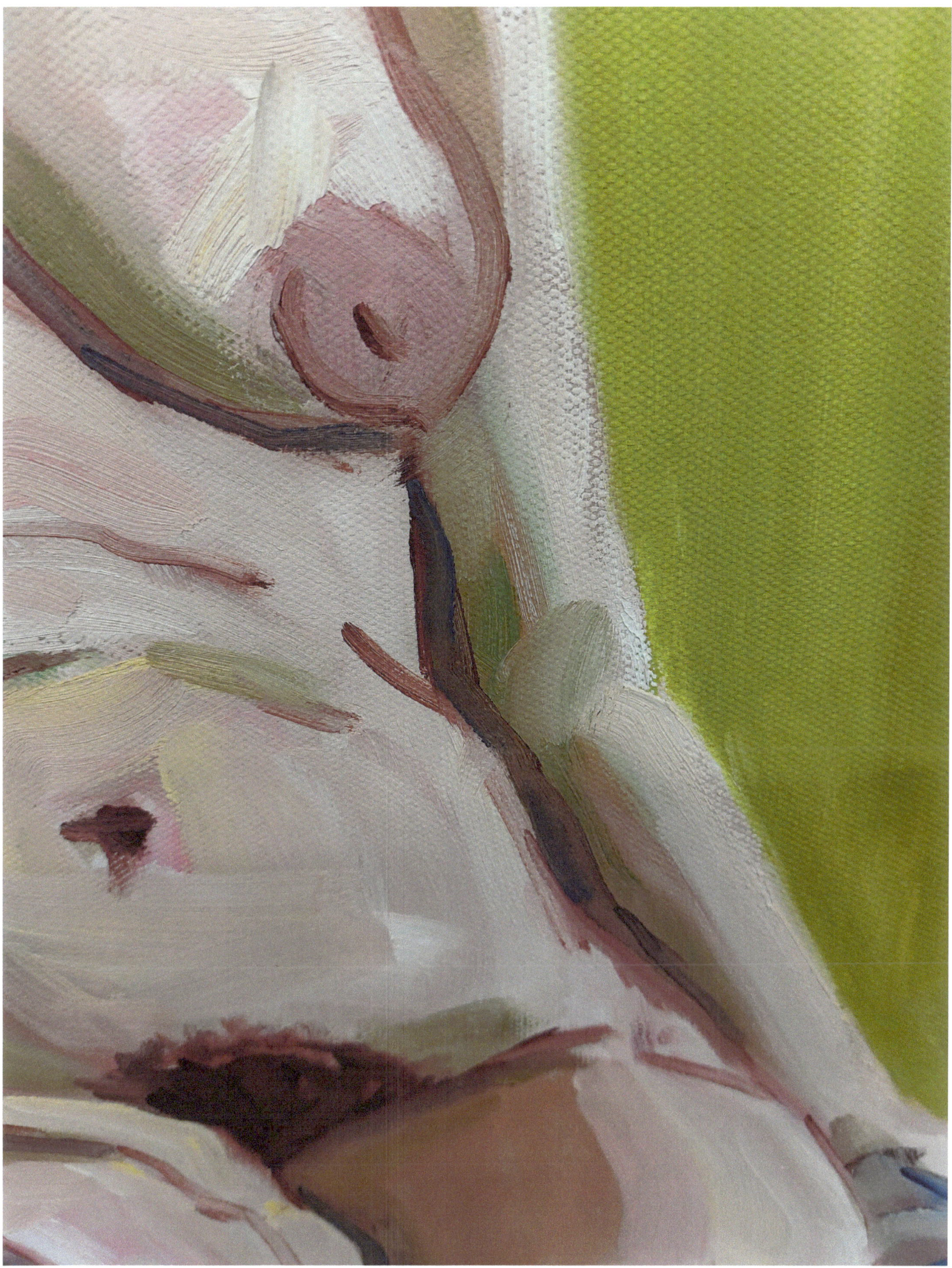

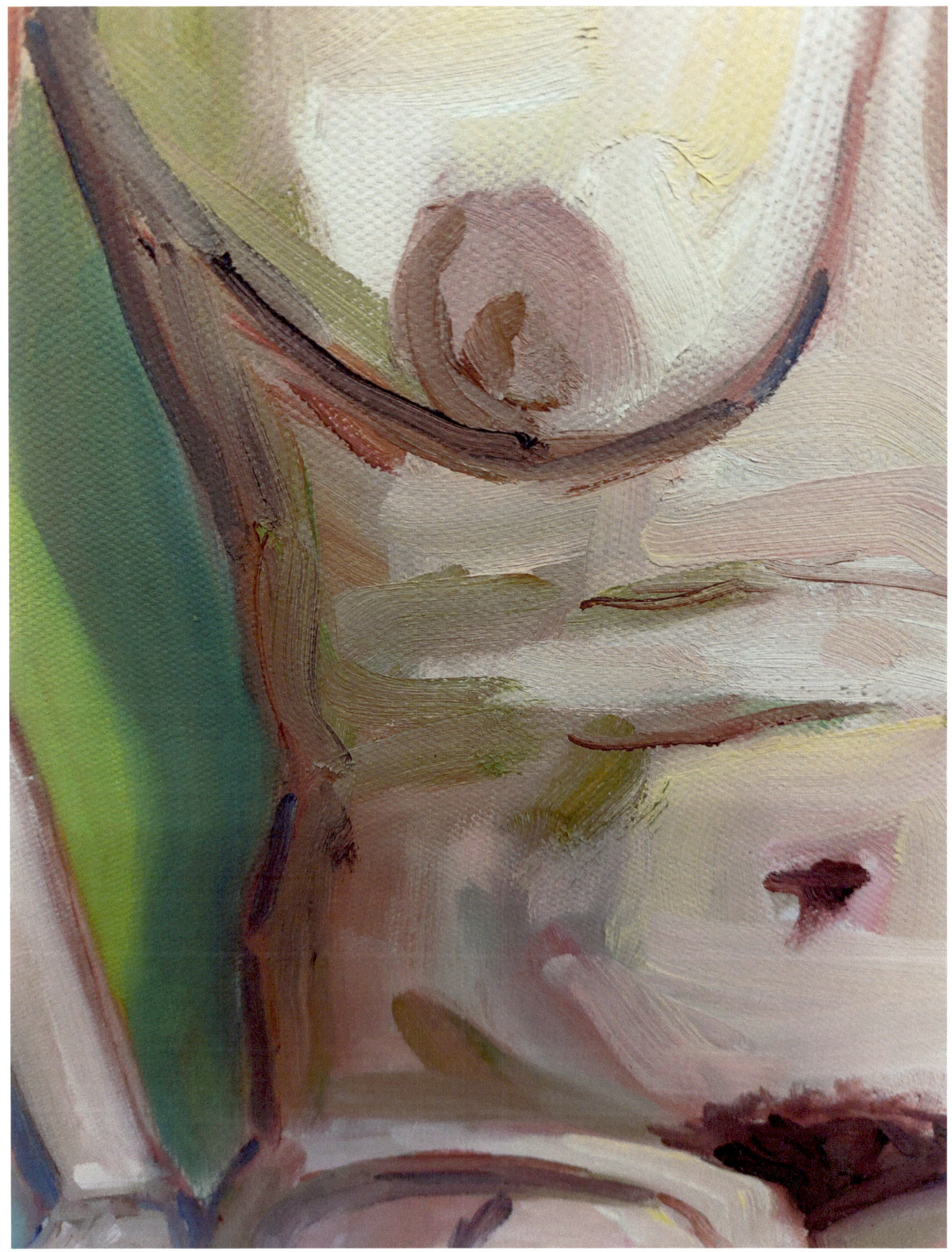

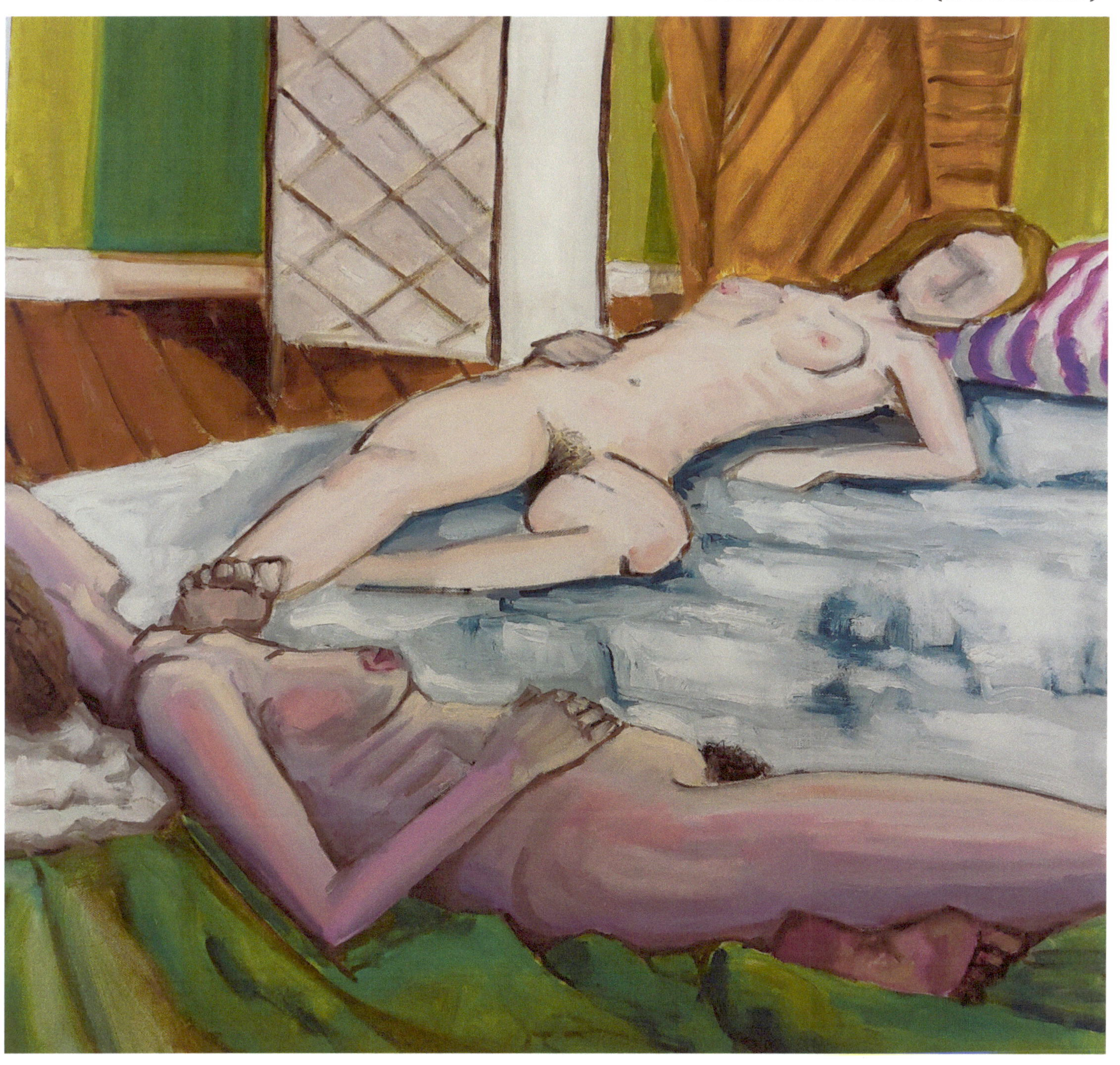

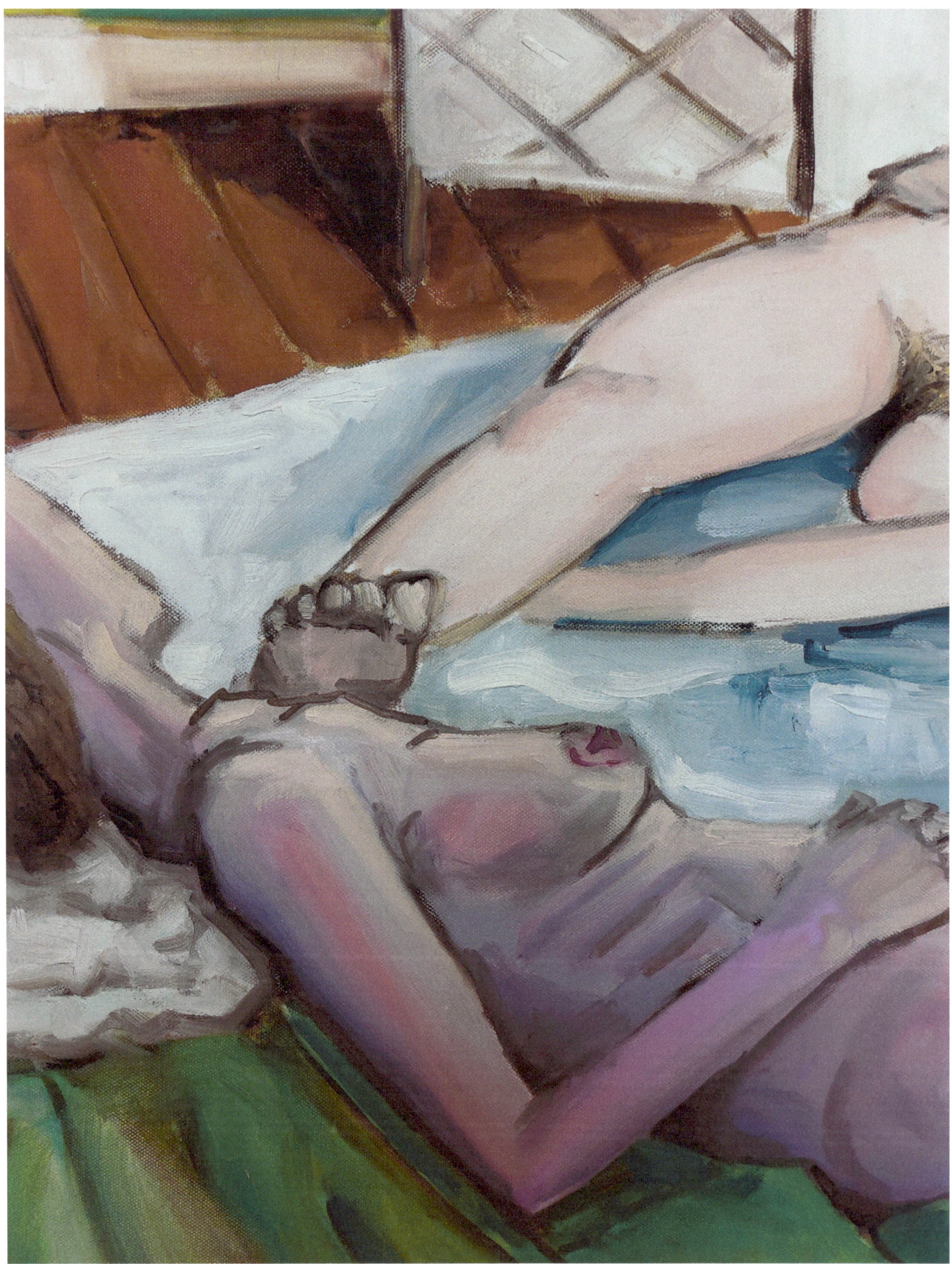

DETAIL - "JULIA AND BRIONY (UNFINISHED)"

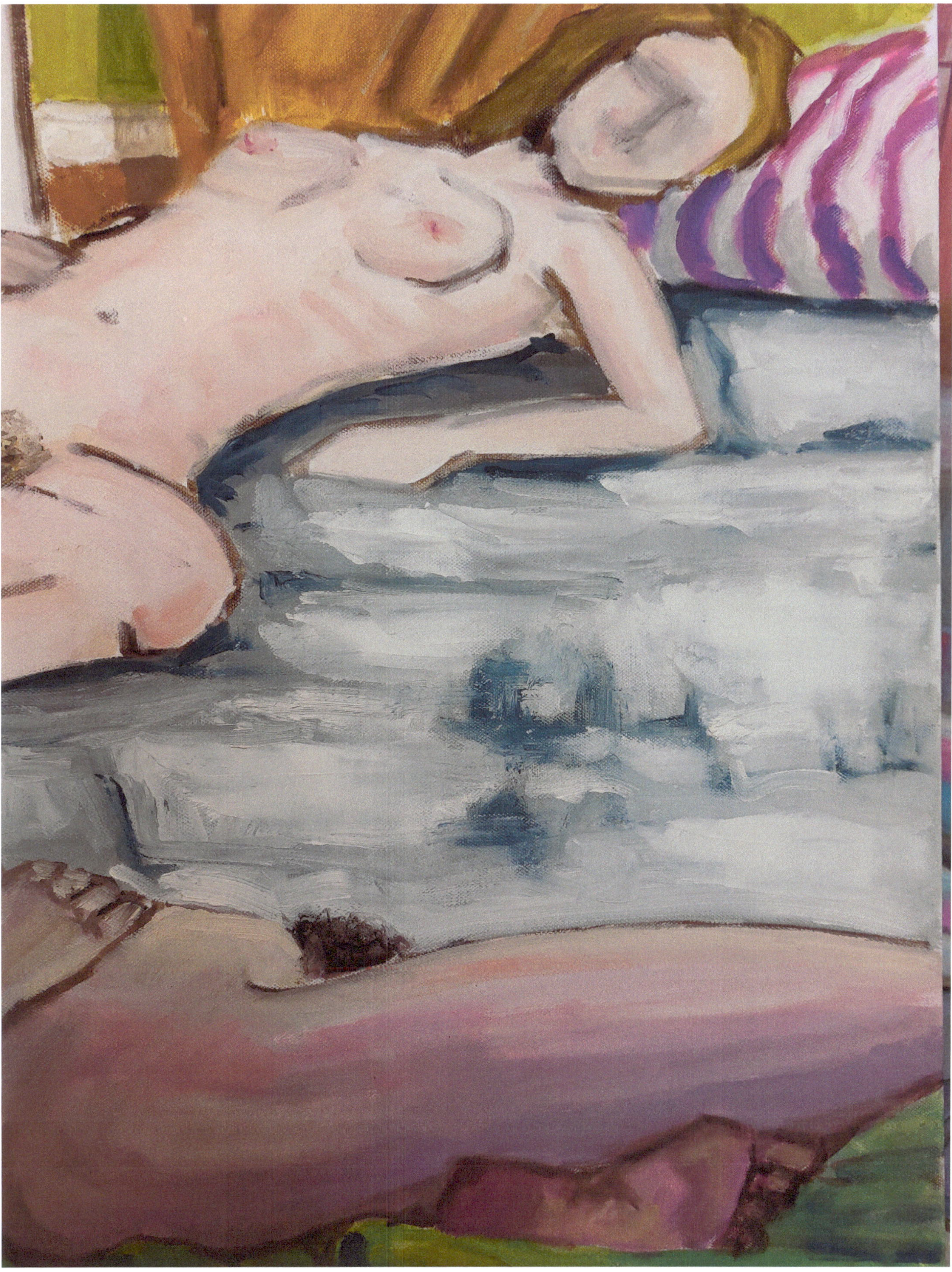

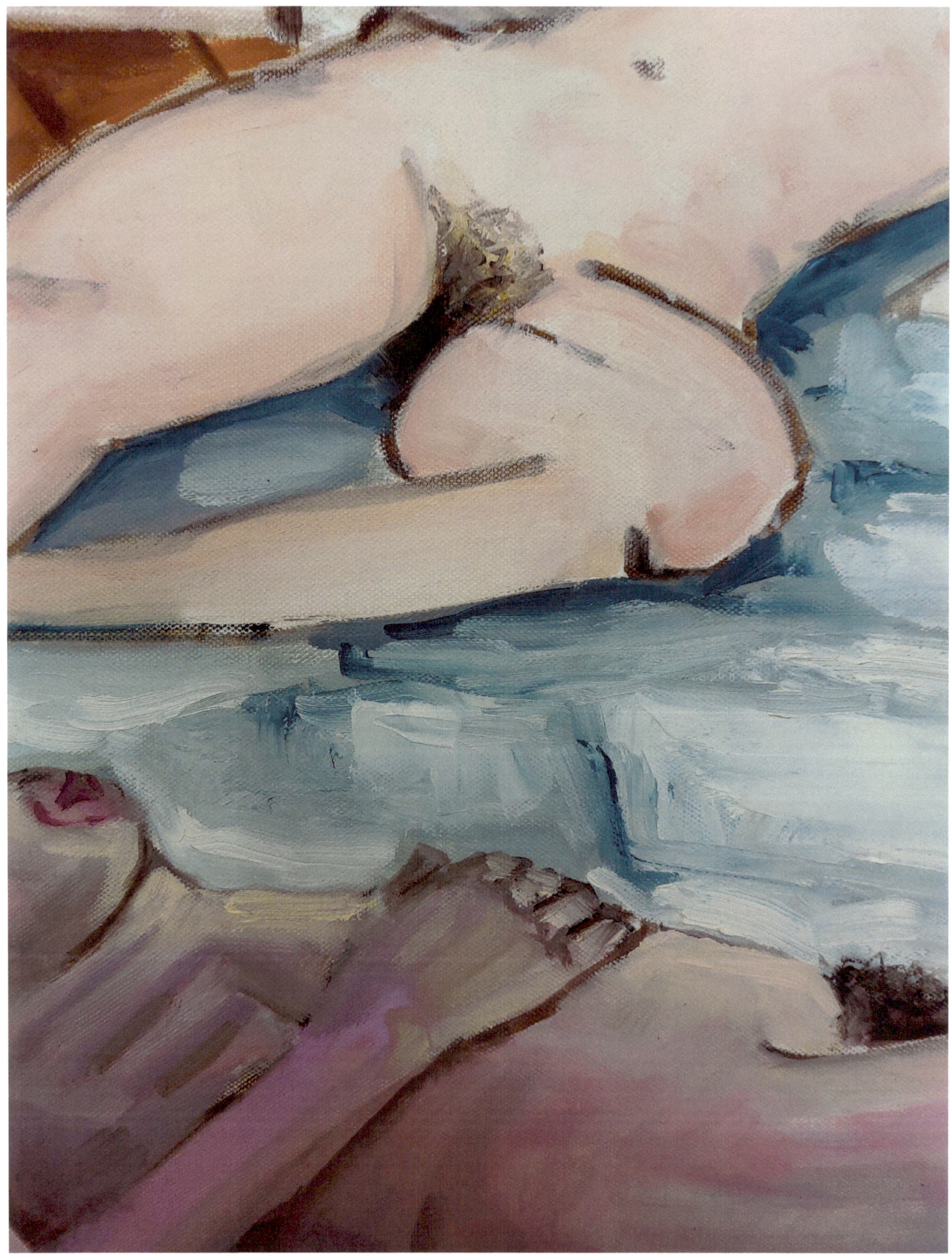

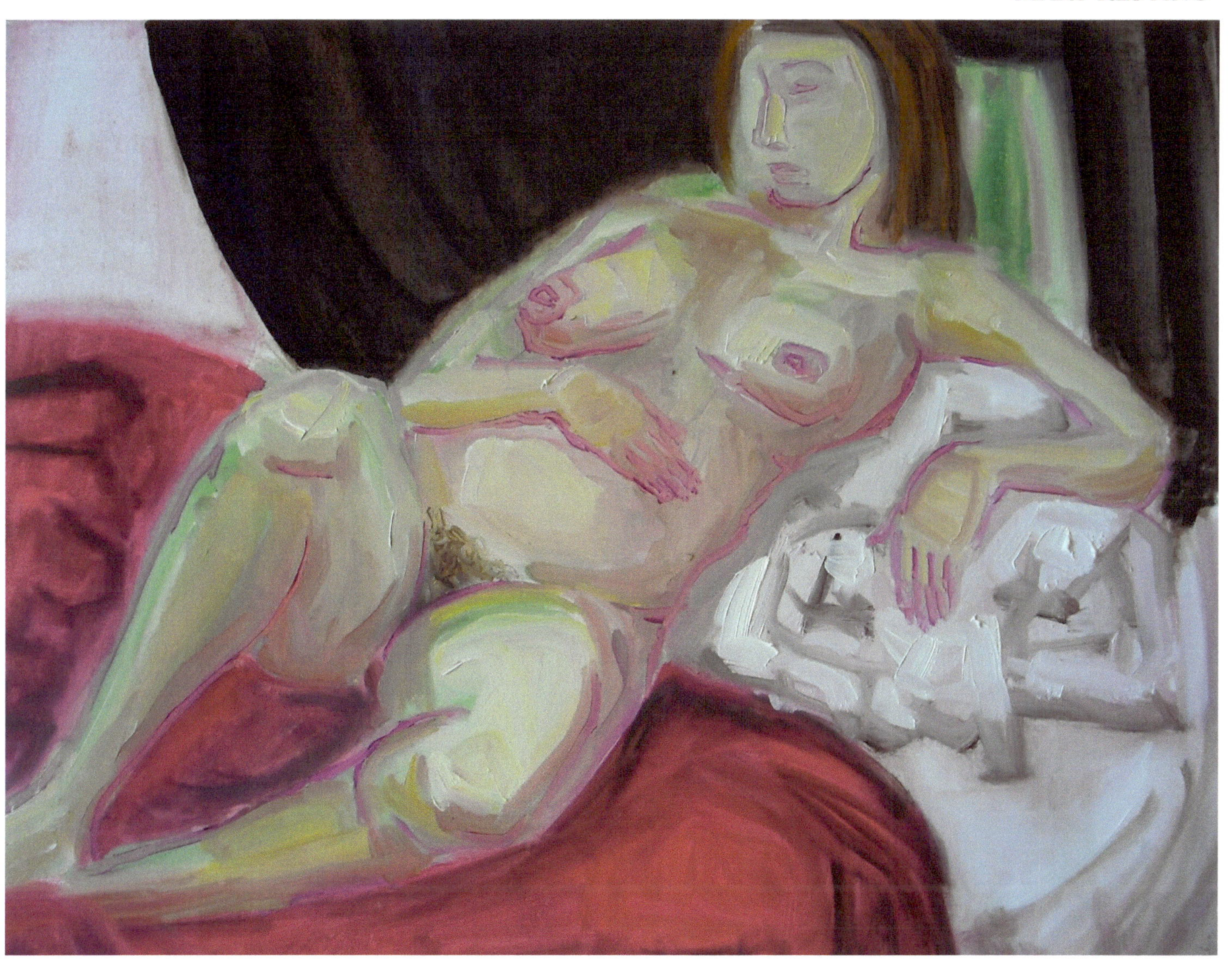

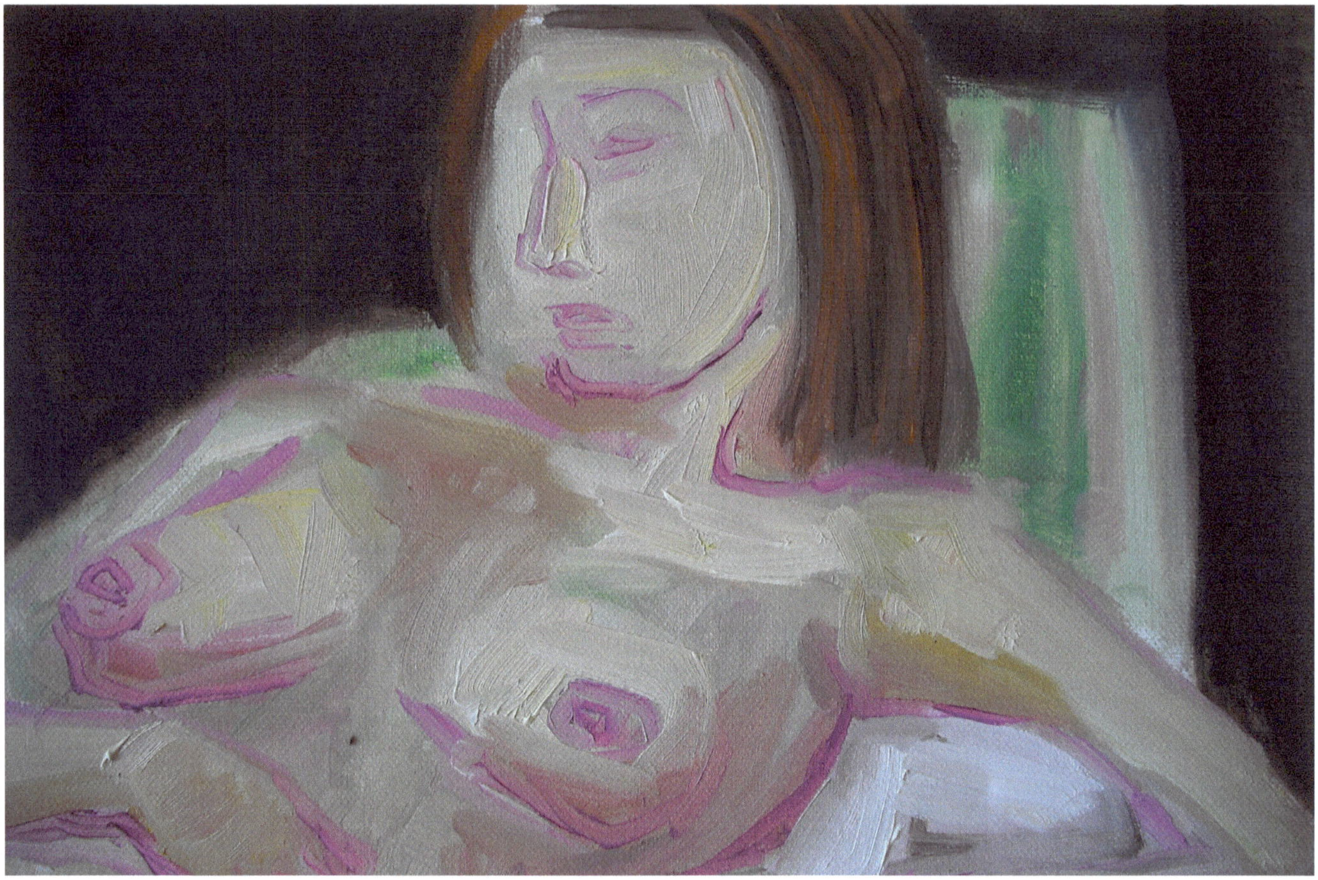

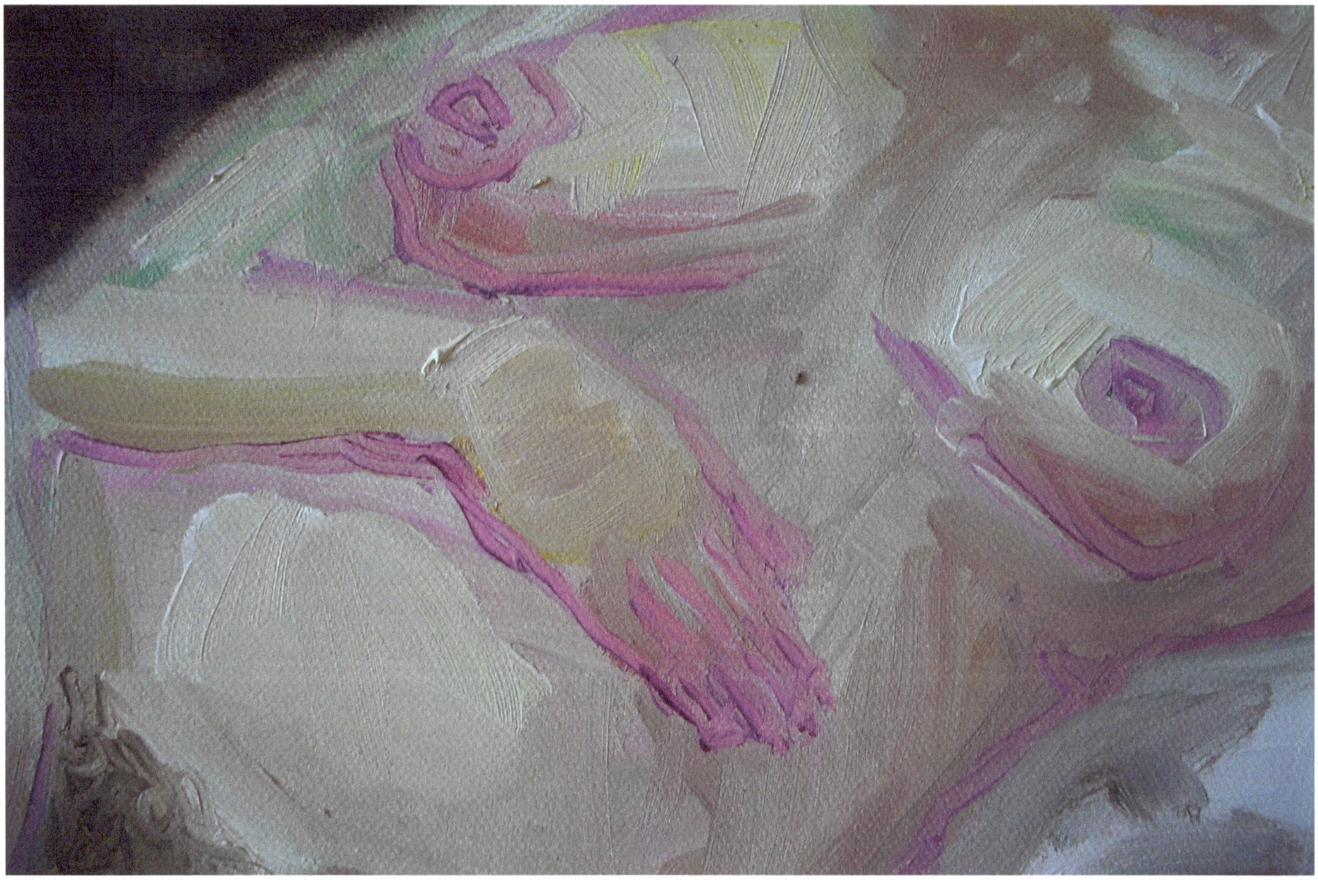

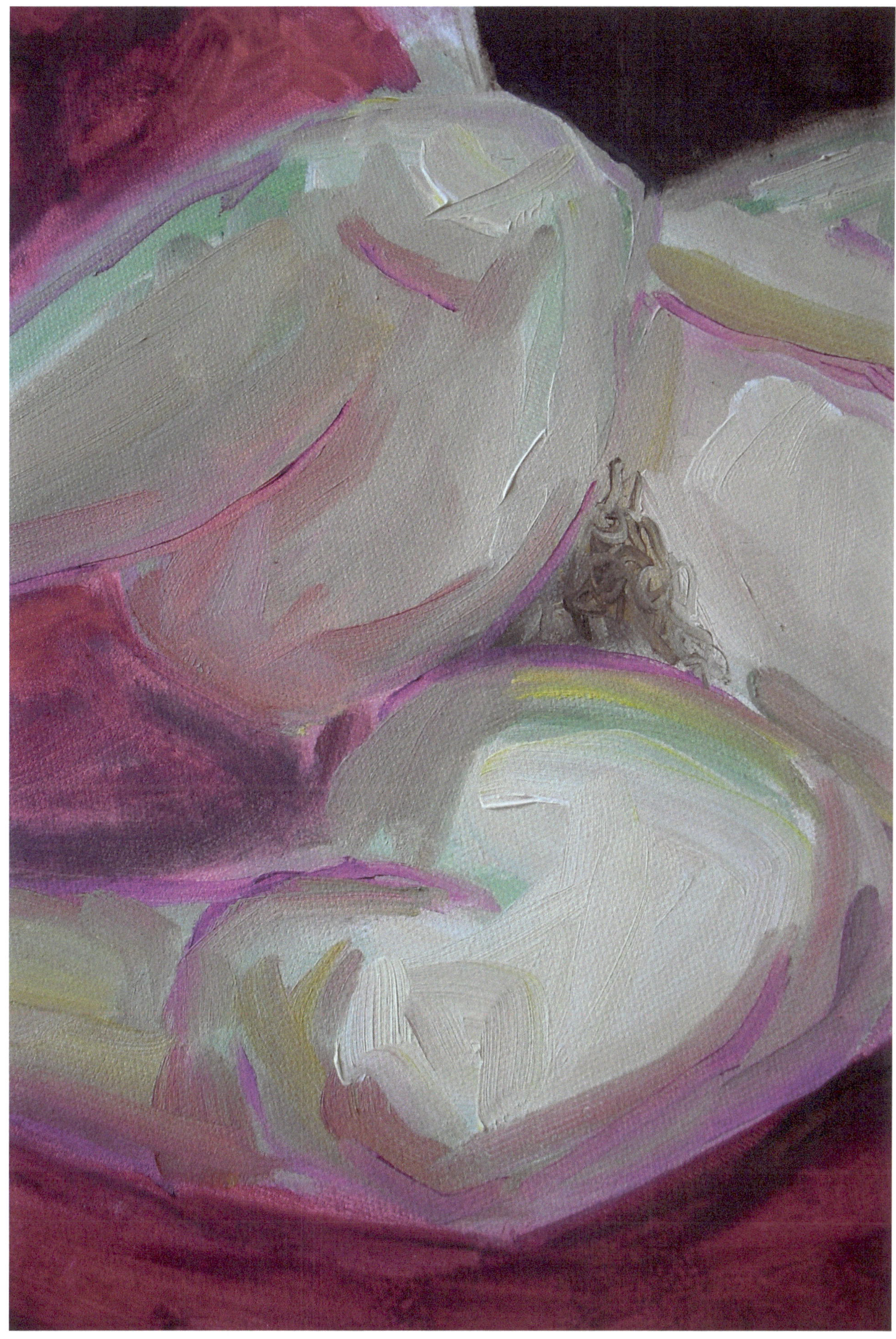

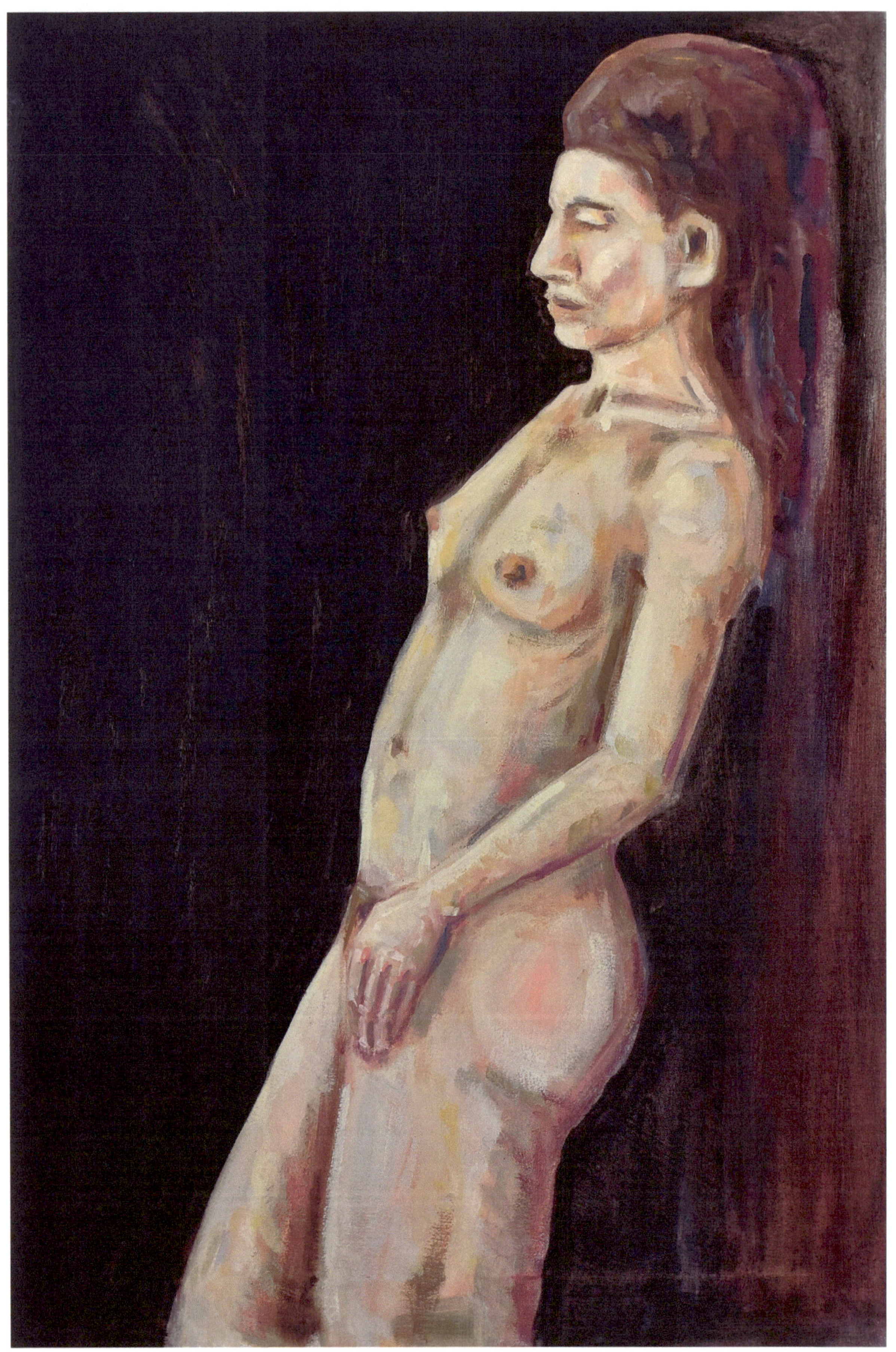

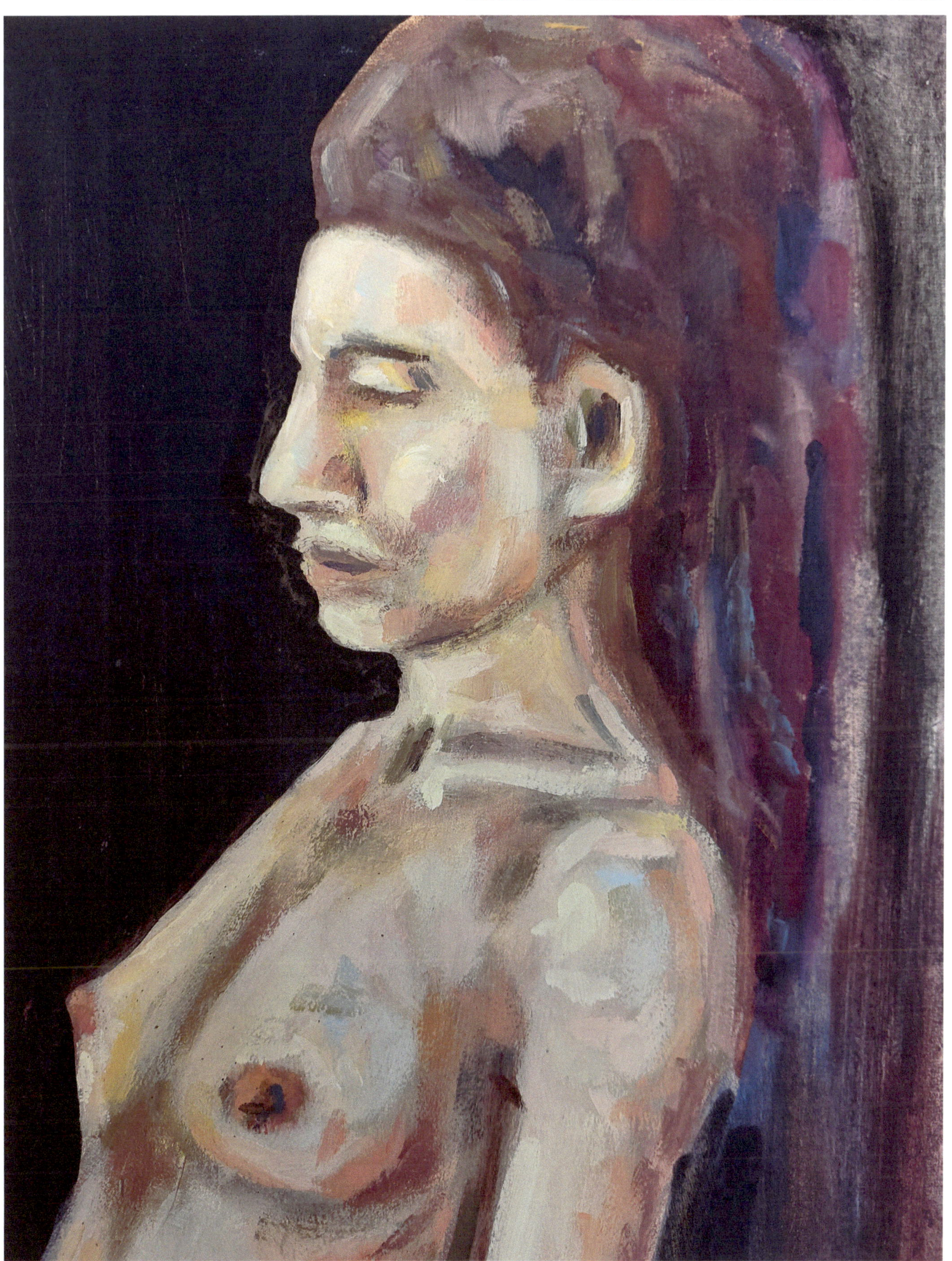

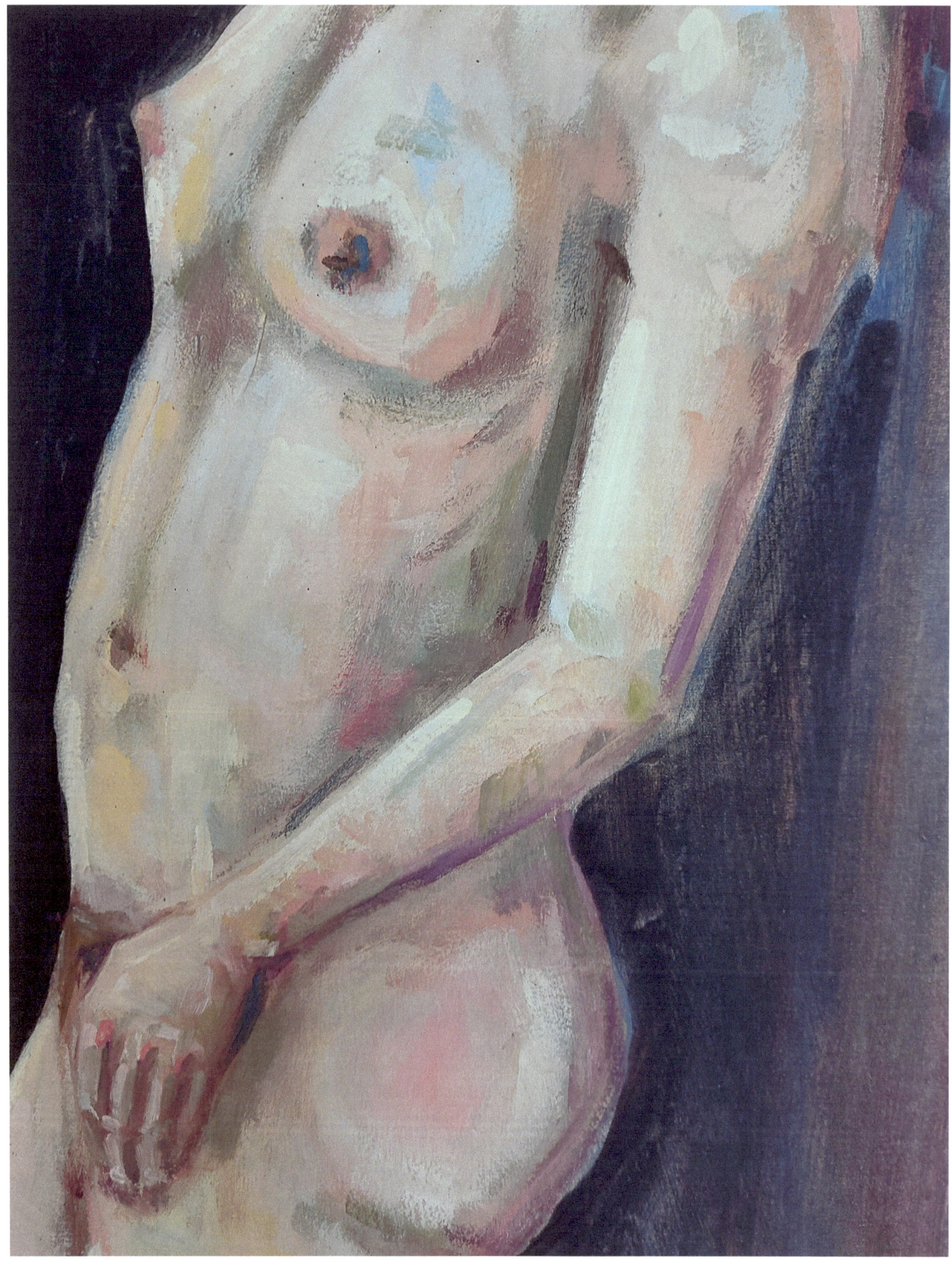

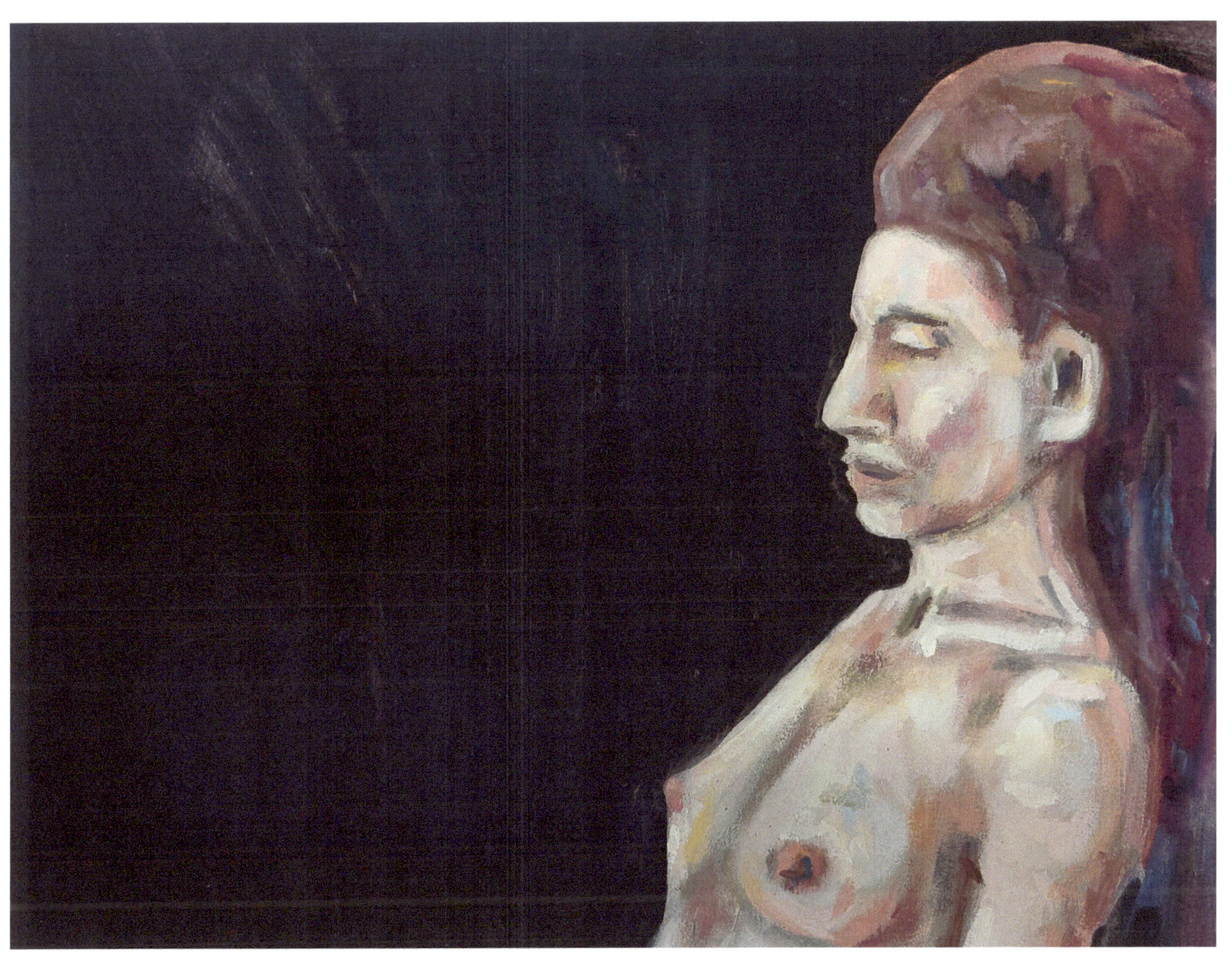

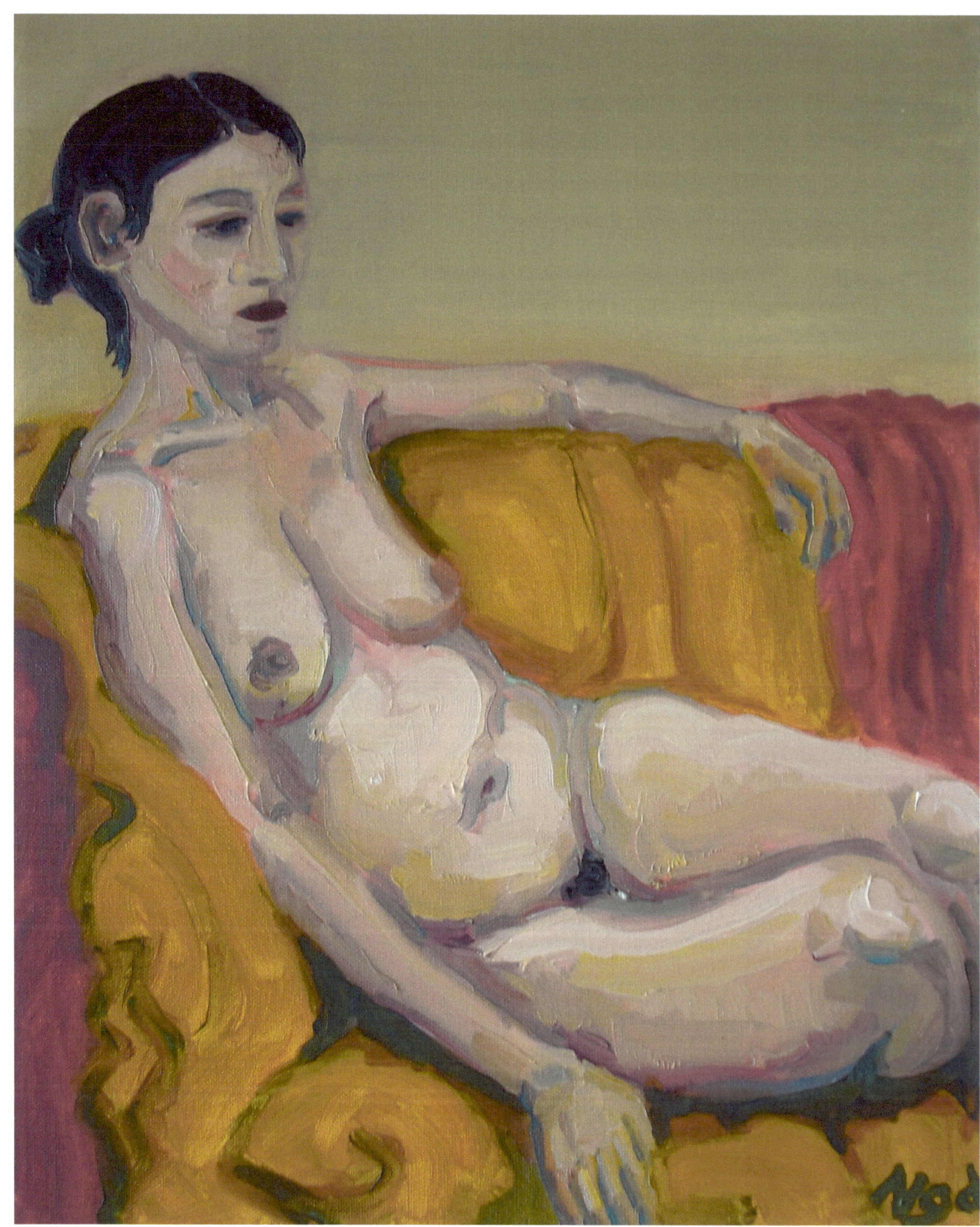

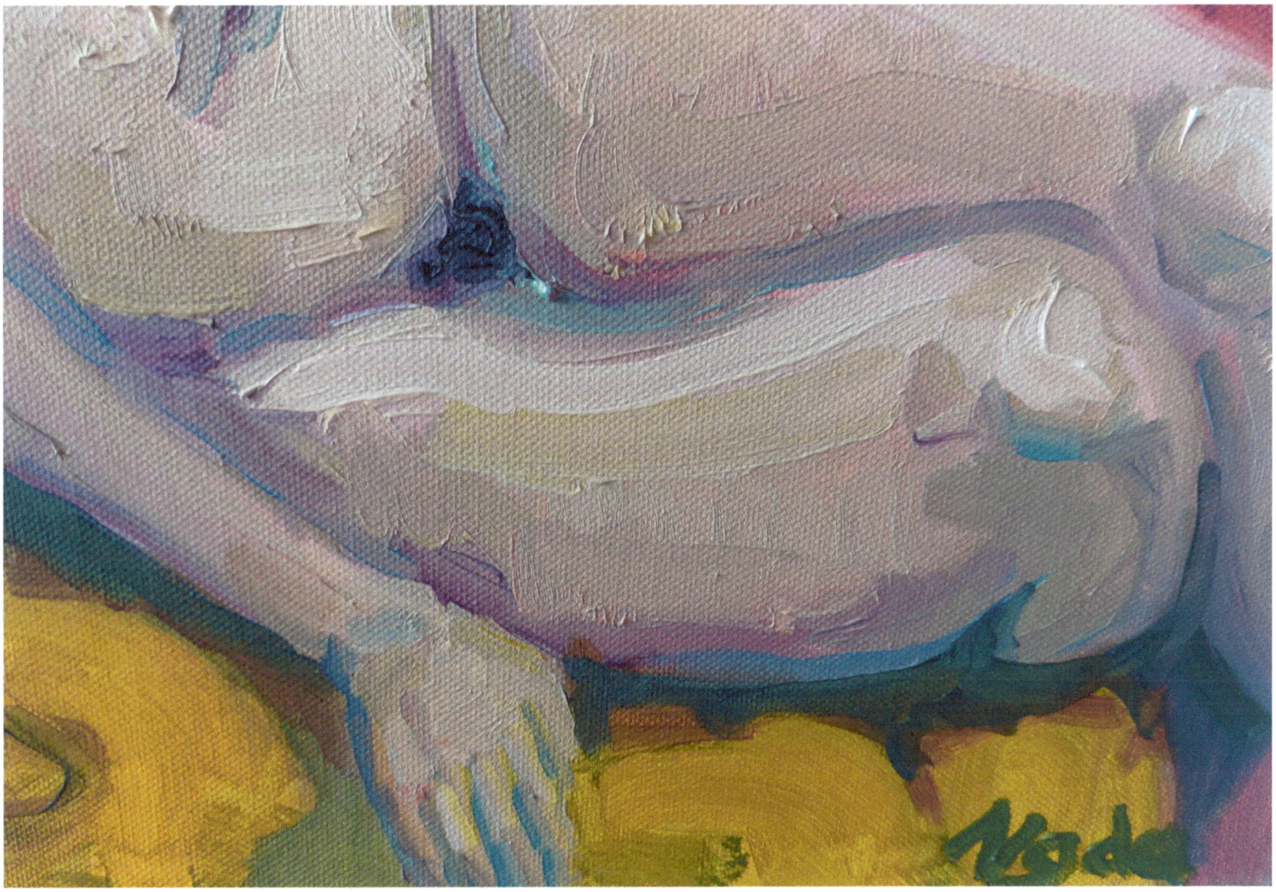

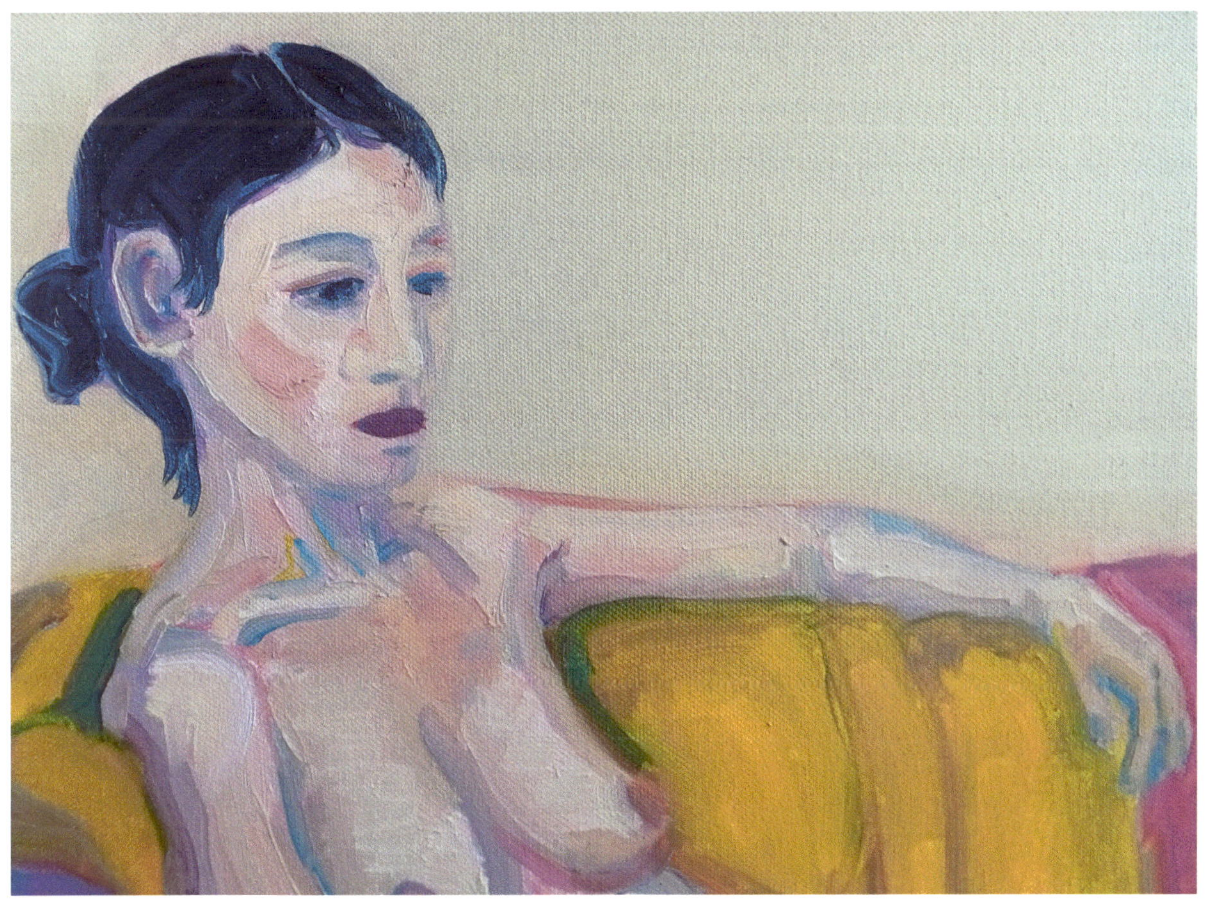

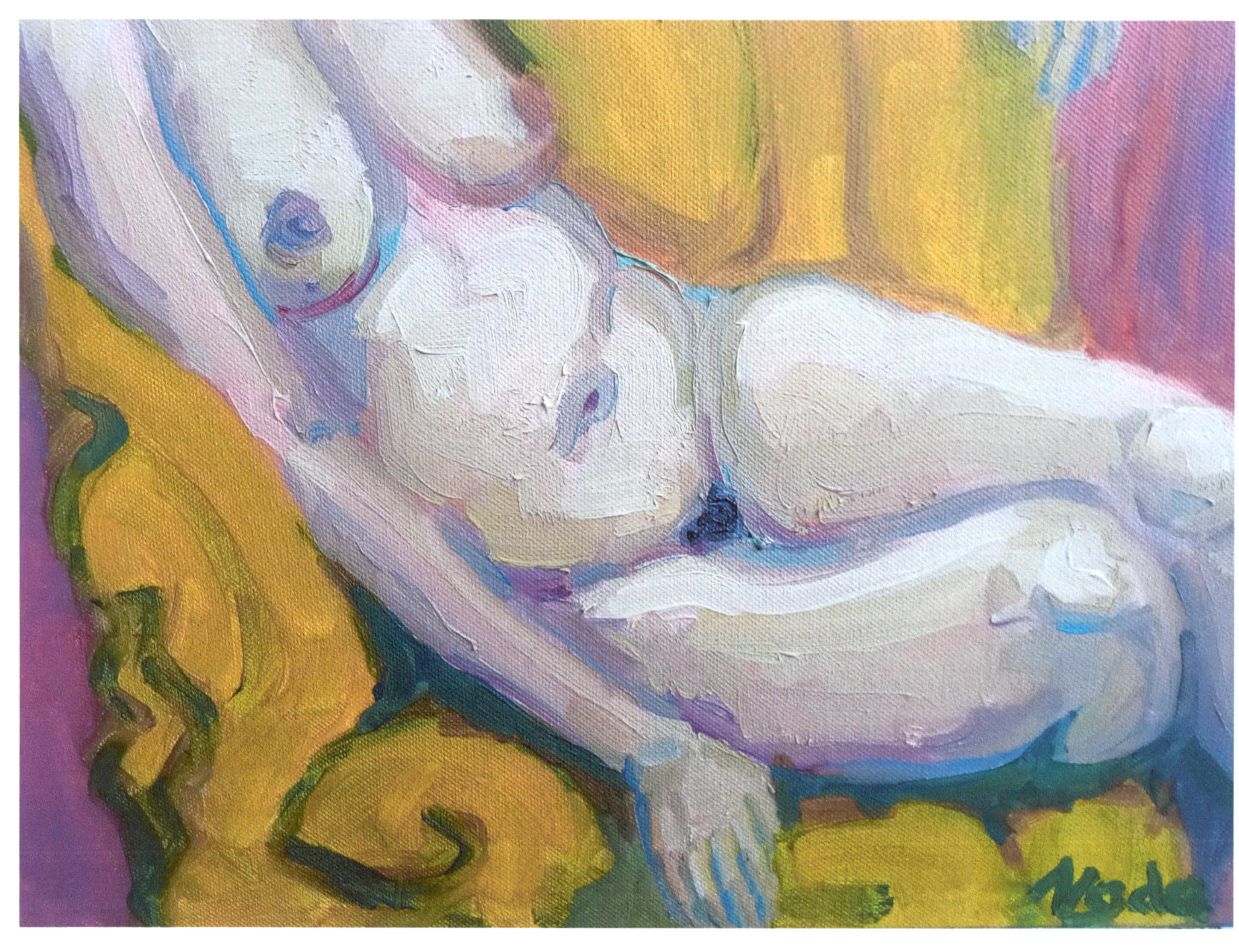

Stephen Najda

Life

-The move to abstraction-

(Oil on canvas)

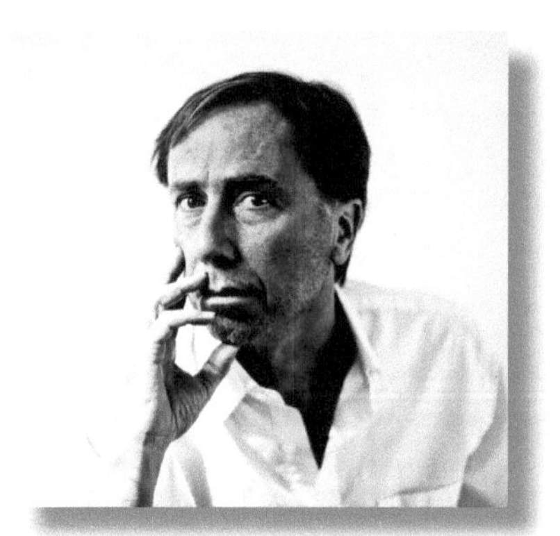

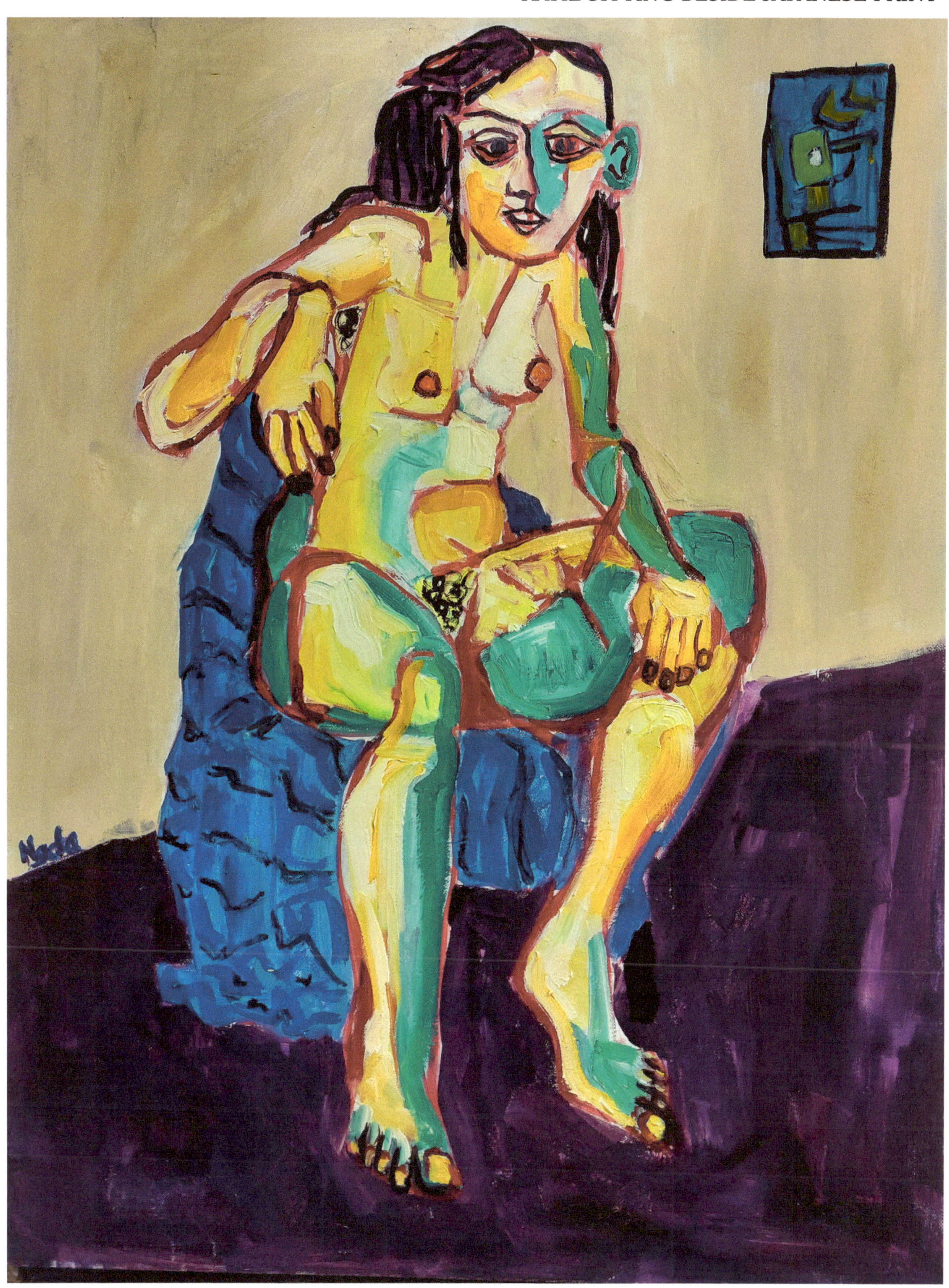

DETAIL "KATIE SITTING BESIDE JAPANESE PRINT"

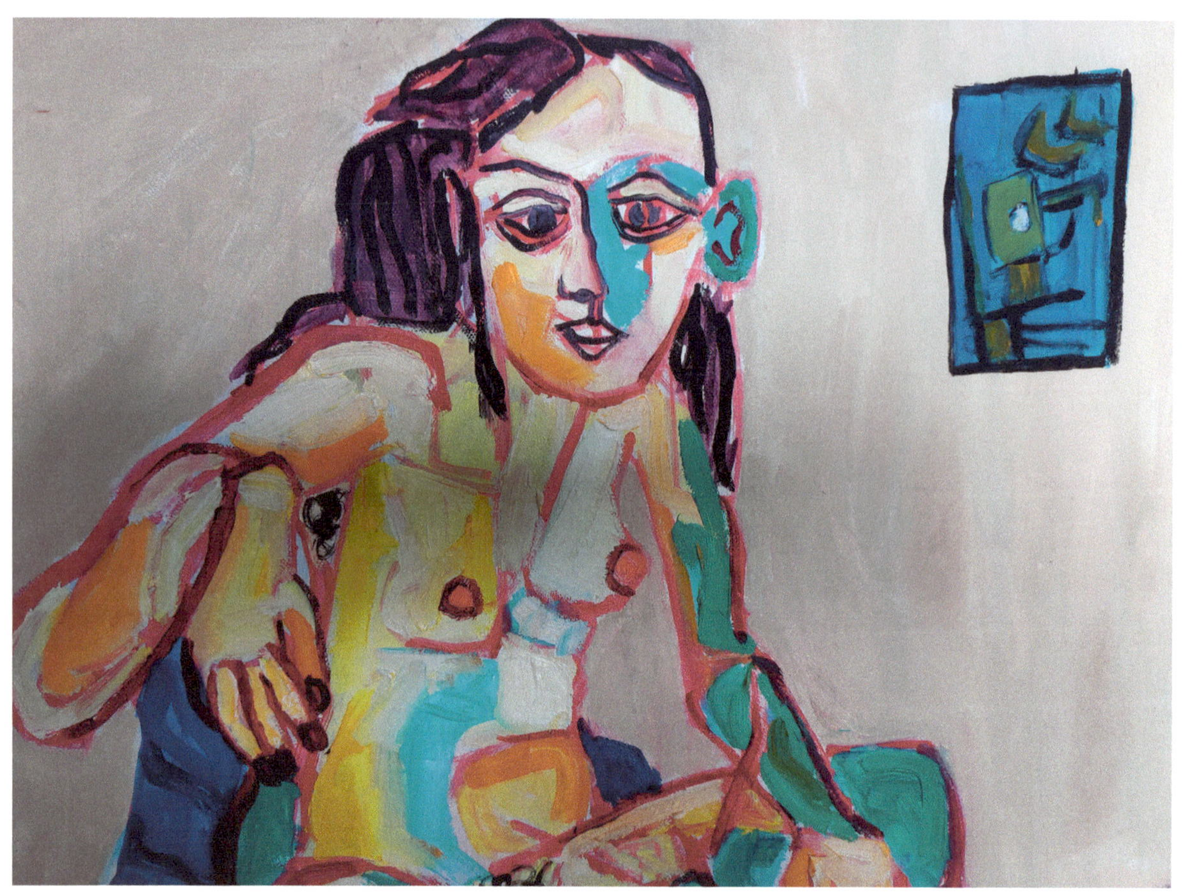

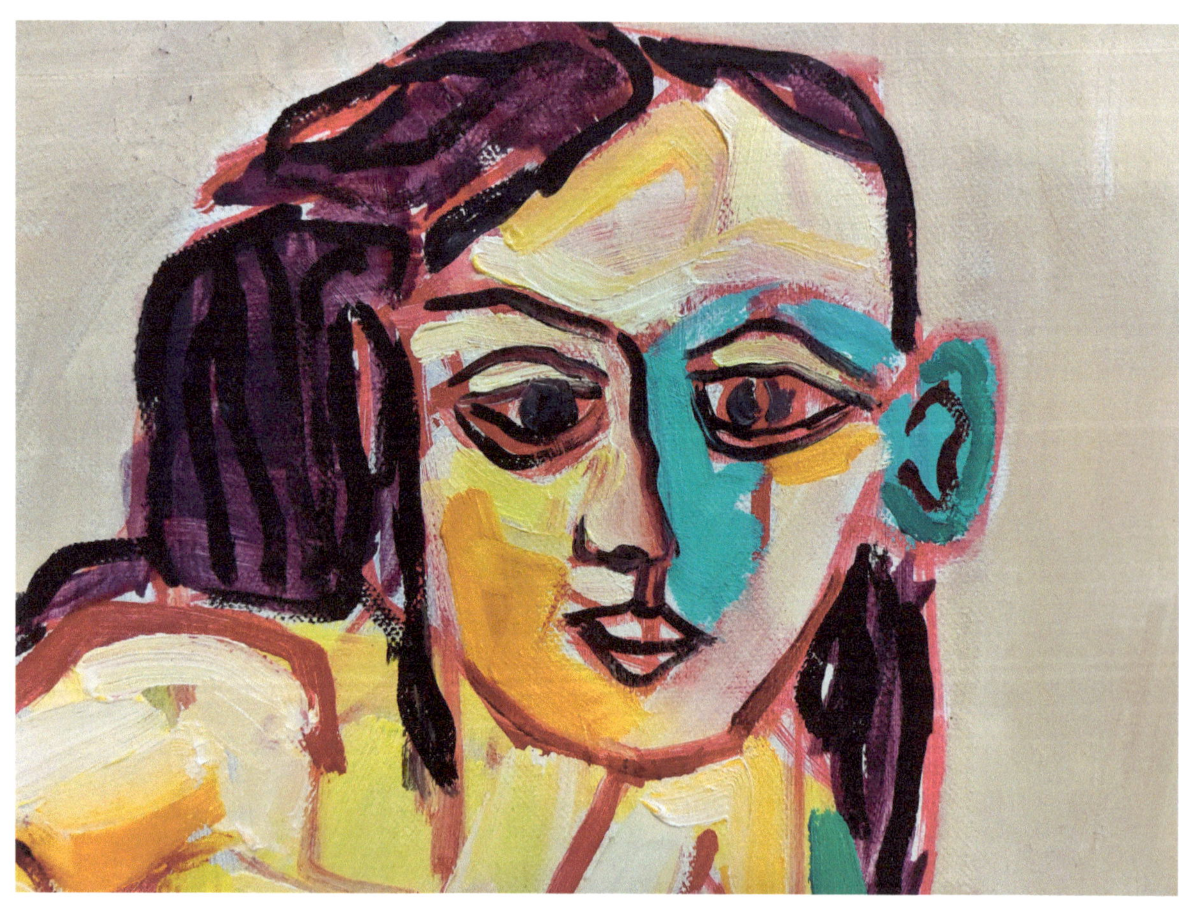

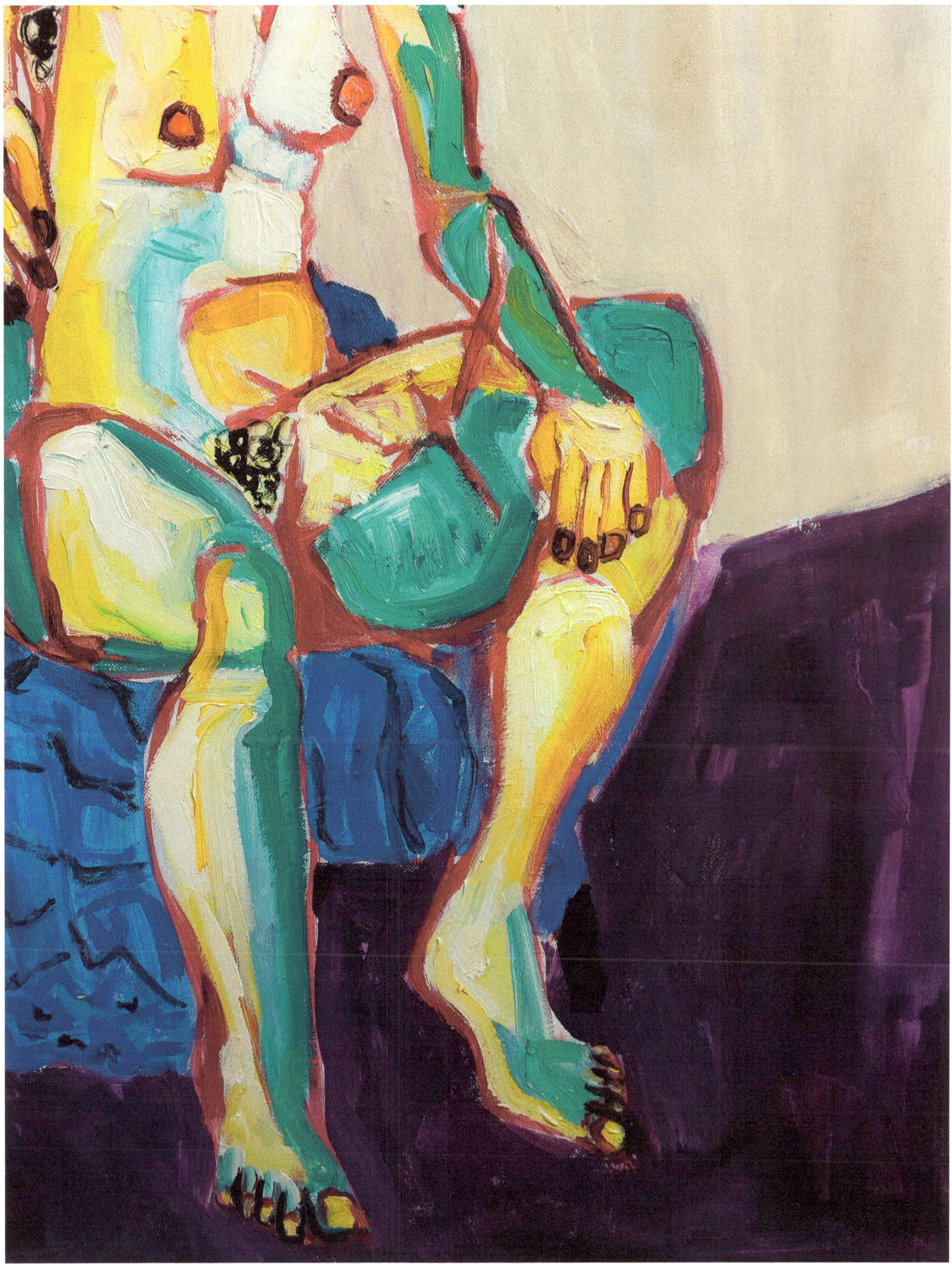

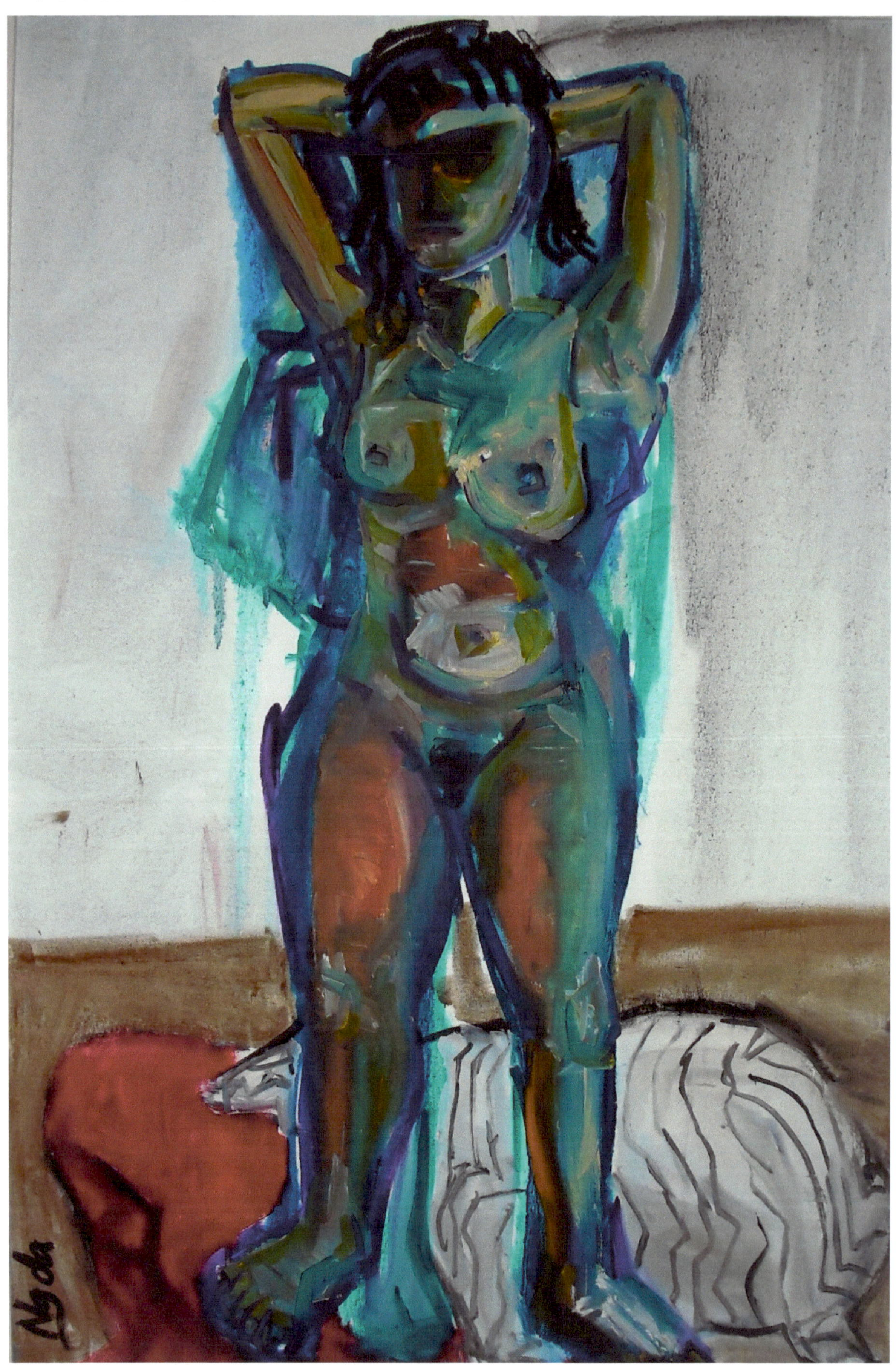

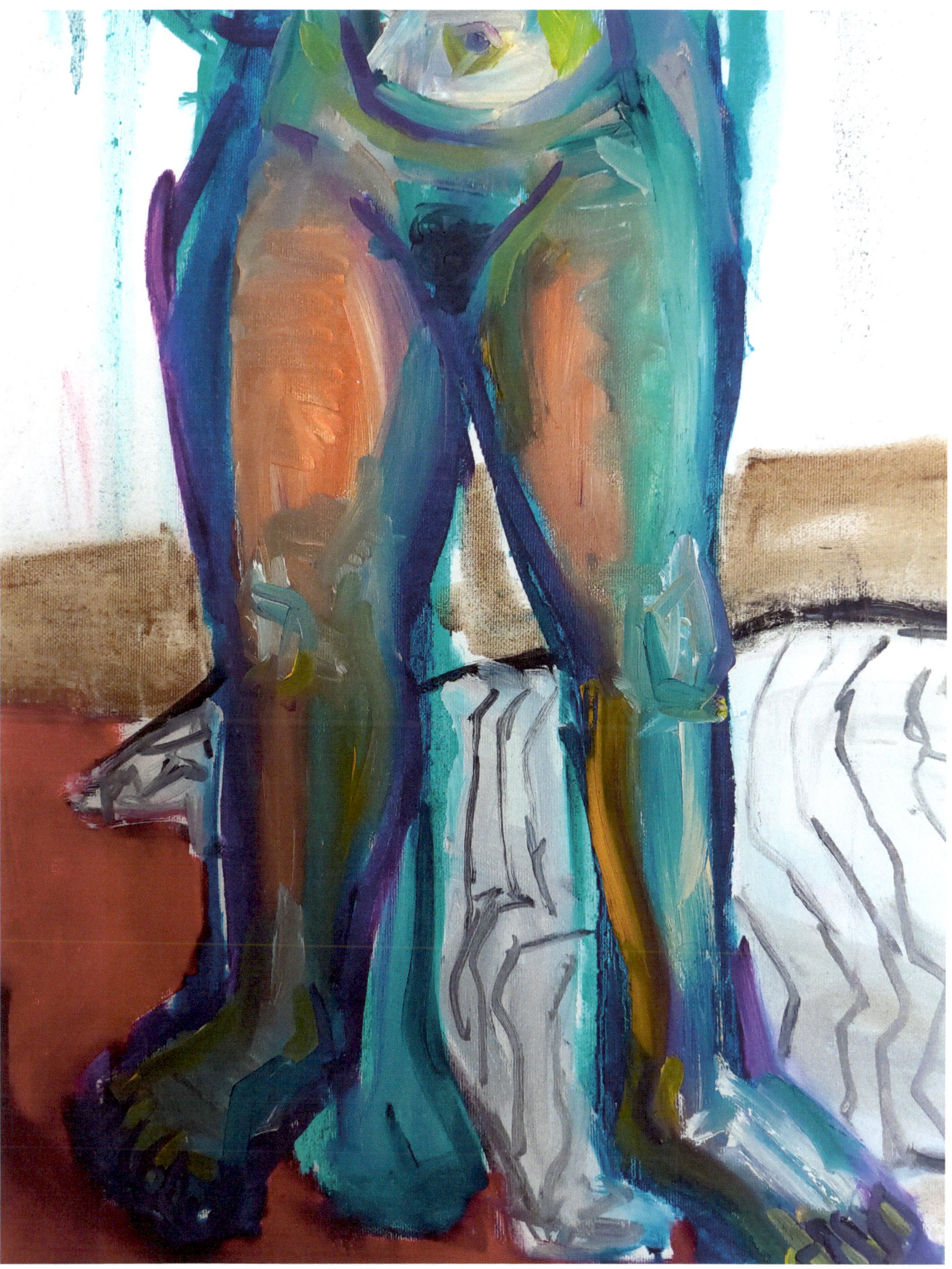

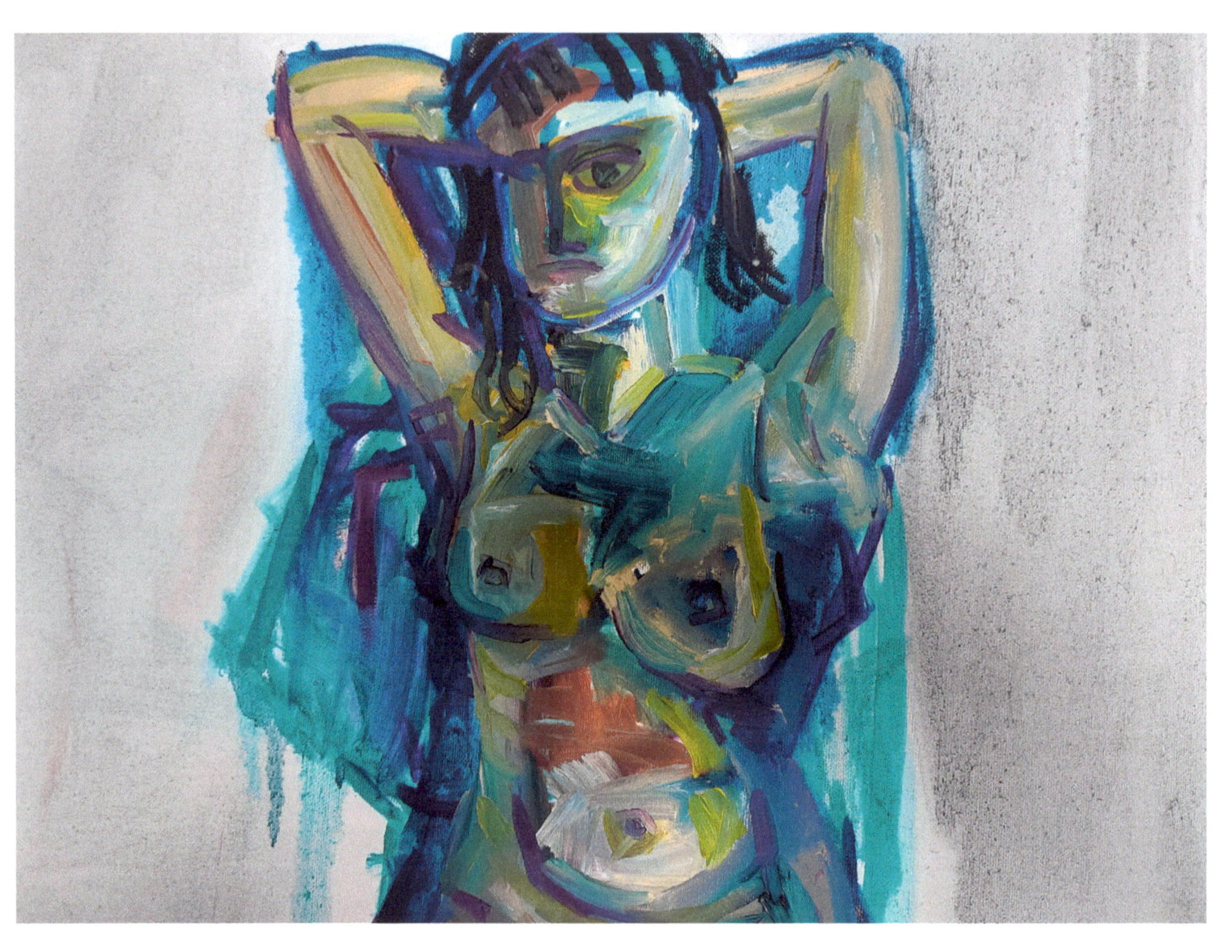

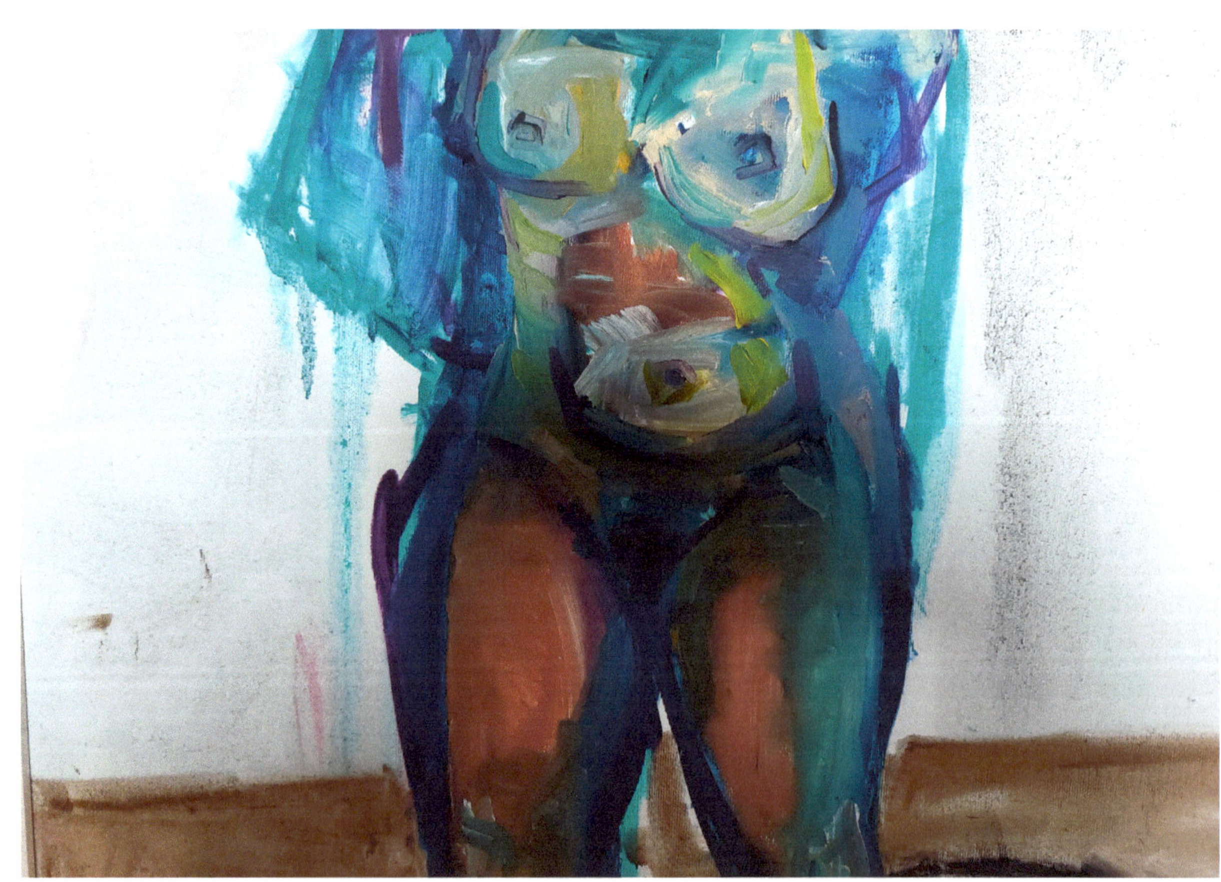

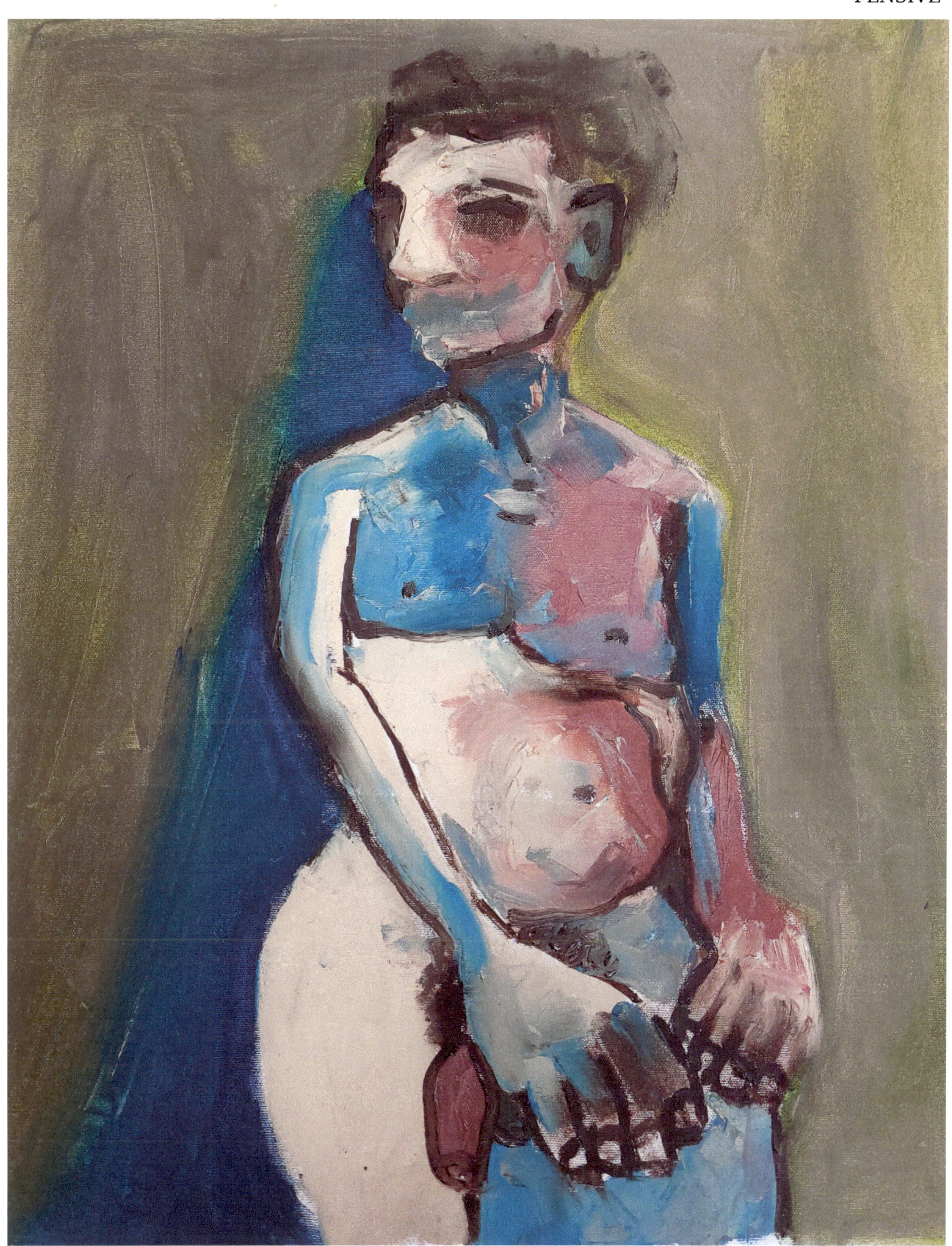

DETAIL - "PENSIVE"

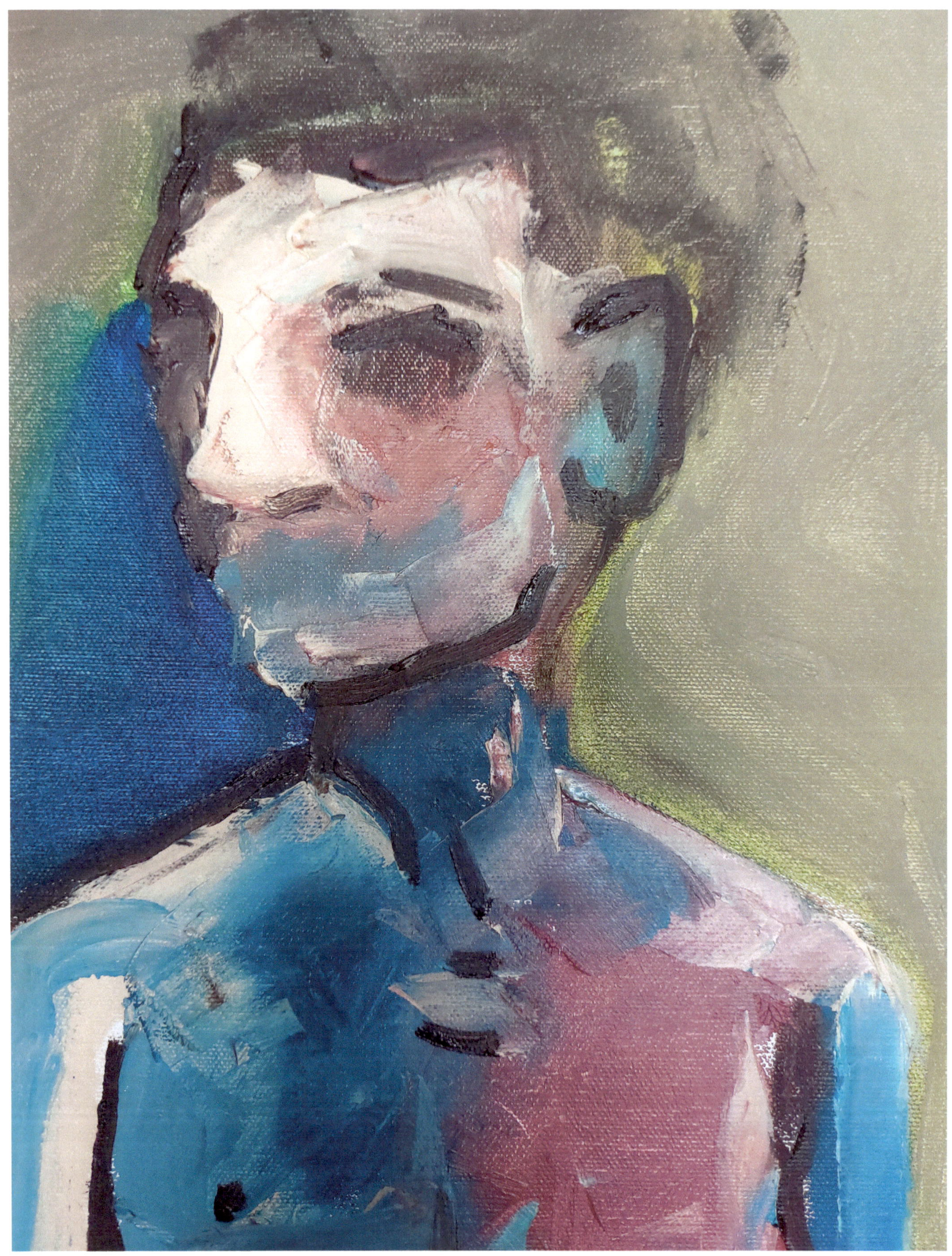

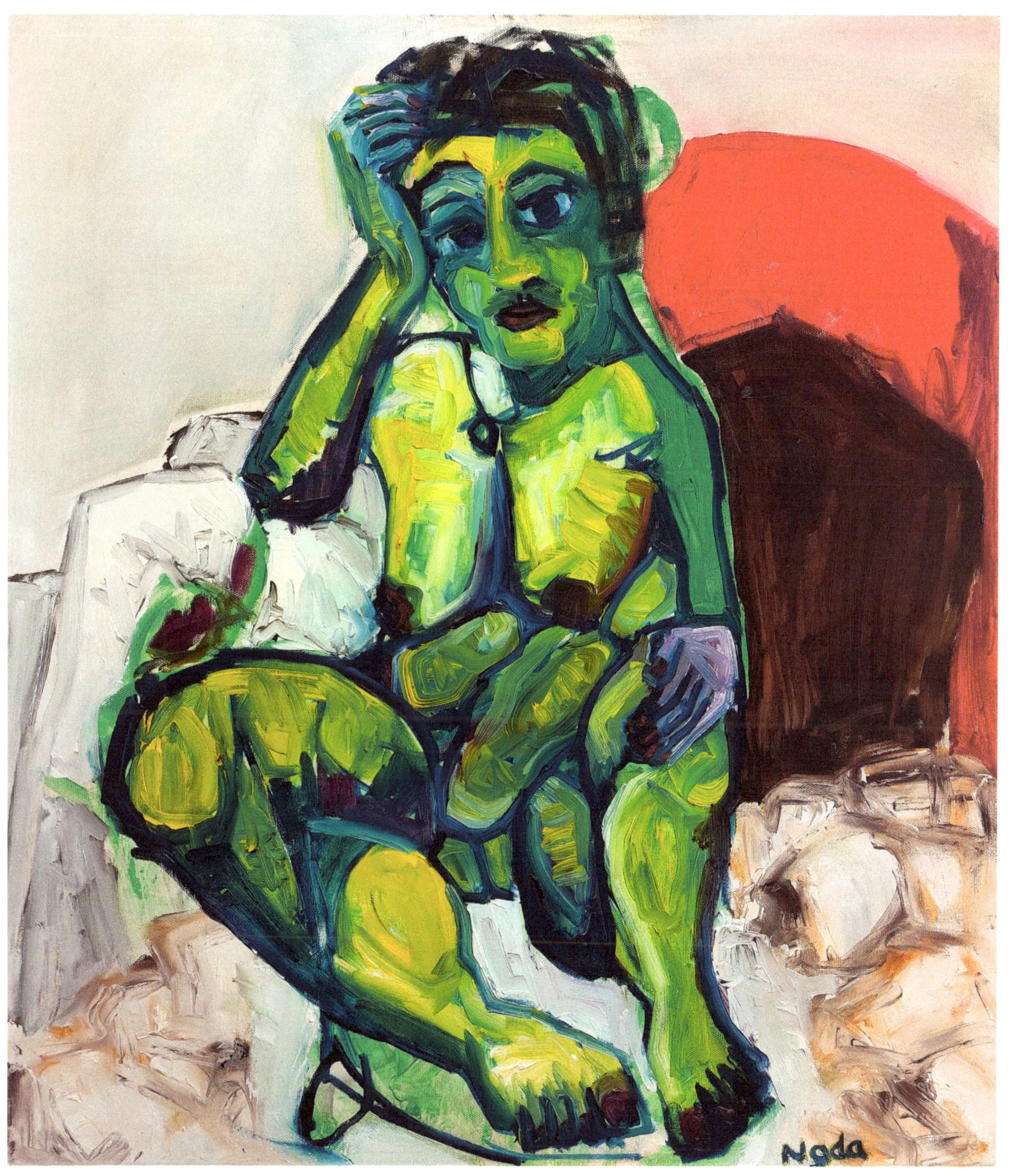

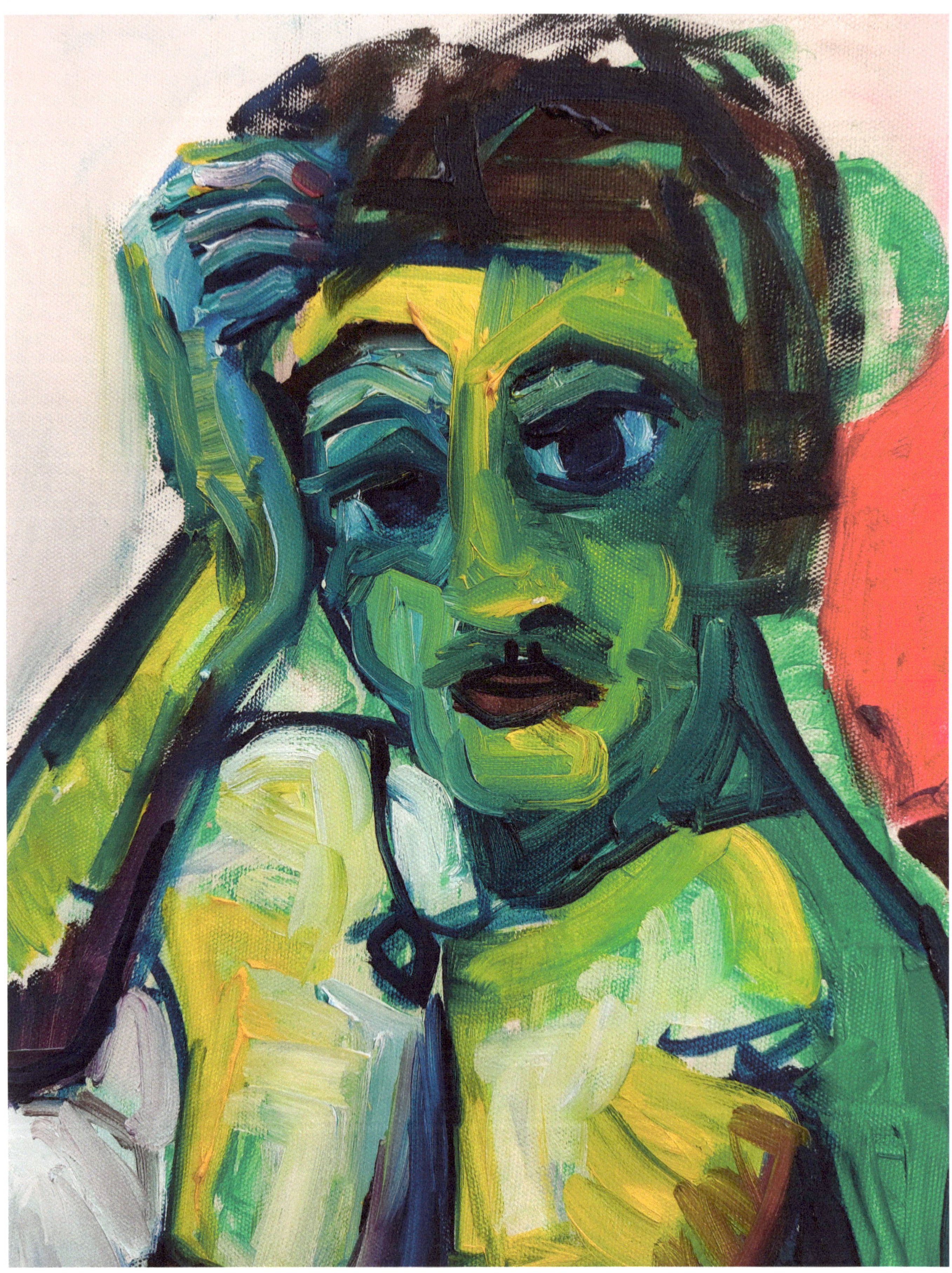

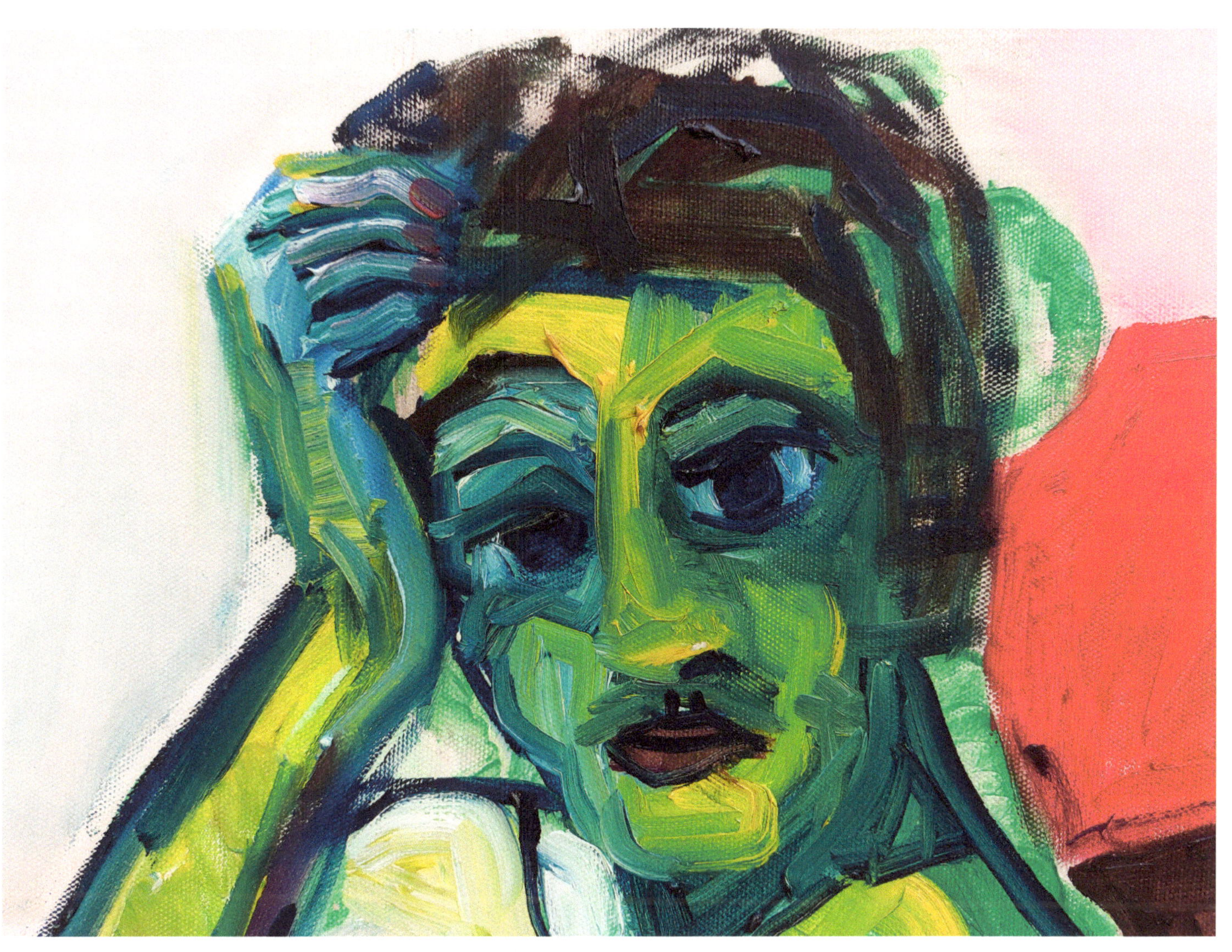

"THE SITTING MAN"

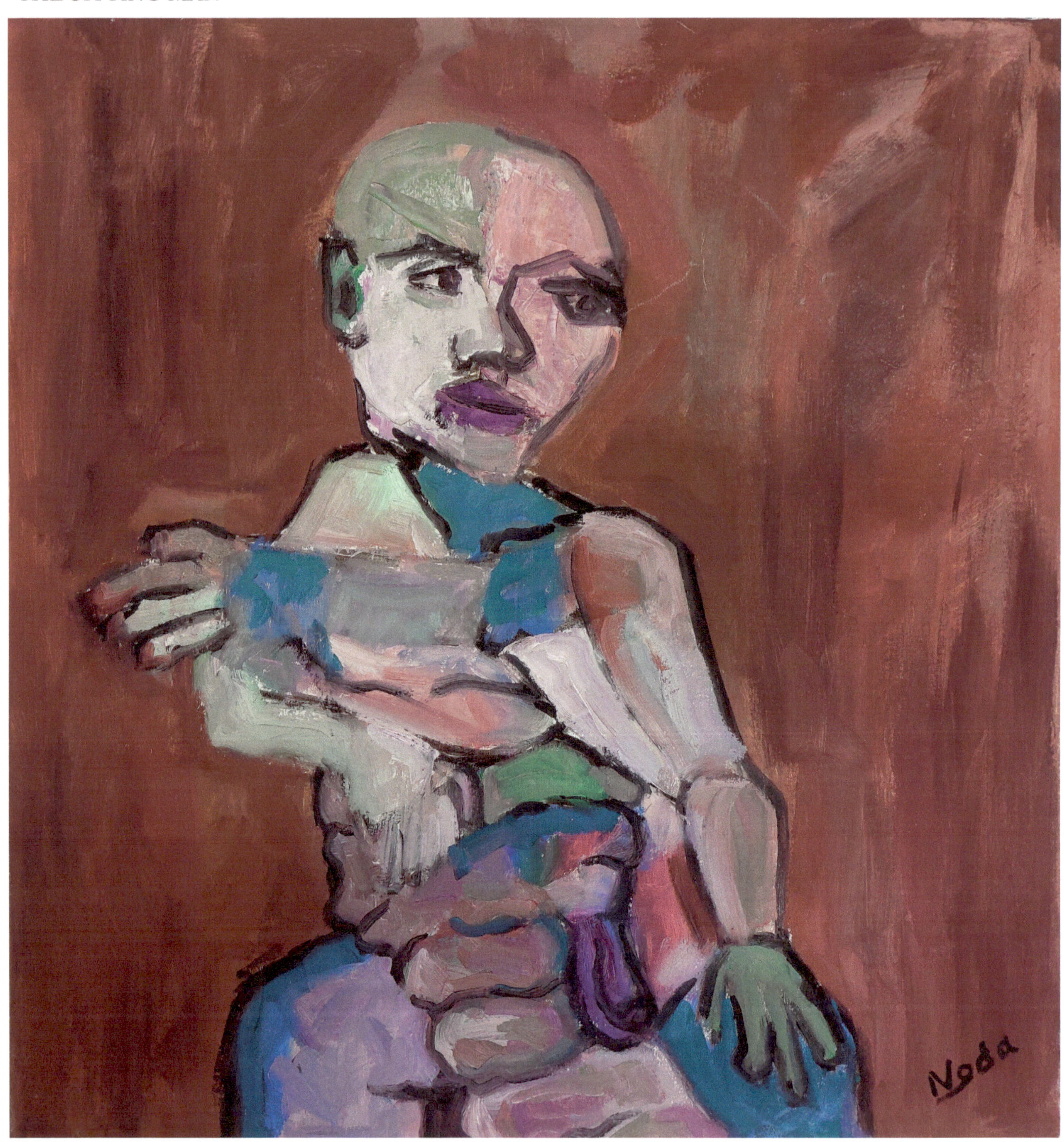

"THE SITTING MAN"

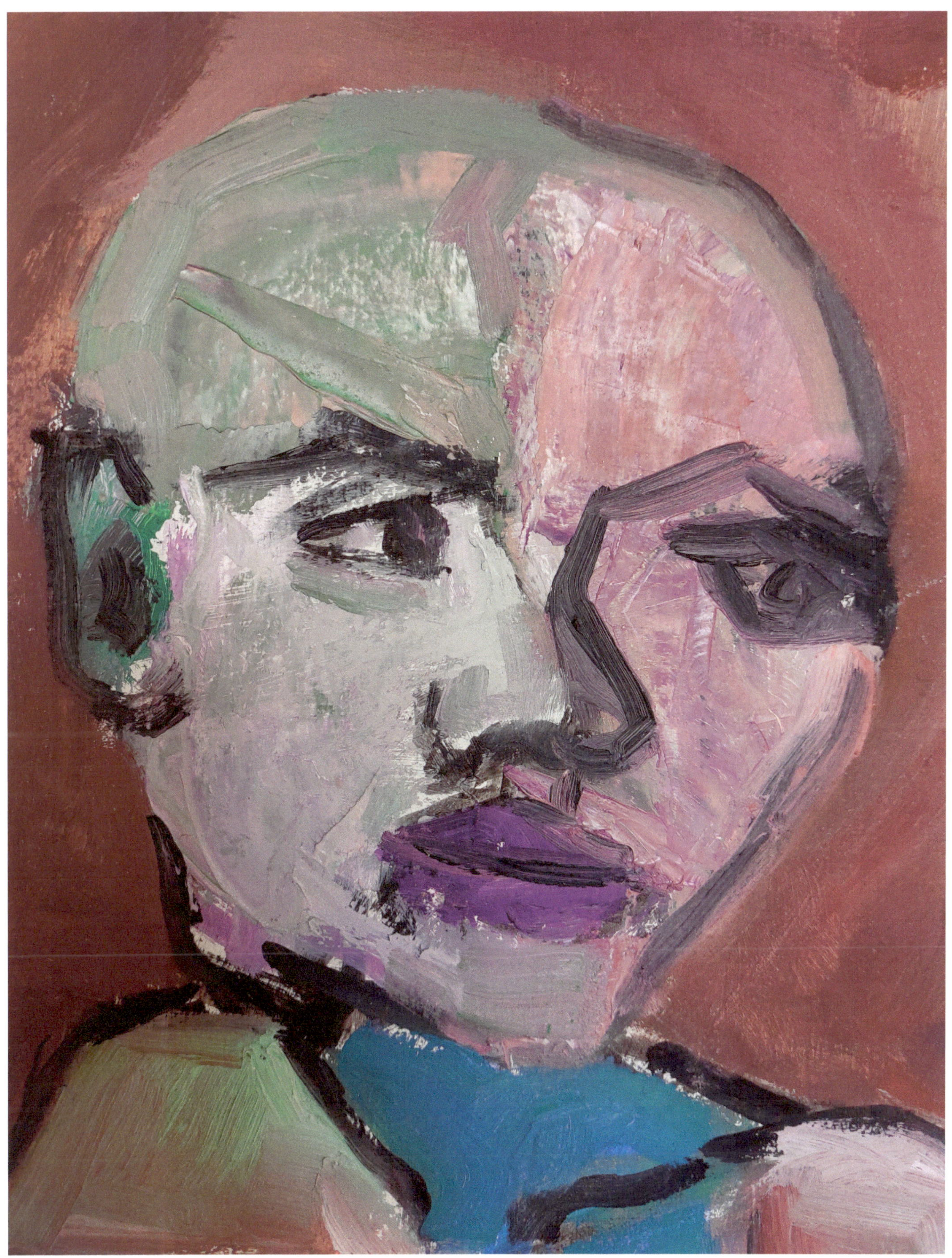

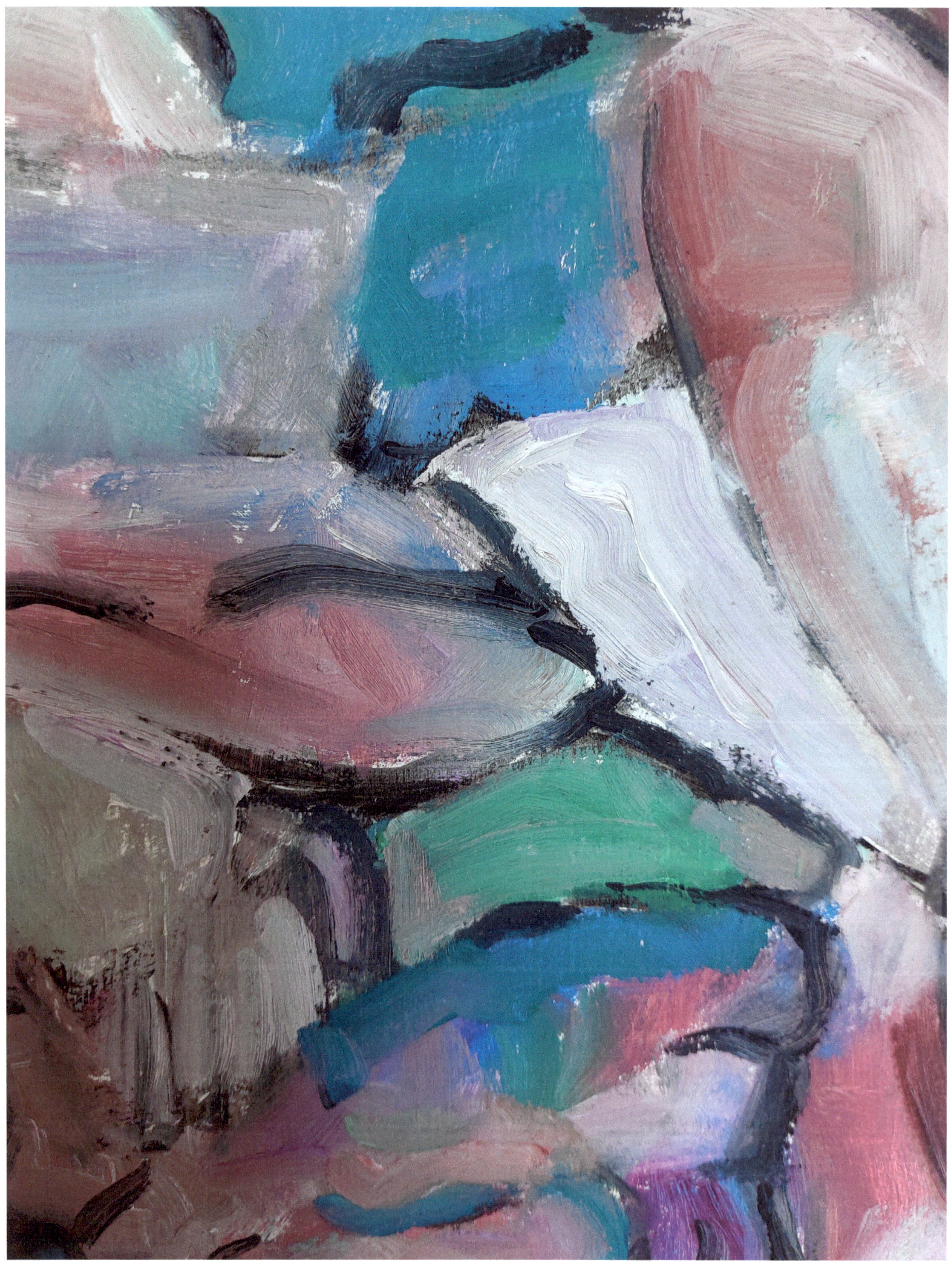

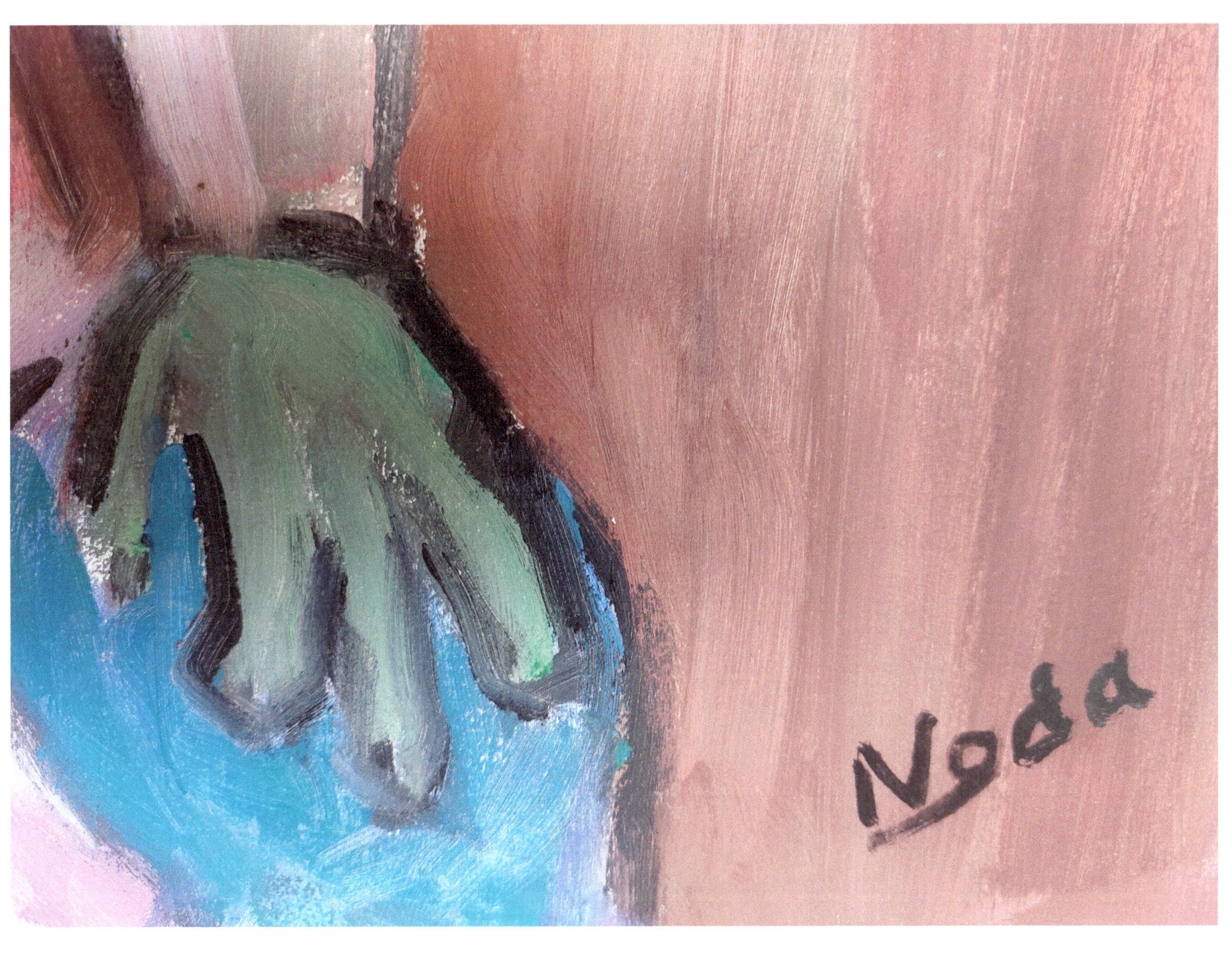Noda

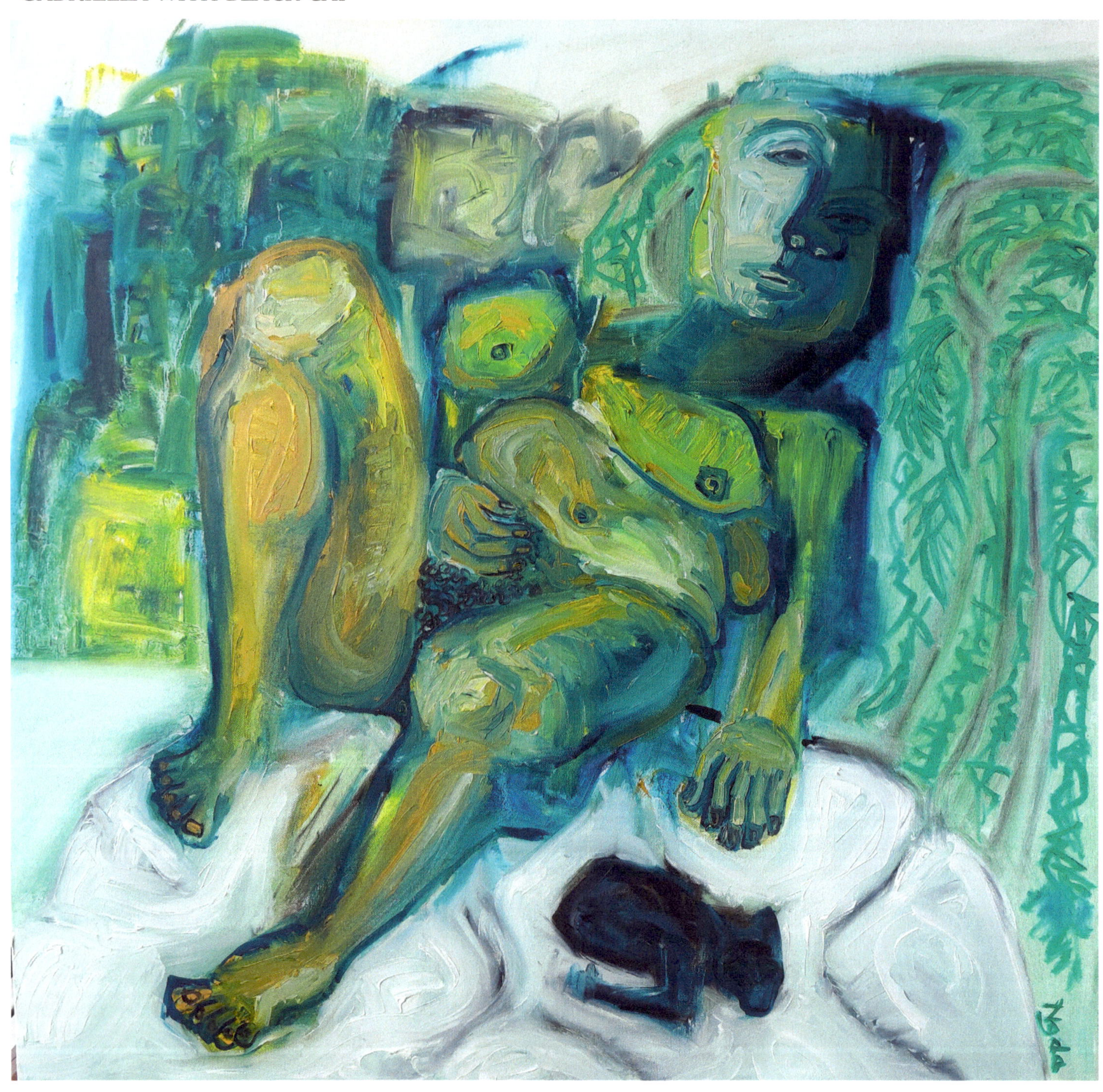

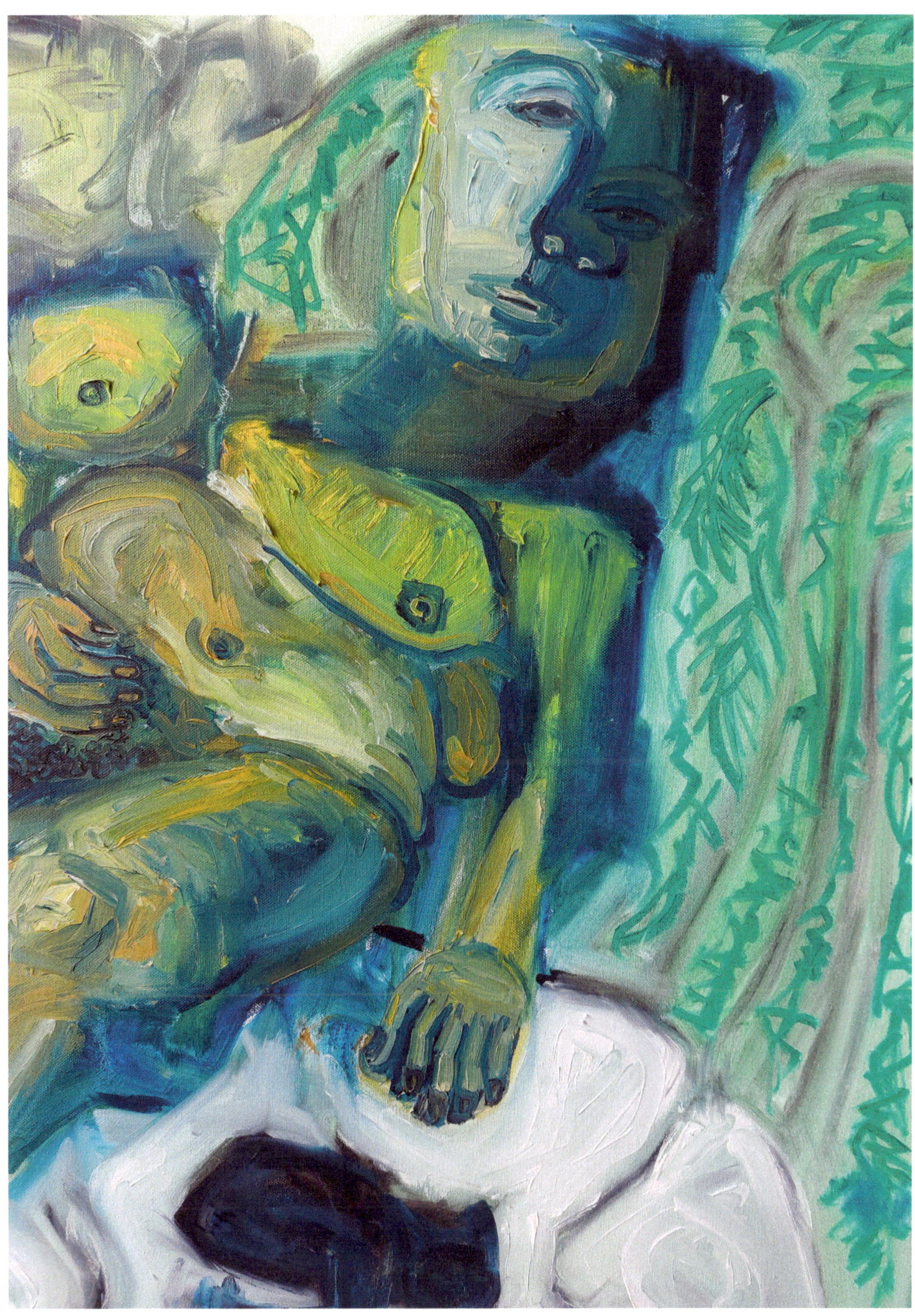

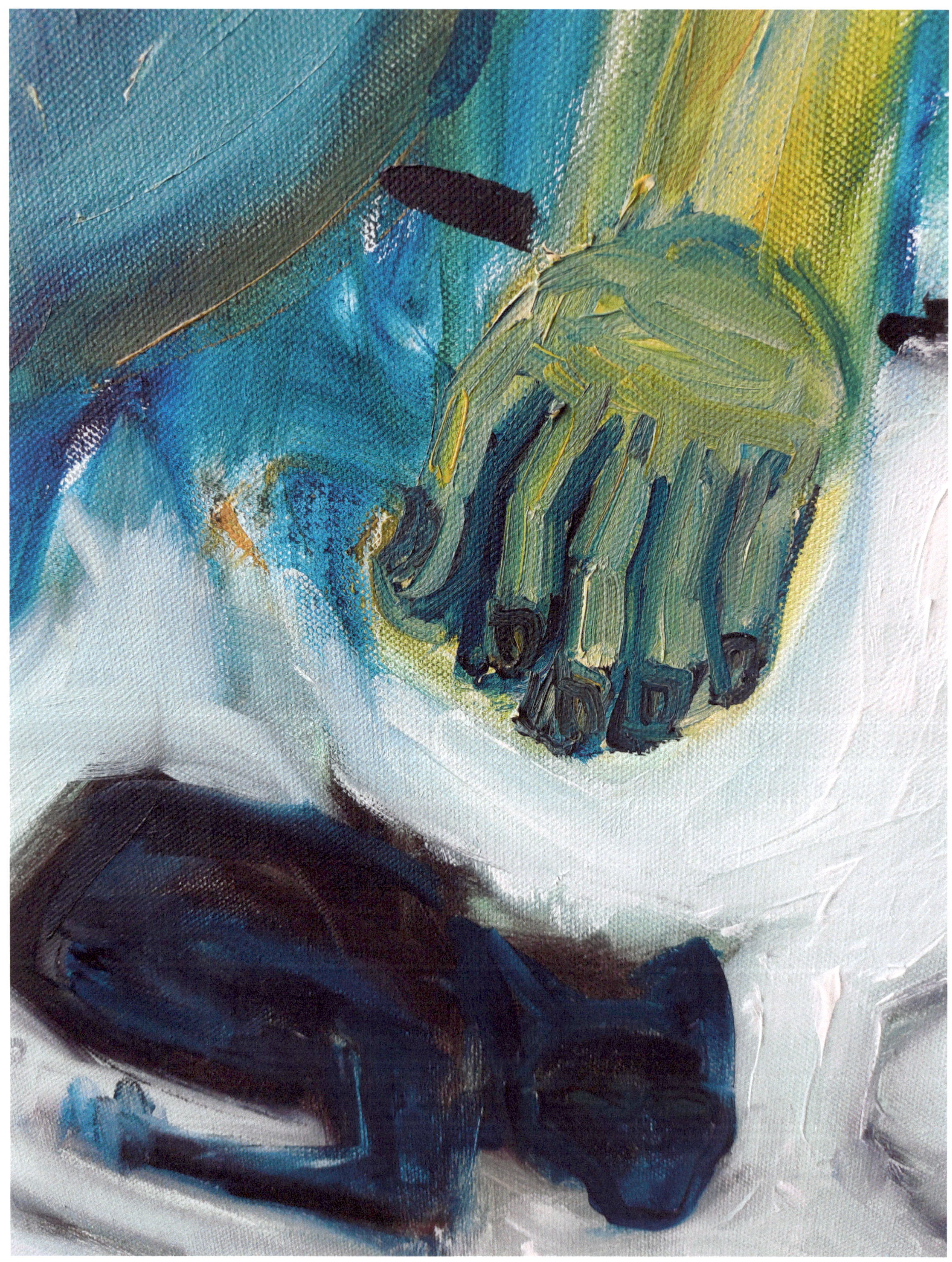

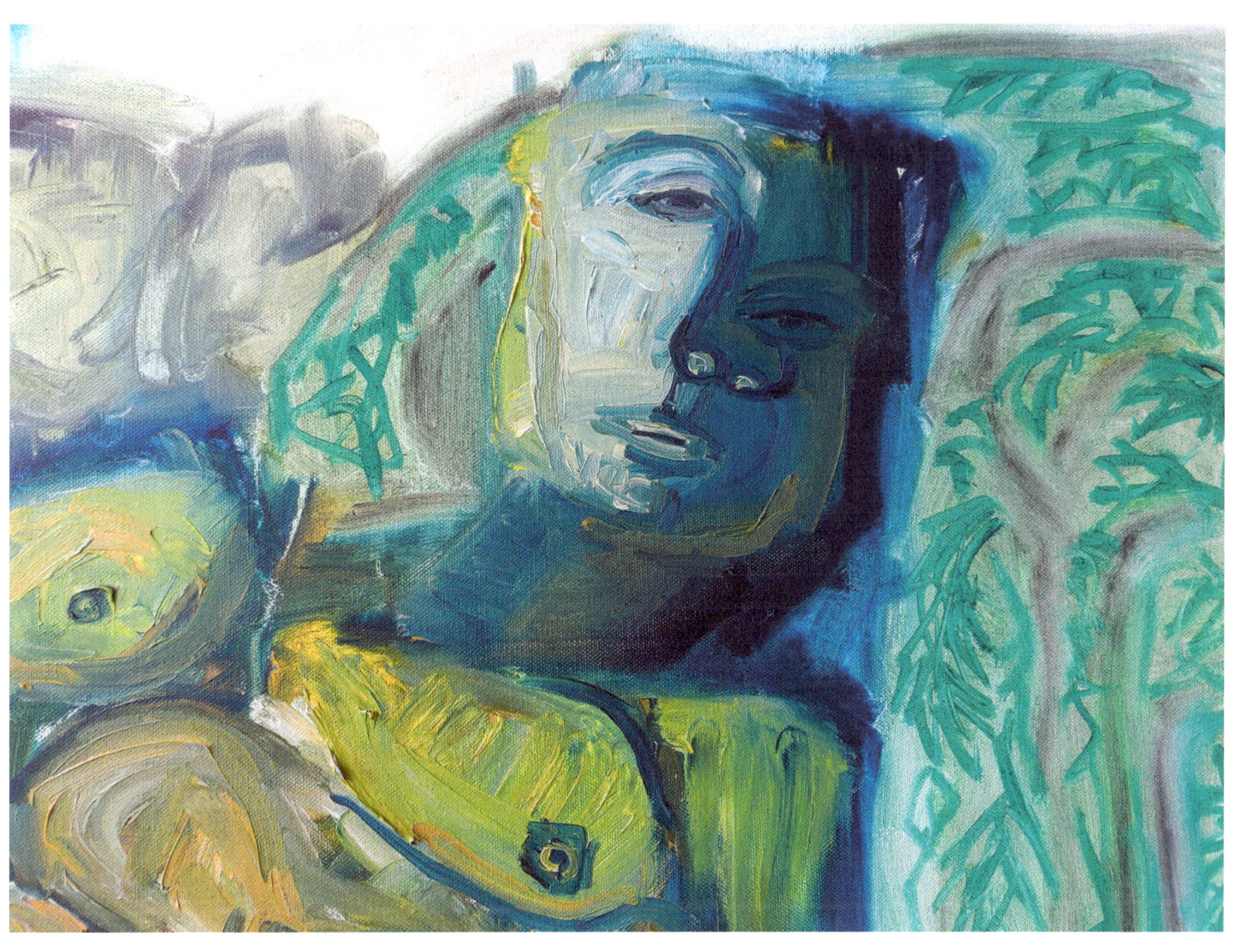

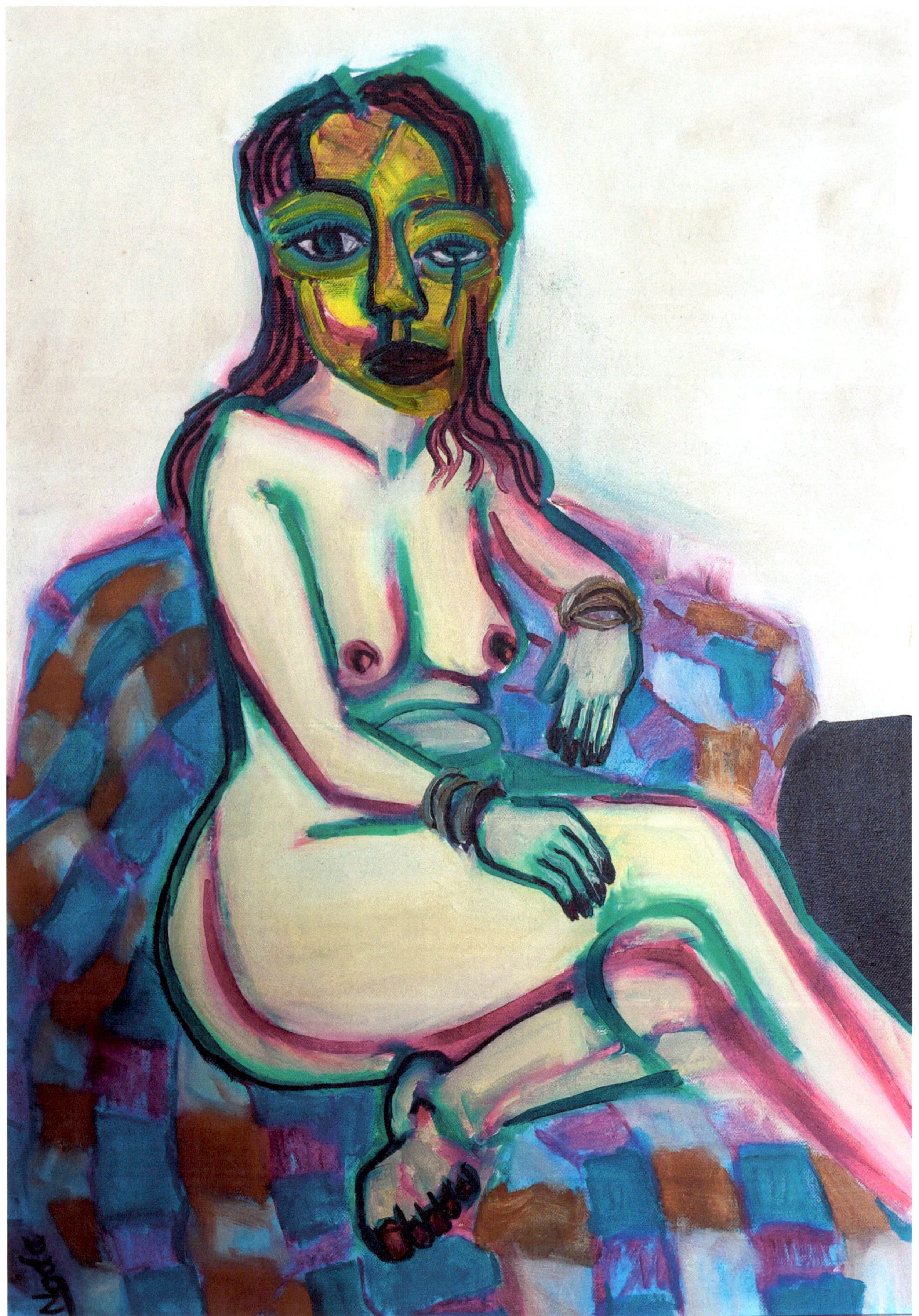

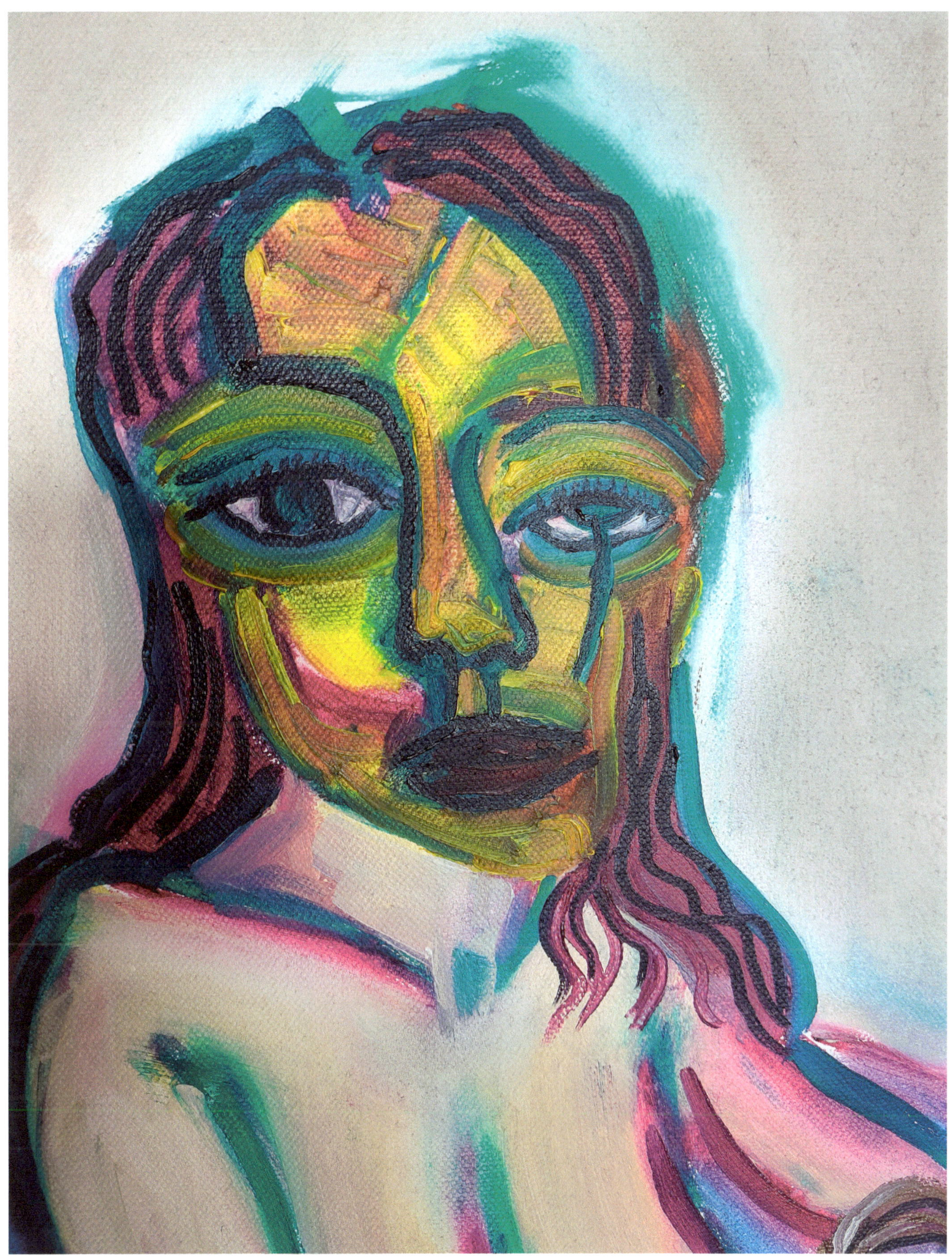

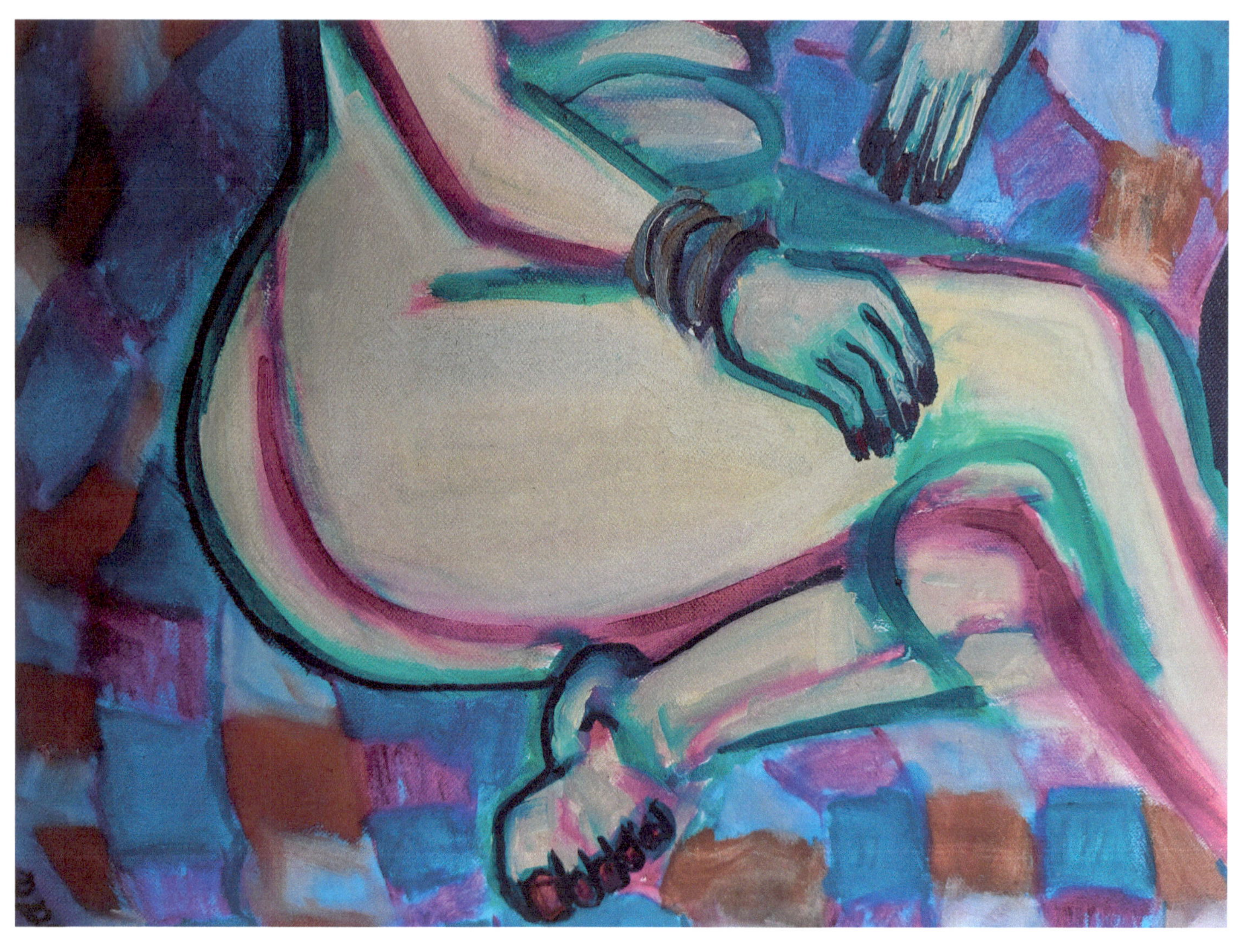

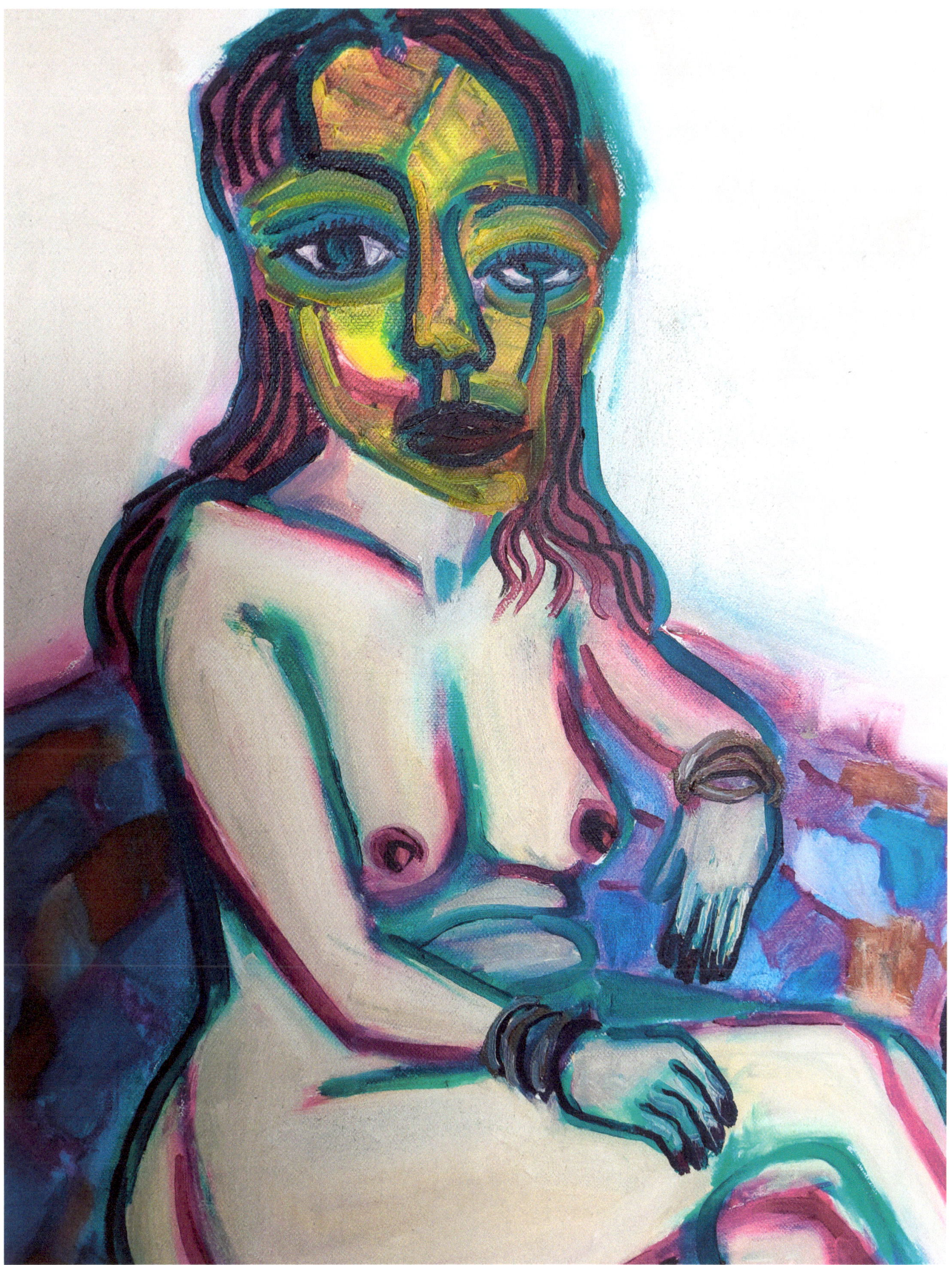

"ROSA"

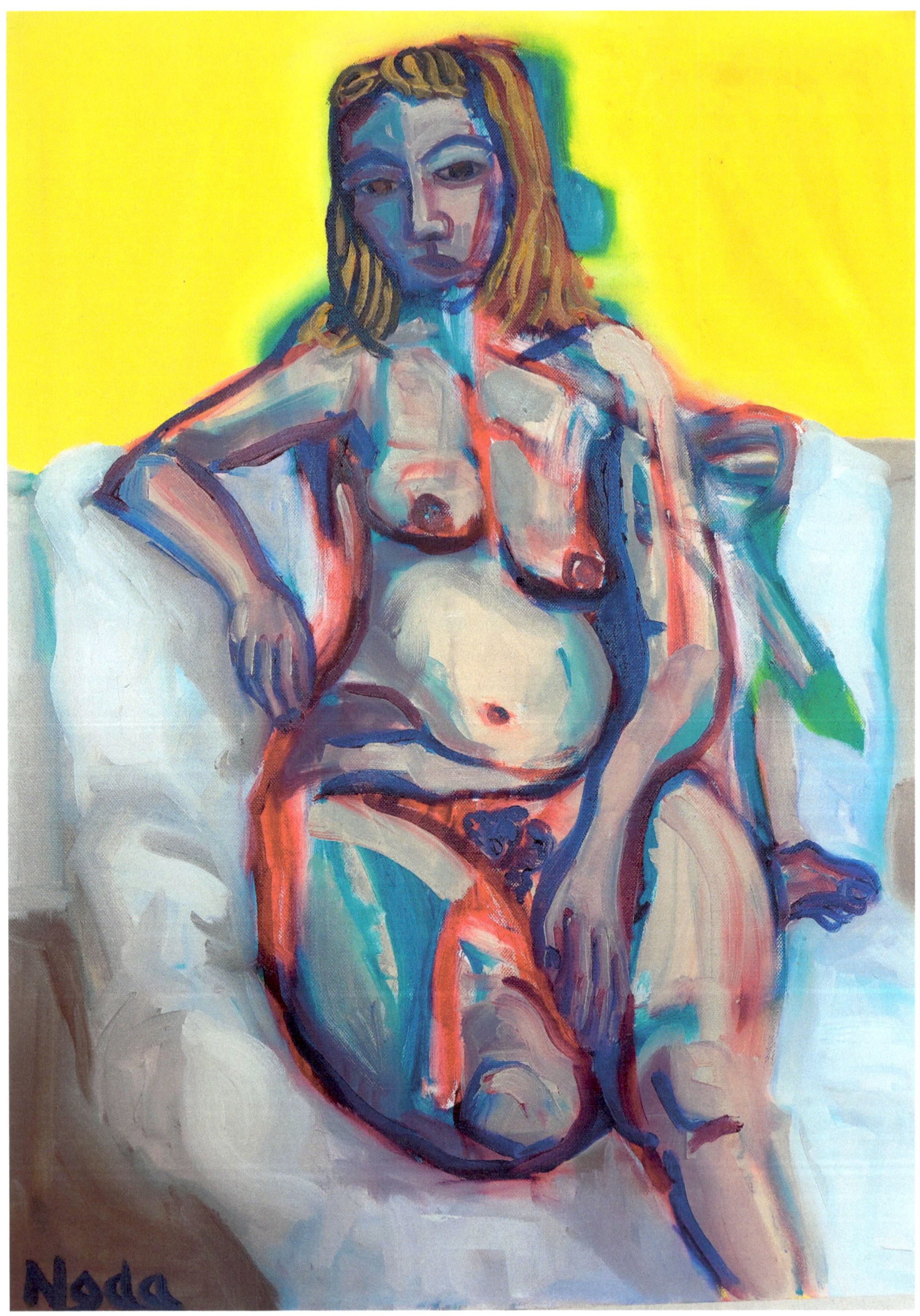

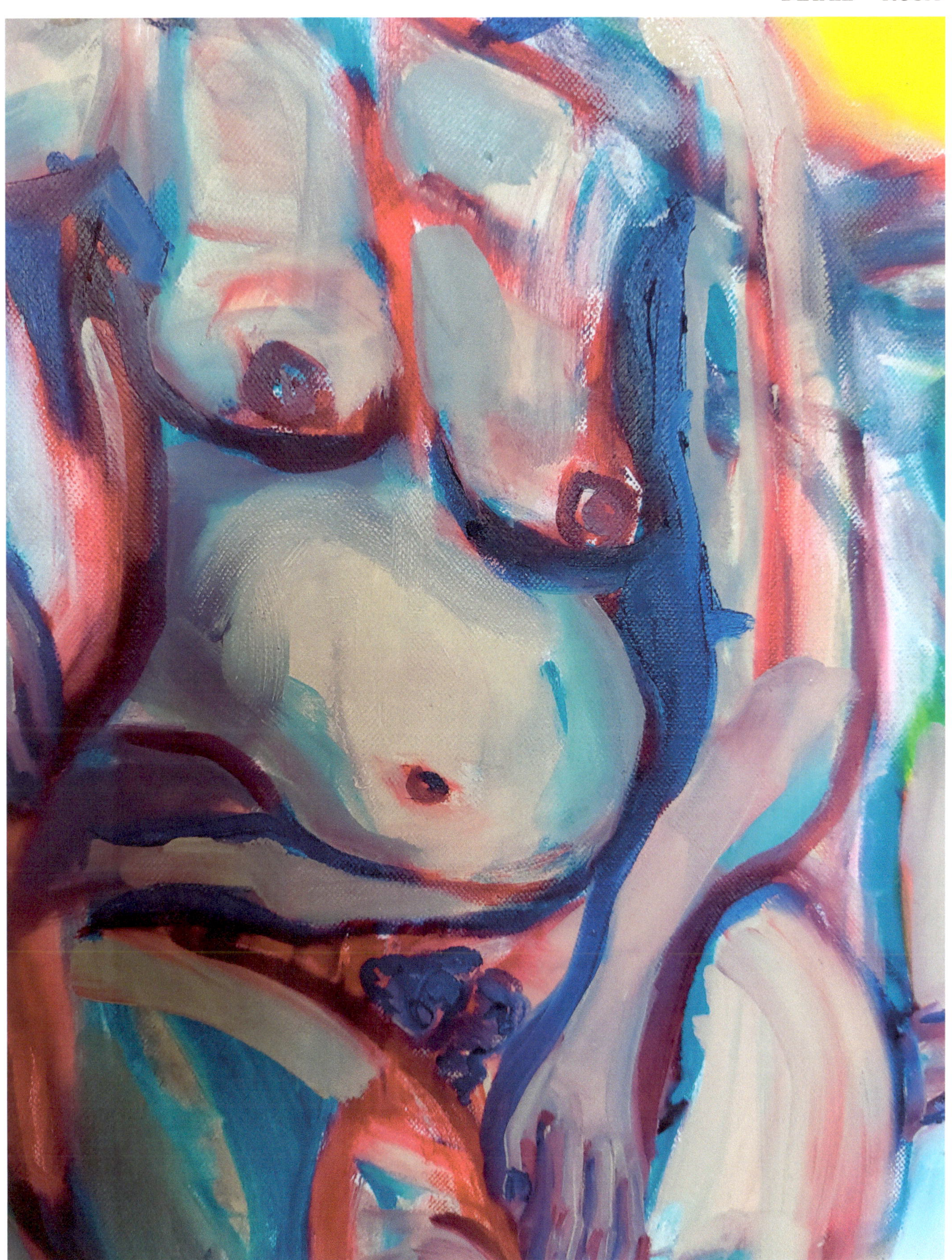

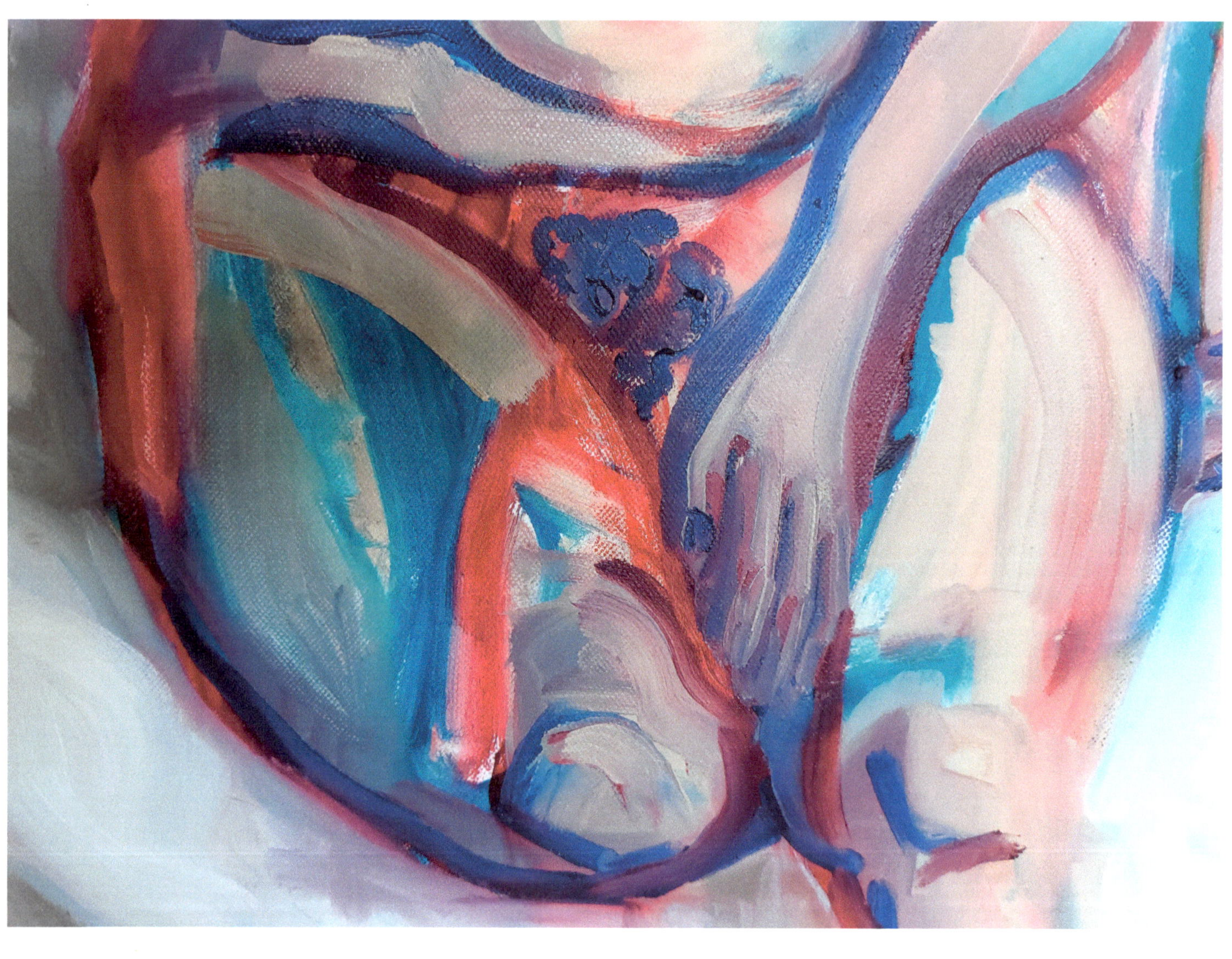

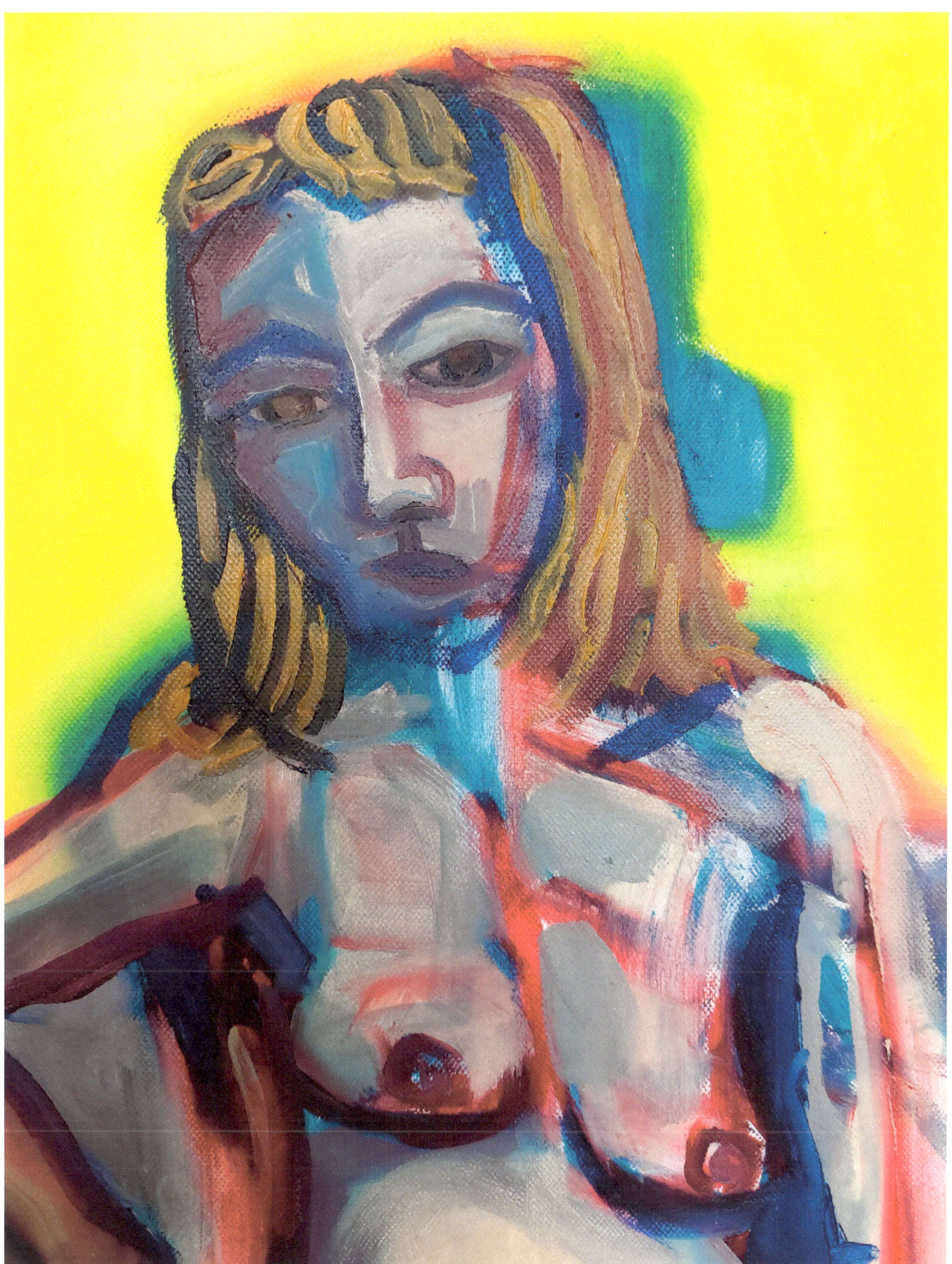

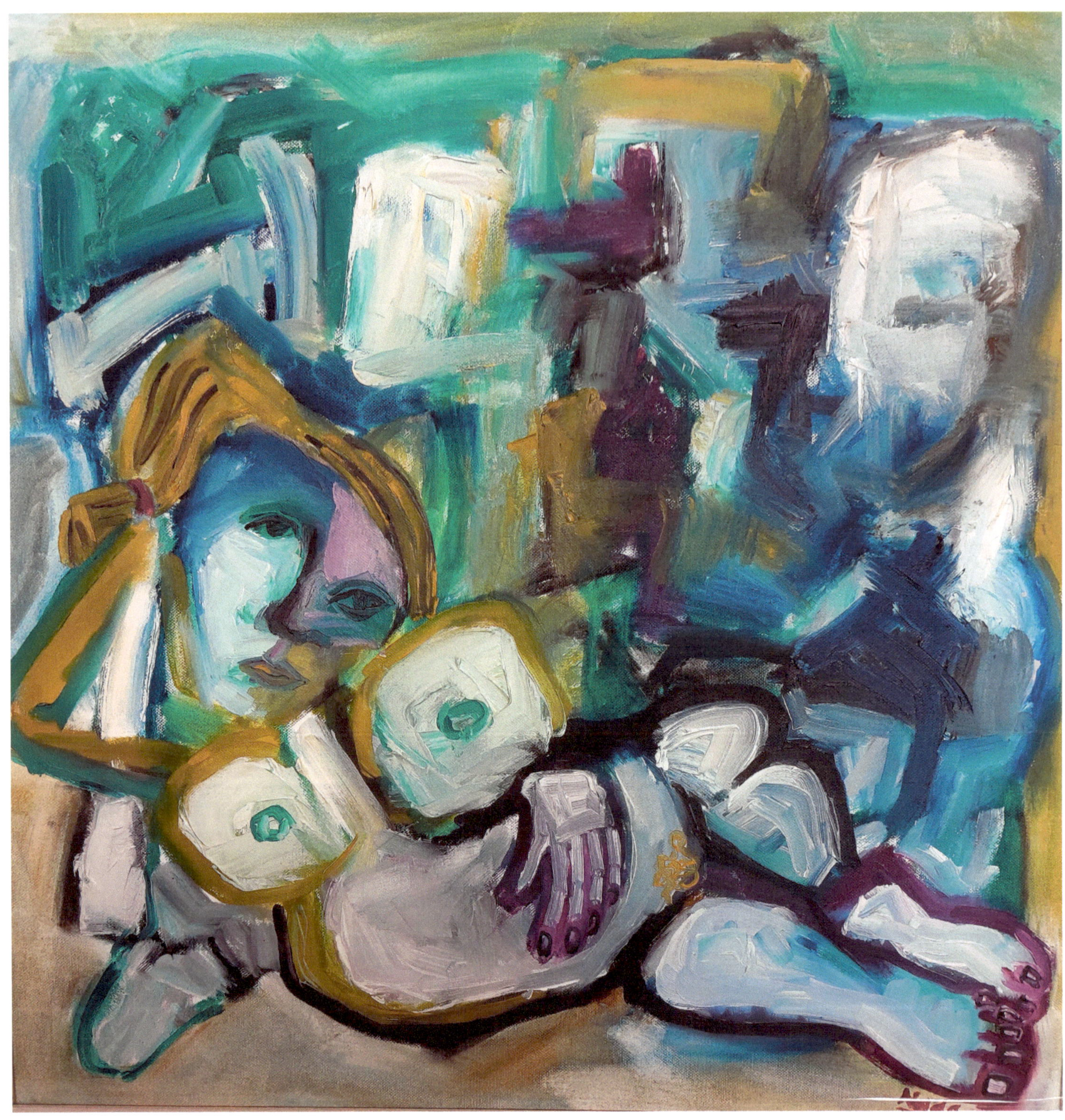

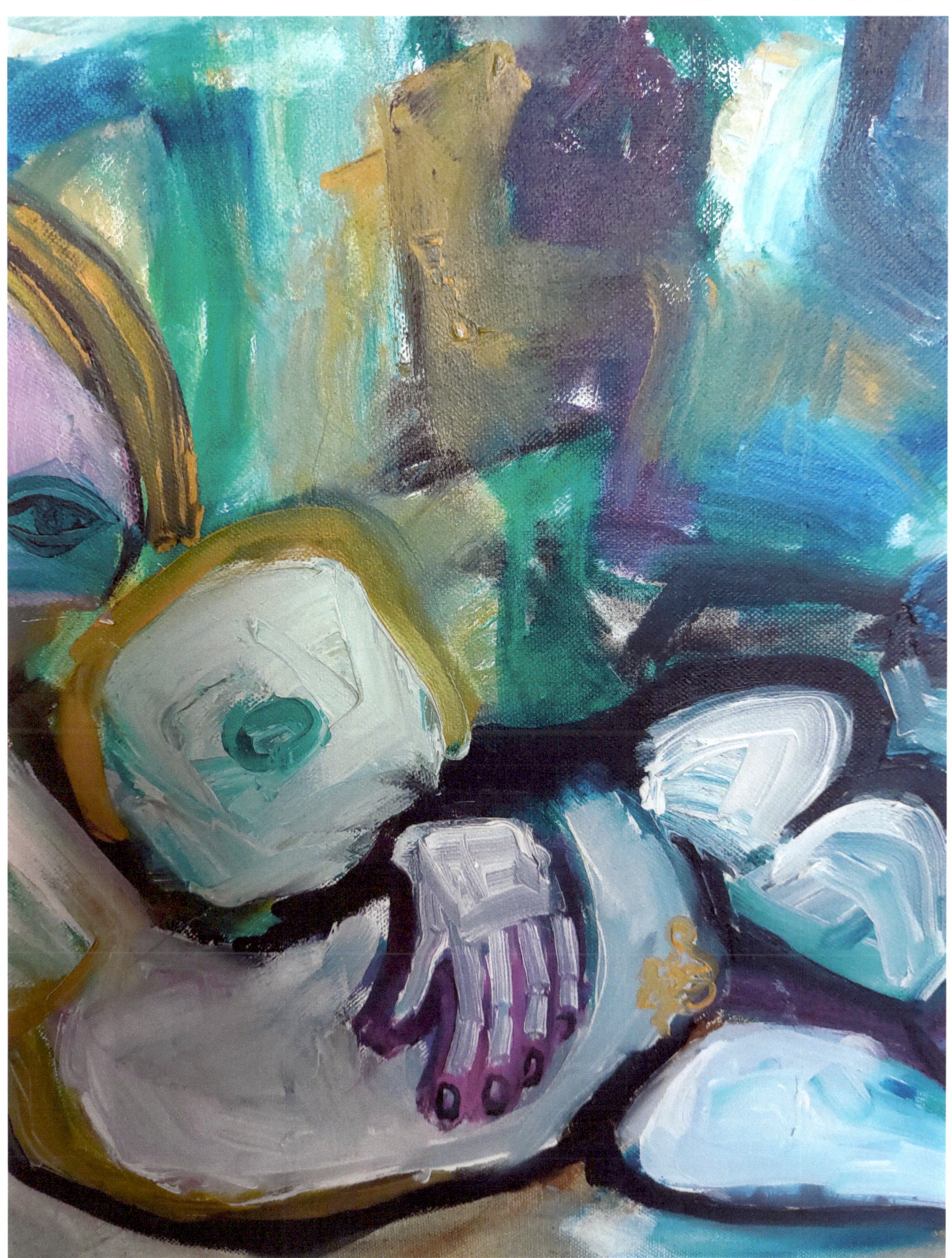

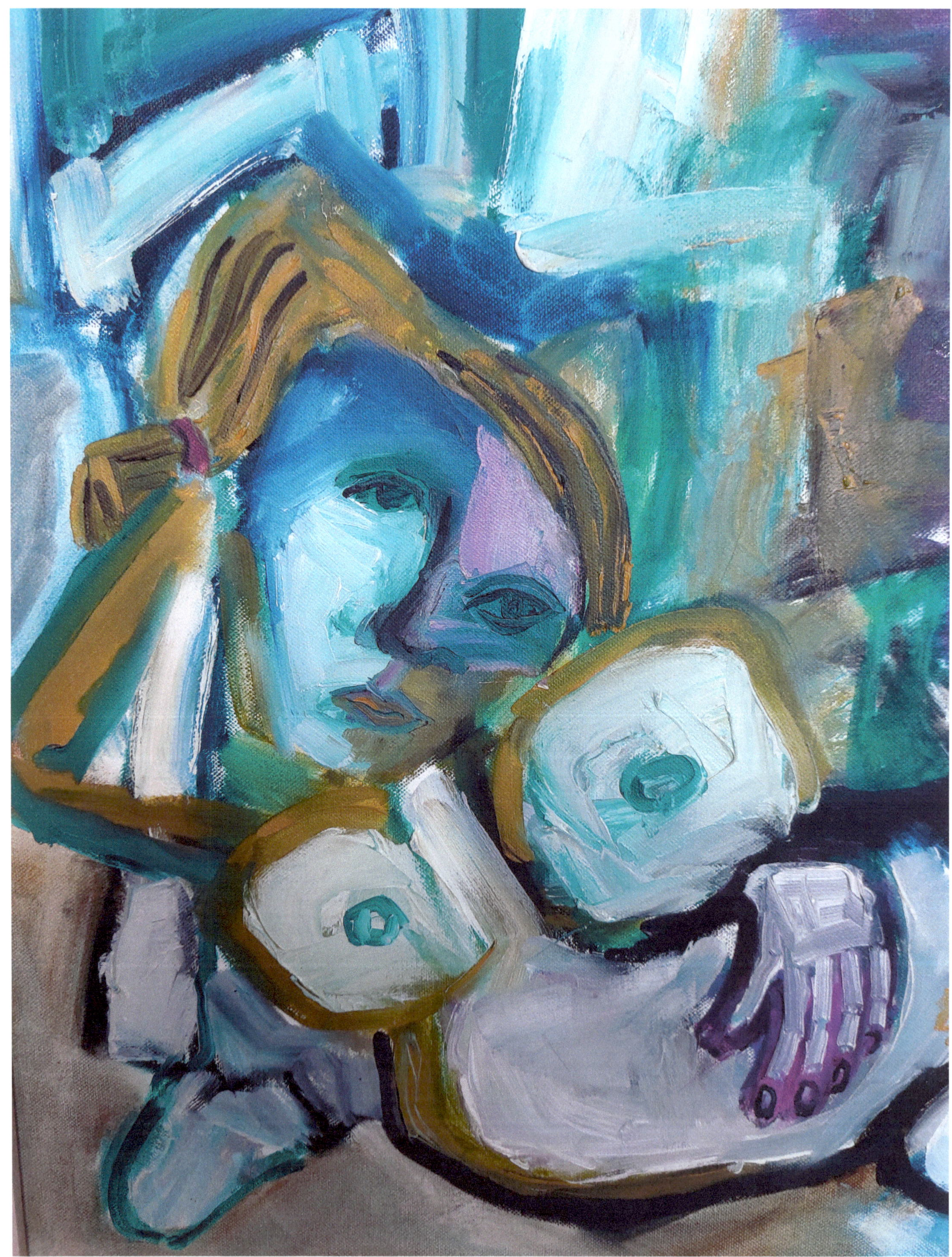

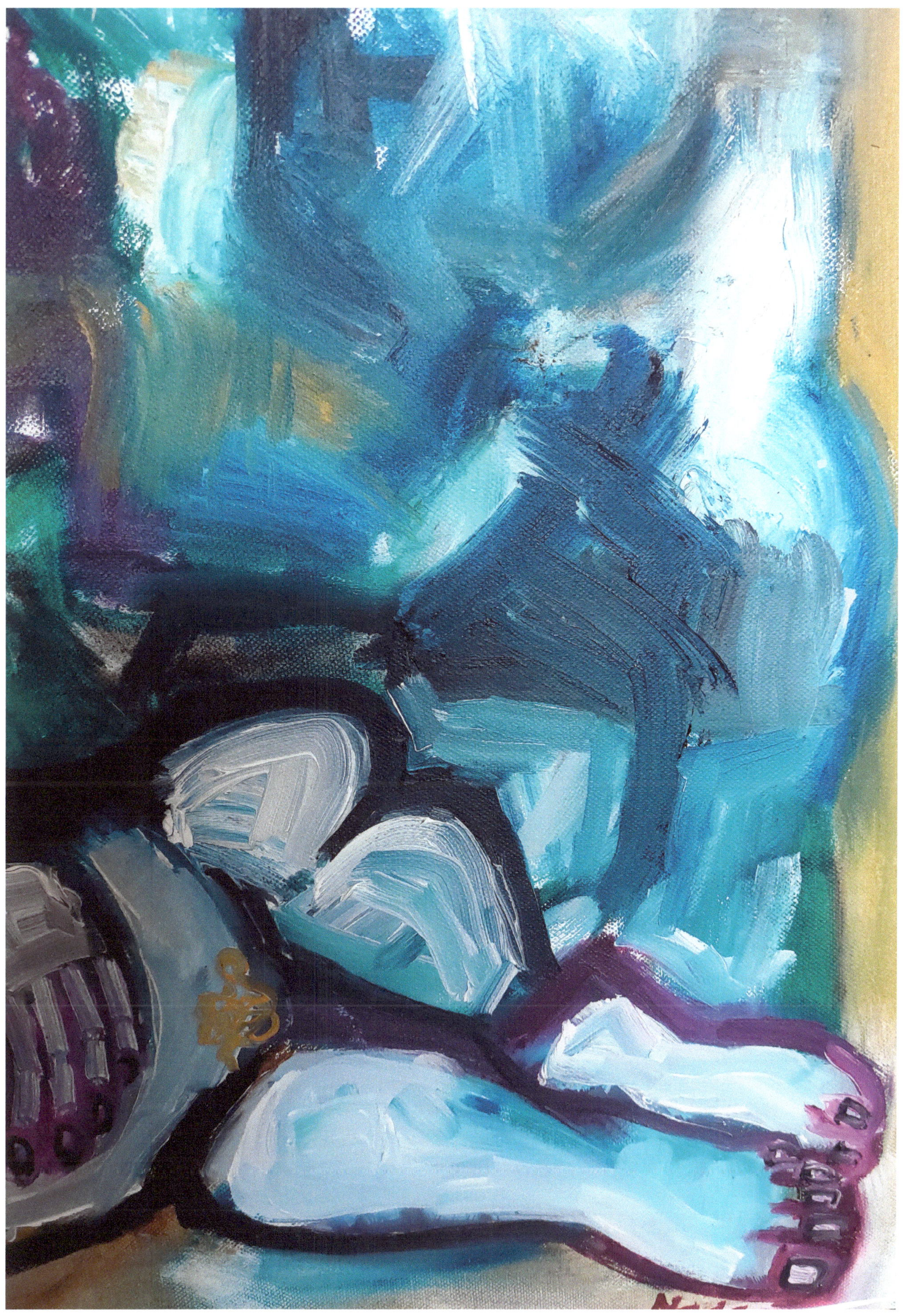

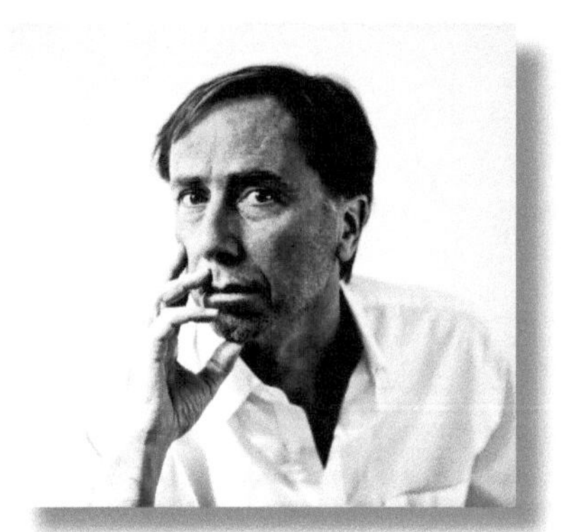

Stephen Najda

On exhibition

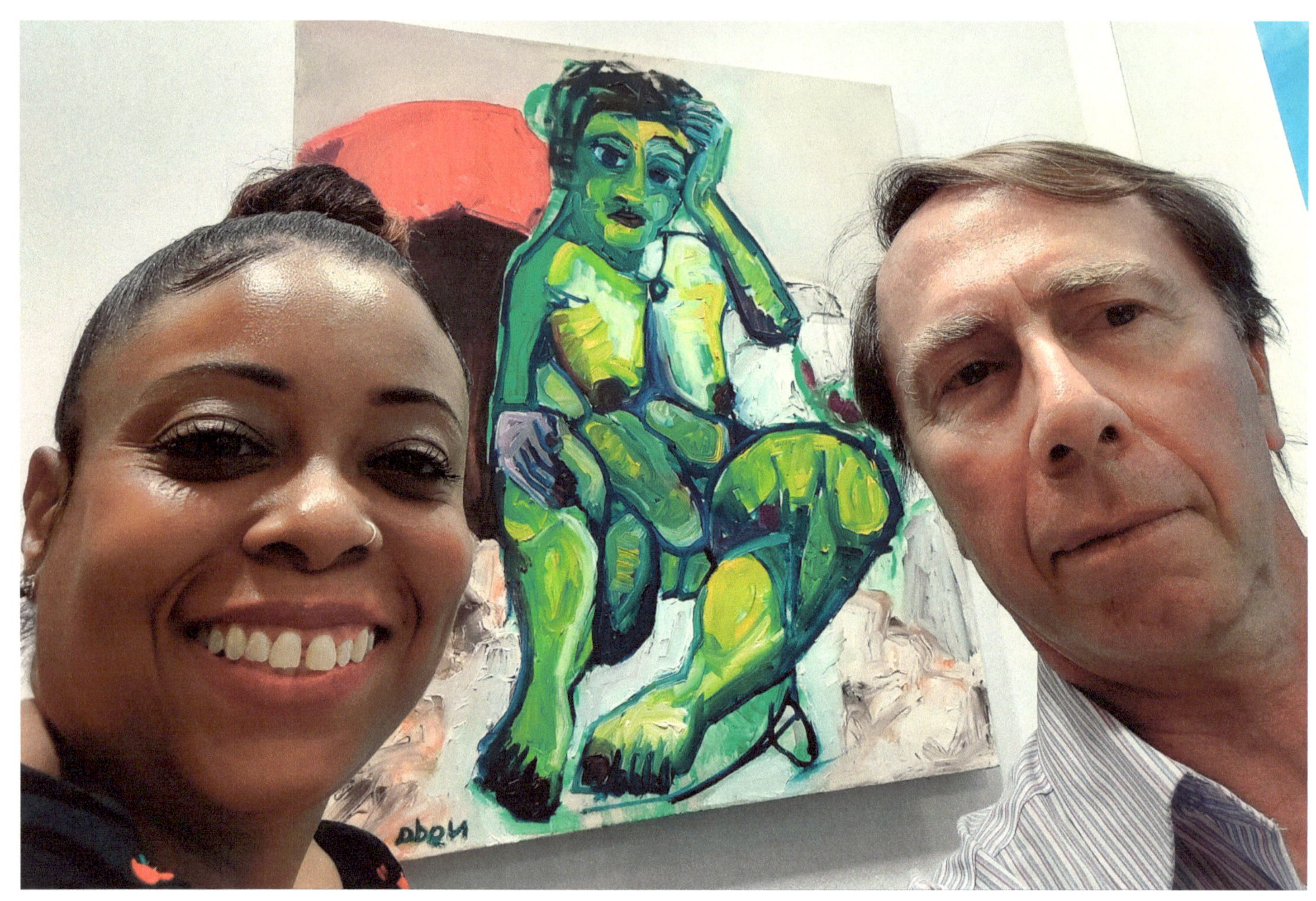

"Mary" at the Salon International D'Art Contemporian, Carrousel du Louvre, Paris with artist Channel Scott and Stephen Najda

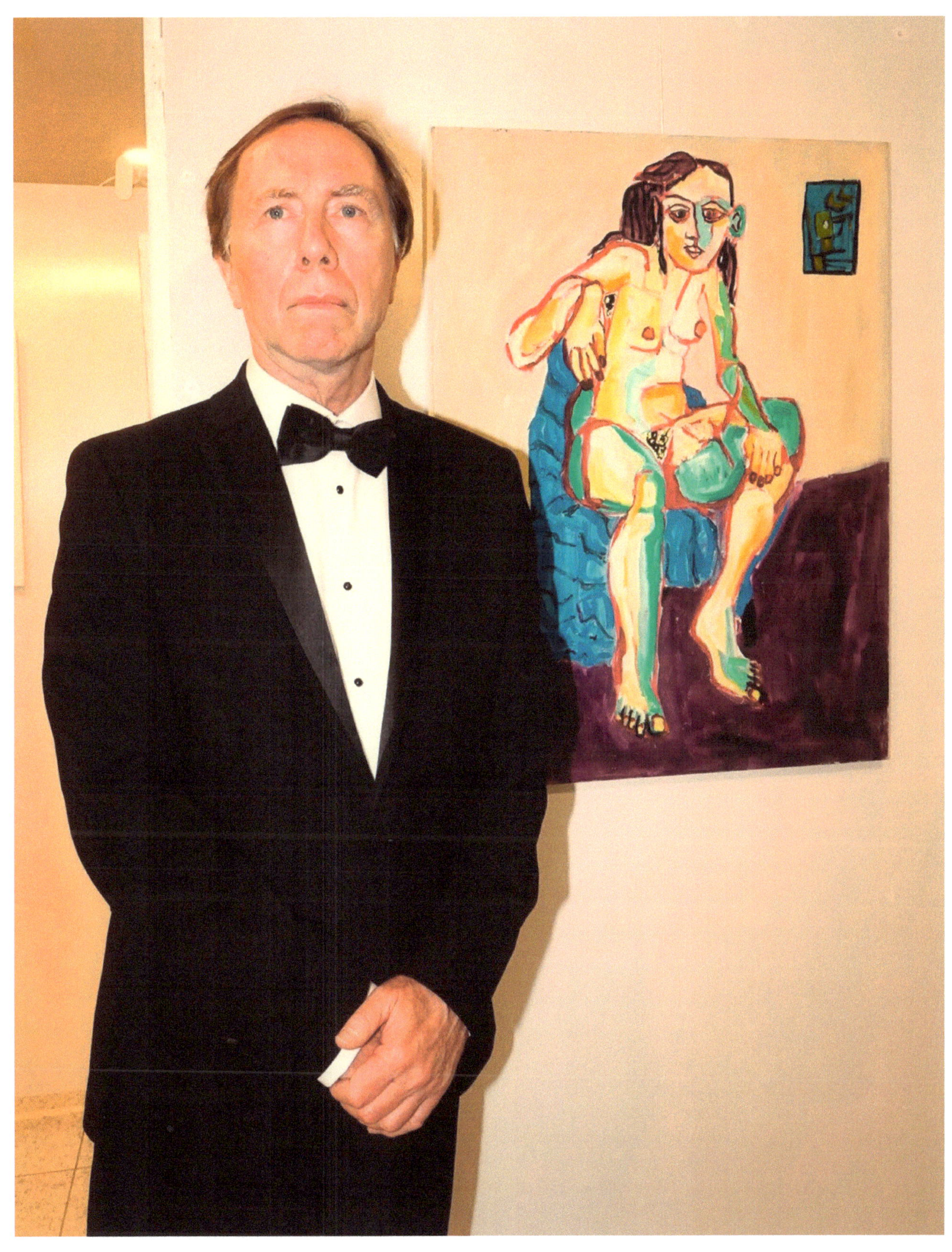

"Katie sitting beside Japanese print" at the Art Cannes
Biennale, Cannes, France and Stephen Najda

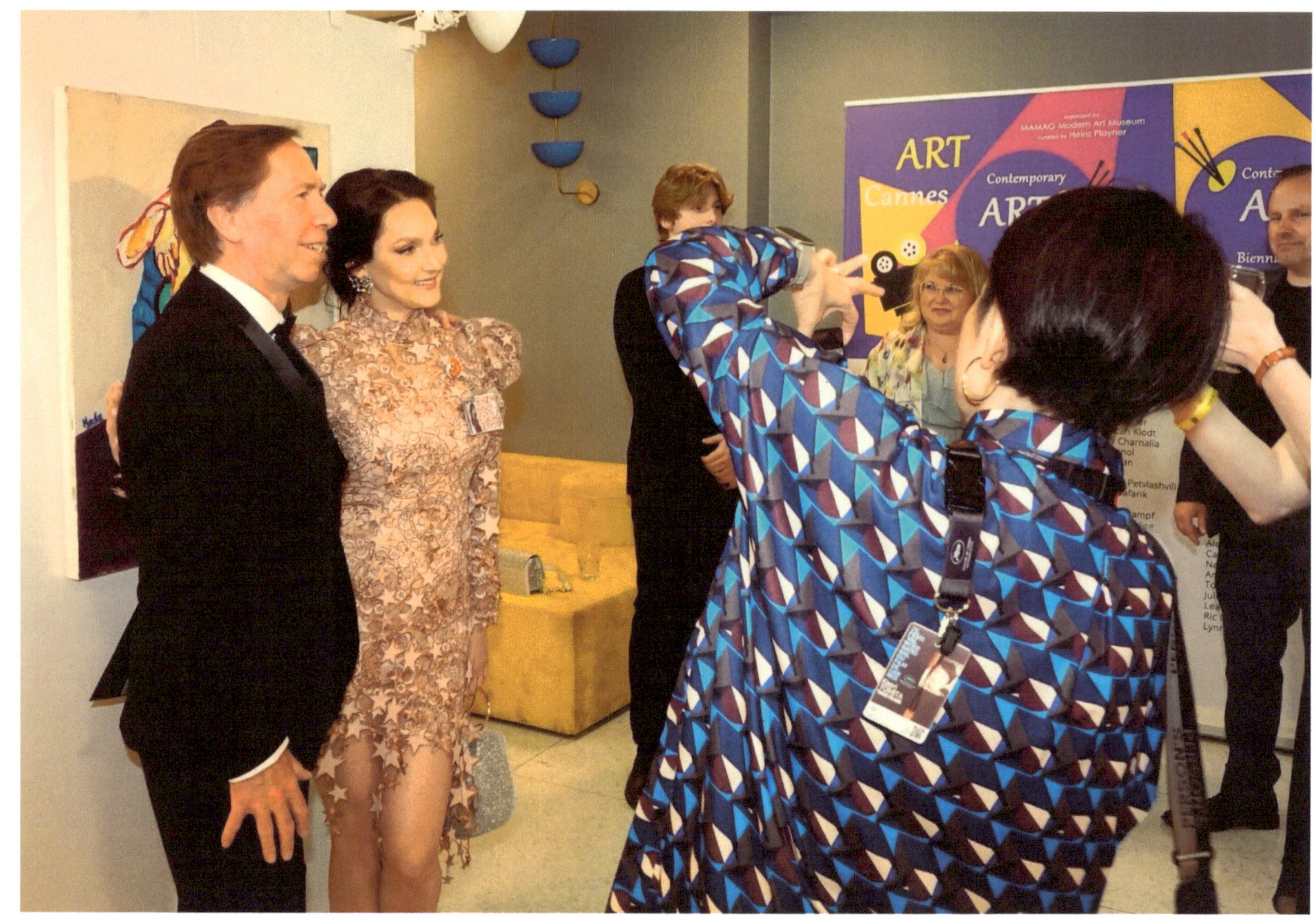

"Katie sitting beside Japanese print" at the Art Cannes Biennale, Cannes, France with artist Irene Van Celestine and Stephen Najda

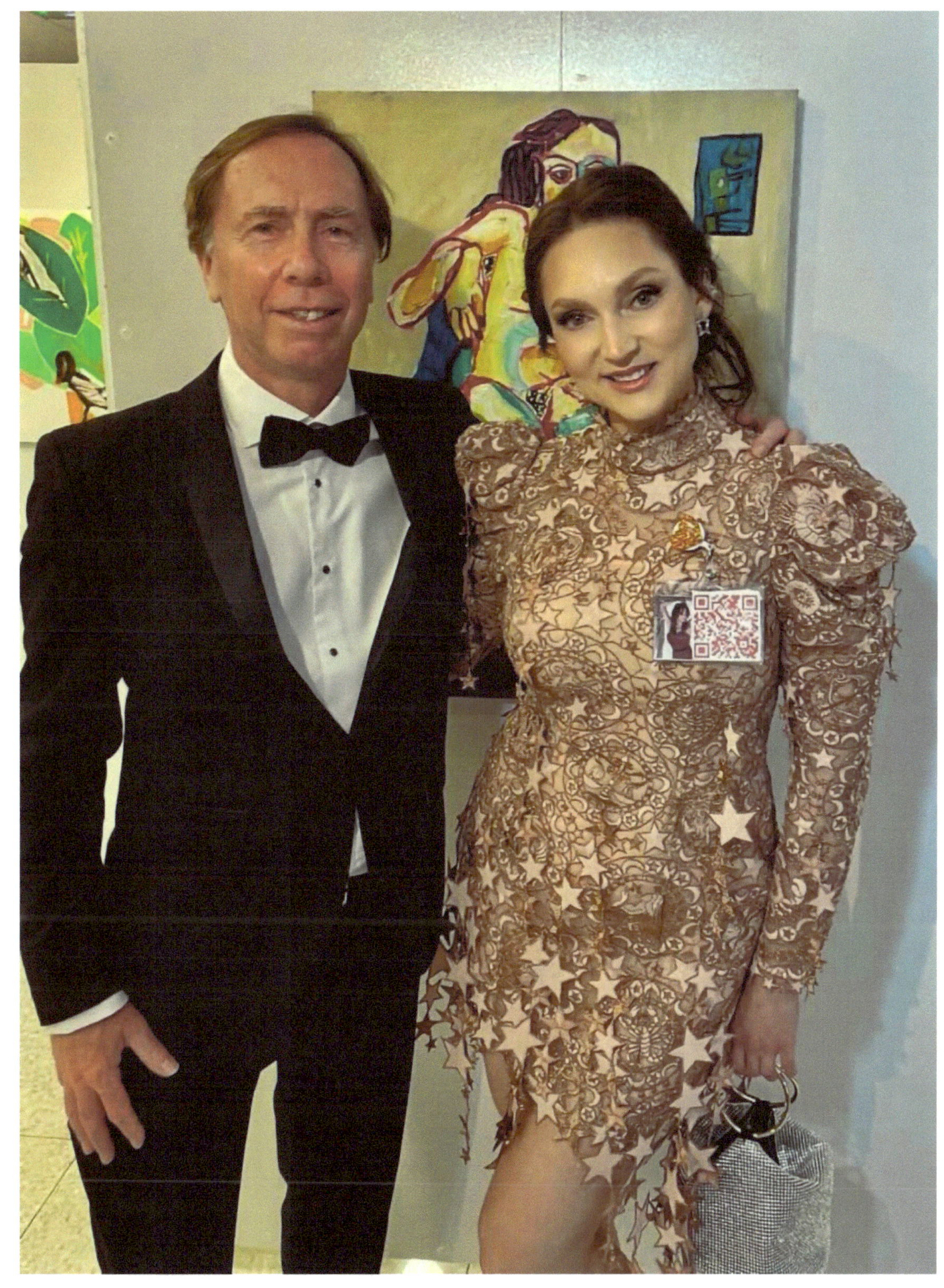

"Katie sitting beside Japanese print" at the Art Cannes
Biennale, Cannes, France with artist Irene Van
Celestine and Stephen Najda

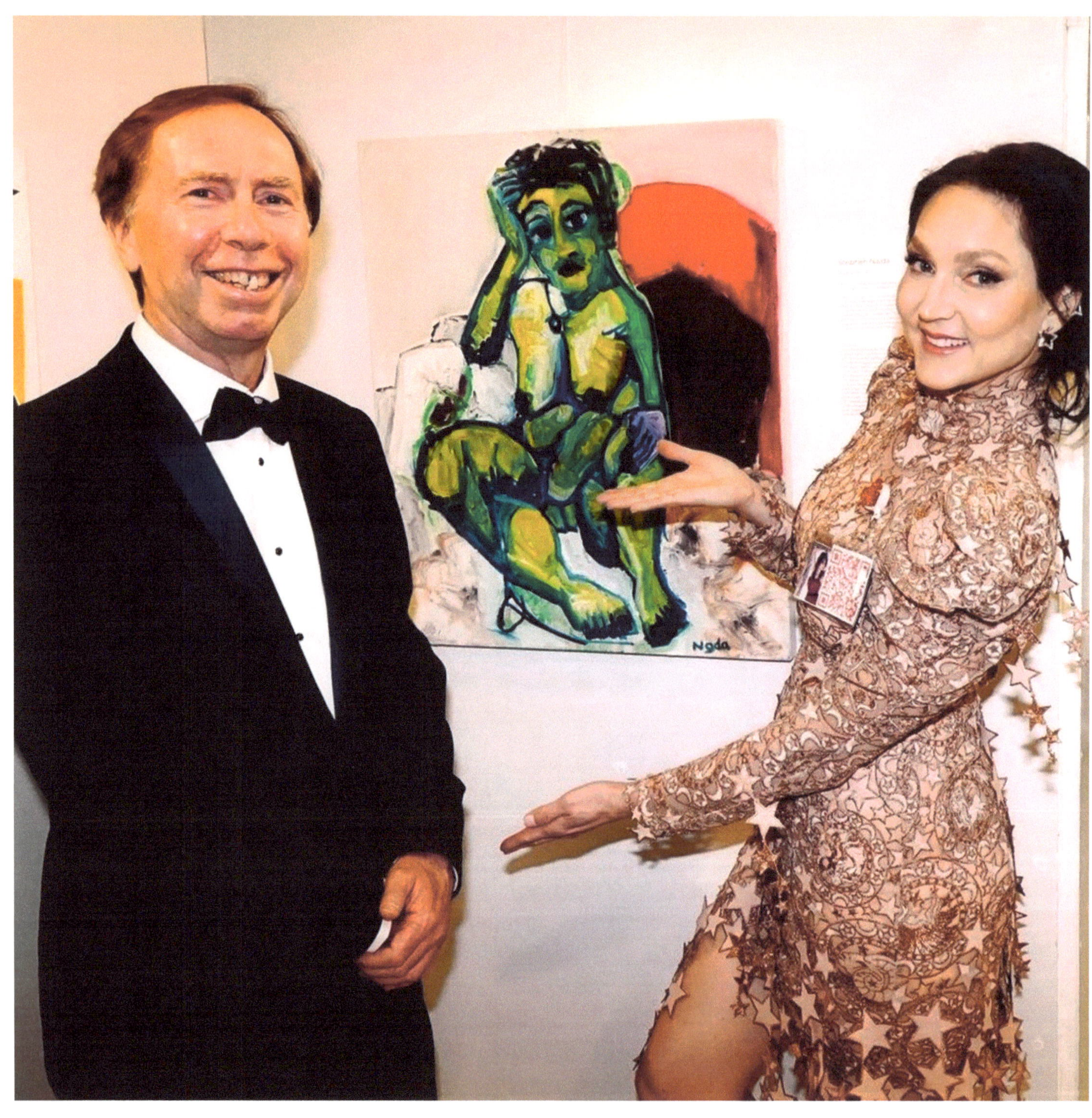

"Mary" at the Art Cannes Biennale, Cannes, France
with artist Irene Van Celestine and Stephen Najda

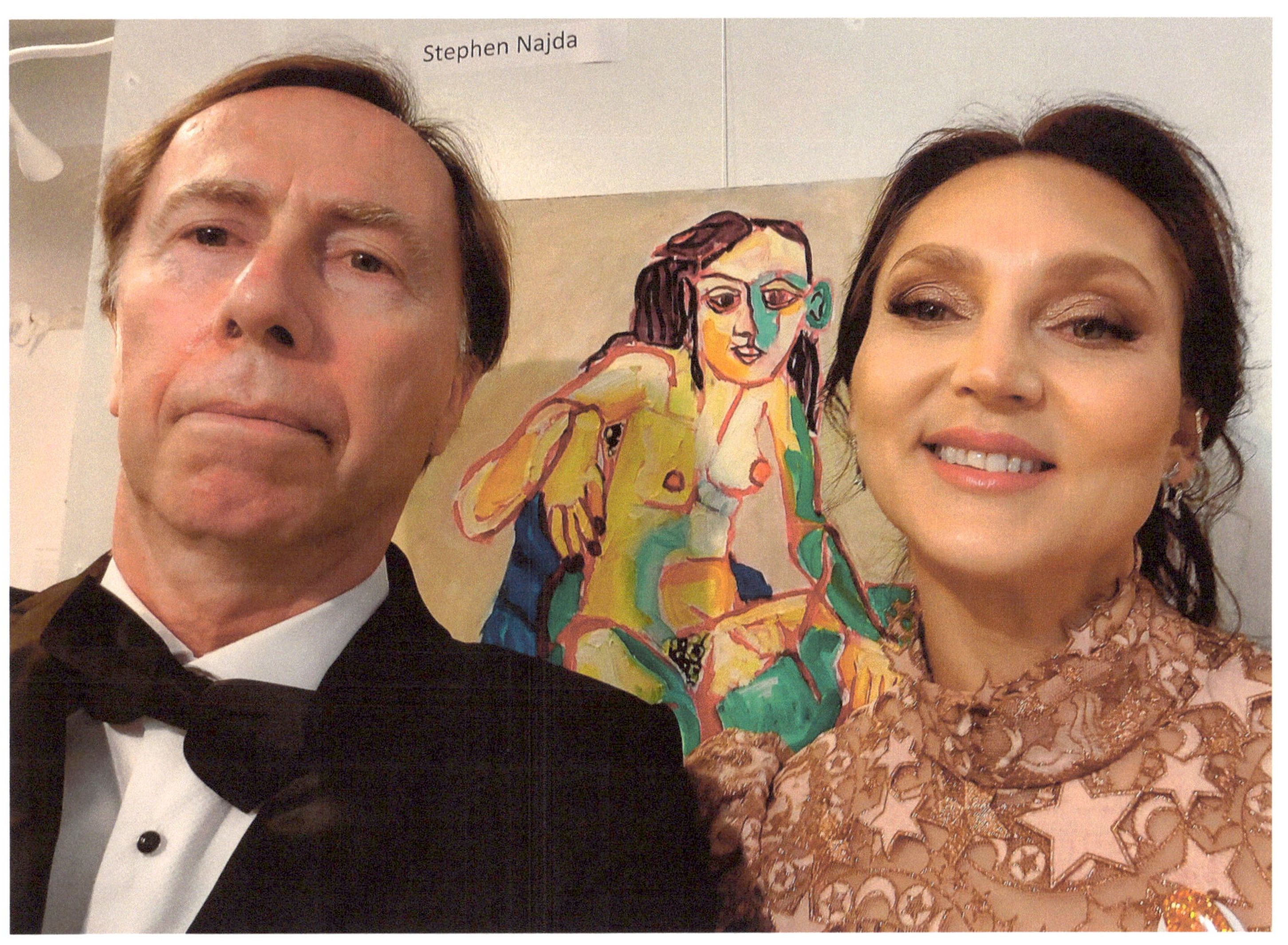

"Katie sitting beside Japanese print" at the Art Cannes Biennale, Cannes, France with artist Irene Van Celestine and Stephen Najda

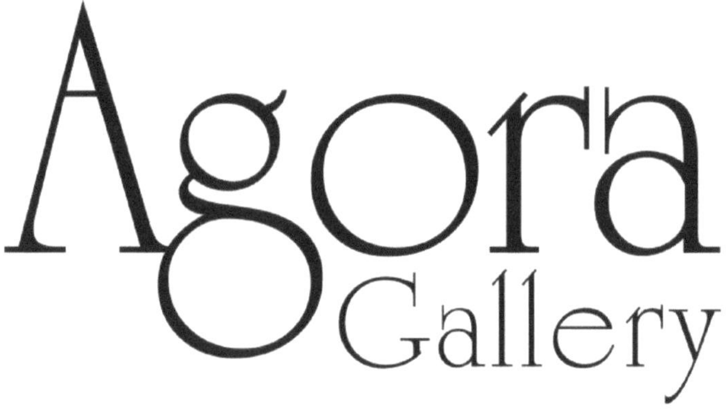

**The artworks were on display at the Agora Gallery
530 W 25th St, Chelsea, New York, USA**

More Artworks by Stephen Najda can be seen:

www.najda.net
Facebook: Najda Art
E-mail enquires: stevenajda@hotmail.com